# Designed for Conquest

## Other Books by Roy L. Laurin

*Acts: Life In Action*
*Romans: Where Life Begins*
*1 Corinthians: Where Life Matures*
*2 Corinthians: Where Life Endures*
*Philippians: Where Life Advances*
*Colossians: Where Life Is Established*
*1 John: Life at Its Best*

# Designed for Conquest

## Roy L. Laurin

**KREGEL PUBLICATIONS**
Grand Rapids, Michigan 49501

*Designed for Conquest,* by Roy L. Laurin. © 1990 by Kregel Publications, a division of Kregel, Inc., P. O. Box 2607, Grand Rapids, MI 49501. All rights reserved.

Cover: Don Ellens

**Library of Congress Cataloging-in-Publication Data**

Laurin, Roy L. (Roy Leonard), 1898-1966.
  [Meet yourself in the Bible.]
  Designed for conquest: biblical models for overcoming life's struggles / by Roy L. Laurin.
     p.    cm.
  Reprint. Originally published: Meet yourself in the Bible. Chicago: Van Kampen Press, 1946.
  1. Bible—Biography. 2. Christian life—Biblical teaching. I. Title.

BS571.L33     1990     220.9'2—dc20     90-36540
                                             CIP
  ISBN   0-8254-3139-5 (pbk.)

1 2 3 4 5 Printing/Year 94 93 92 91 90

*Printed in the United States of America*

# Contents

# *Preface*

LIFE IS AN experience to be lived and not merely a theme to be discussed. The Bible presents the answers to our personal problems not only in lofty principles but also in the experiences of the men and women who make up its cast of characters.

*Designed for Conquest* is an effort to make the Bible come alive in terms of people and experiences, rather than doctrines and ideas. It is a portrayal of real experience lived by flesh and blood characters, rather than a classroom discussion.

Here is life by experience. It is a series of biographical sketches and character studies showing how its men and women faced and conquered their problems.

The author is grateful for the permission to use quoted material and poems. Acknowledgment is given as far as it was possible to do so.

Stimulating thought-starters and helpful ideas for the subject matter of this volume are gratefully acknowledged from such sources as, W. M. Taylor's *Bible Biography*, George Matheson's *Bible Portraits Series* (republished in 1987 by Kregel Publications), also *Genesis: A Devotional Commentary* by W. H. Griffith Thomas (republished in 1988 by Kregel Publications).

# Introduction

THE BIBLE IS full of people. It is full of men and women who lived in life situations quite similar to our own. The age and place make little difference for human experience is an unvarying thing from generation to generation. Beneath the various colors of our skins lies a similarity of character and condition that is amazingly changeless.

Since the Bible goes back into antiquity and deals with a vast span of time it is qualified to speak as no other book can or does. Across its pages tread the races, nations and people of over four thousand years. It includes war and peace, prosperity and poverty, barbarity and civilization, creation and re-creation. It is as modern as it is ancient and as human as it is divine.

Somewhere in the Bible you can meet yourself for in it there is to be found a person just like you. You will find someone with experiences, troubles, weaknesses, and problems just like yours.

This is so because the Bible covers every possible situation that can arise in life. While this is not always true specifically, it is so generally.

In literature there are but thirty-six dramatic situations which all drama and literature are based. Repeated efforts have been made by Goethe and others to develop more than these thirty-six basic dramatic situations but without success. Similarly there are but twenty-six letters in the English alphabet from which our language is formed. There are but seven notes in the musical scale from which all music is written. There are but three primary colors from which all painting is done.

Life is like this too. There are certain invariable and unchangeable life situations. These can be tabulated and counted and include such situations as fear, inferiority, frustration, anxiety, pride, jealousy, anger, sorrow, sickness, poverty, adversity, ambition, futility, doubt, death, handicap, temptation and so on. For these basic situations the Bible offers basic solutions.

In giving these solutions the Bible does not present its truths of life in cold capsules of ethics or philosophy or religion. They are presented, among other ways, through men and women of flesh and blood who actually faced these situations in life on this earth. Finding the person who fits your experience, you will meet yourself.

When you meet yourself in this person in the Bible you will find that the way to meet life for that one who is like you is not tucked away in some corner of comfort or enshrined in some place of artificial piety, but will be found in the swift stream of life.

We shall thumb our way through God's great Book of Life, the Bible, and walk across its pages. As we meet some of its people we are going to stop, for one of them will be you. We will inquire concerning their experience and find out the secret of their conquest.

In each case the end of life is conquest. We are not left suspended in doubt about what life means. We are not tantalized by an impractical ideal. We are not lifted into theoretical clouds with our feet left dangling over the solid earth. Instead, we will find that life is liveable by the highest virtues and principles in the most difficult places.

# 1
# Noah
## The Conquest of Circumstances

NOAH IS WITHOUT doubt one of the greatest of the great characters of all time. He is seldom appreciated to the full limit of his stature because we have enveloped him in a fog of ridicule. He is looked upon as some sort of a crepe-hanging reformer and people imagine him to have been some dour-faced, bewhiskered old fogey who lived in the hills apart from the rest of men. This is untrue, for I am quite sure that Noah was not afflicted with some quirk that made him odd and strange. He is paying the price of individuality, for he stood against the stream of evil and corruption in his generation and dared to be different.

The background of the deeds and acts of Noah's life is described in these Bible words: "And God saw that the wickedness of man was great in the earth, and that every imagination of the thoughts of his heart was only evil continually. And it repented the Lord that he had made man on the earth, and it grieved him at his heart" (Gen. 6:5, 6). Again it reads: "The earth also was corrupt before God, and the earth was fined with violence. And God looked upon the earth, and, behold, it was corrupt; for all flesh had corrupted his way upon the earth" (Gen. 6:11, 12).

In the midst of this general corruption and violence stood one man. He did not stand with it but against it. He grieved over it. He protested against it. He plead with the people to turn from their wickedness. Let any man stand up and out against the sins and derelictions of his generation and he will be branded as a crank. No one can stand against the world and yet stand in with the world.

Jesus knew this when He said to His disciples, "If the world hate you, ye know that it hated me before it hated you." Jesus refused to accept the status quo and marked out for judgment those who were misusing their privileges and corrupting the world.

Noah was not a visionary dreamer. He saw the danger of the present. He saw the uncleanness of the cities and the people. He saw their present wickedness and their present danger. He was not dealing with future perils but present problems.

It is high time that we should be like Noah and concern ourselves with some of the present problems of the world. It is unfair to our fellowmen to dangle a future hope that has no promise of present relief.

Noah was not a bombastic reactionary. His name, Noah, means "rest" and it suggests that he was a quiet man. Consequently, no one looked for any opposition from him. They expected that he would loyally follow their plans. They planned on his piety to profit them and expected his prayers to bring them good. Yet this man stood out— "a solitary figure against a multitude."

Noah is a supreme example of a man who conquered his circumstances. Let us inquire into these circumstances and the conquest Noah made of them.

To begin with, Noah's generation was materialistic. It was the generic fruit of Cain who was a deist. They had a religious conception which made God a racial convenience. He was neither reverenced nor respected. They did as they pleased and went the limit of their desires. Consequently they followed the flesh and not the spirit.

They gloried in human might and physical virtues. We read that "there were giants in the earth in those days . . . the same became mighty men which were of old, men of renown."

World War II resulted from the same conception. Hitler, and Mussolini before him, glorified the physical. He talked about supermen and a superior race. He regimented youth in cults of physical science. He militarized the nation. With the increase of the human came the decrease of the divine. Presently the only god of the Germans was the god of the German spirit recreated out of the folklore of the nation.

Noah refused to compromise with this religious philosophy. He believed and later preached of a God of integrity and righteousness; a God who created man, not one created by man. In other words, Noah refused to follow the popular religions and ideologies of his time.

Then there was social corruption. It was so general that the account says that "all flesh had corrupted his way upon the earth." It reached its worst phase in the marriage relation for they "married and were given in marriage" a phrase which means that the sanctity of marriage was completely disregarded and it was treated only as a physical convenience.

It was against this that Noah stood, but just how was it possible for him to conquer his circumstances?

First of all, he kept himself clean. It is said that he walked with God. "Noah was a just man and perfect [upright] in his generations, and Noah walked with God" (Gen. 6:9). Just what does it mean for a person to walk with God. Obviously it does not mean in God's physical presence, but it does mean in the consciousness of God's presence. It means agreement of purpose for "how can two walk except they be agreed?" It means the same direction, for the one who walks with God is not going in the opposite direction. It means purity of life, for "what fellowship hath righteousness with unrighteousness?" It means communion which draws strength from the divine source.

> Give me thy strength for my day, Lord
> That wheresoe'er I go,
> There shall no danger daunt me
> And I shall fear no foe;
> So shall no task o'ercome me,
> So shall no trial fret,
> So shall I walk unwearied
> The path where my feet are set;
> So shall I find no burden
> Greater than I can bear,
> So shall I have a courage
> Equal to all my care;
> So shall no grief o'erwhelm me,
> So shall no wave o'erflow—
> Give me Thy strength for my day, Lord,
> Cover my weakness so.*
>
> —Annie Johnson Flint

Besides, Noah was a man of faith. Of him it is written: "By faith Noah, being warned of God of things not seen as yet, moved with fear, prepared an ark to the saving of his house; by the which he condemned the world, and became heir of the righteousness which is by faith" (Heb. 11:7). No person can conquer his circumstances unless he is a person of faith. Faith is that force which can make it possible for us to withstand the terrific pressure which our circumstances often put upon us. In Noah's case his circumstances were not changed. Noah's faith did not change his generation simply because such a change without the consent and desire of the people would have been arbitrary and would have profited them little. However, Noah's faith saved him and his family from the corruption and consequences of his circumstances.

Faith gave Noah an understanding of what would be the end of the corruption of his generation. It also gave him the means by which he escaped the consequences of that corruption in the flood. Had Noah merged himself with his circumstances he would have been lost. Because he dared to stand apart and live above them he was saved from the thing that destroyed the people. This was because faith gave Noah a God's-eye-view of life. A God's-eye-view of life sees the future as well as the present. Without it we see only the value of the present. It was because of Noah's faith that he "prepared

---

\* Evangelical Publishers, Toronto, Canada.

an ark to the saving of his house. Be it noted with great care, that Noah so profoundly influenced his family that he saved them as well as himself. He had little influence on the people of his generation but he did influence his family. Better that a man be the means of influencing his family and be respected at home than that he should rule a kingdom. The first responsibility he has is to his home.

Along with these reasons for Noah's conquest of his circumstances is the fact that he was a man of ideals as well as a man of God and a man of faith. In fact, because he was both a man of God and faith he was also a man of ideals. It could not have been otherwise. Because of these ideals Noah did not succumb to the evils of his circumstances. He was a man in the best sense of that term. He was a man's man because he was God's man.

To say that a man is rich or clever or popular is not necessarily saying that he is good, for a man may be great without being good.

"When Professor Joad, the English philosopher, was conversing with a certain Indian sage, Joad happened to say something in praise of one of the technical marvels of our generation. 'Yes,' replied the sage, 'you can fly through the air like birds and swim in the sea like fishes, but how to walk upon the earth as man you do not yet know!'

"Nor do we. The truth is that the black ruins of Coventry, Cologne and Milan; the staccato of machine guns, the roar of bursting bombs and the cries of innocent children—these are but the symptoms and symbols, the accents and accompaniments of the failure of men. Human ingenuity, unillumined by the wisdom of God, has managed to make a neighborhood of our world. But a neighborhood without brotherhood is hell. Man has failed—let no one deny it."

Our individual circumstances may be different from Noah's in both their details and extent, but they are just as real and can be just as threatening to our peace and happiness and they are none the less conquerable. Noah was not a superman. His superiority came because of qualities that are available to every one of us. He was simple enough and humble enough to trust God. He became good enough and strong enough to live above the popular tempo of life.

Yes, the Bible is full of people and Noah is one of them and perhaps he will furnish just the example your life needs.

# 2
# *Abraham*
## *The Conquest of the Unknown*

ABRAHAM IS THE Bible's first great pioneer. He represents the spirit of adventure, not under the stimulus of ambition so much as under the guidance and direction of God. He fulfilled the purposes of God. He lent his life to God's plans and did not live for the selfish accumulation of things.

Abraham was also a builder. He follows, in the history of the Bible, the names of those who attempted to build a vast human kingdom without God, but Abraham became a builder with God.

Abraham was what we call a visionary; not an impractical one, but one whose visions were more than dreams of hope. In league with God he could hear God talk to him. He heard God speak out under the stars. While still in his home city of Ur he heard God speak to him. These experiences were the foundation of his future. He heard God say this: "Get thee out of thy country, and from thy kindred, and from thy father's house, unto a land that I will show thee: And I will make of thee a great nation, and I will bless them that bless thee, and curse him that curseth thee: and in thee shall all families of the earth be blessed" (Gen. 12:1-3).

This was the basis and beginning of Abraham's pioneering. It was the beginning also of his goodness, his greatness and his usefulness. Such a beginning, similar but not identical, must be true of us if we are to live usefully and profitably. An experience with God is an appointment with destiny. It is the crossroads at which we change our direction of life.

The basis of this experience was faith. Abraham's life and experience sets forth the Bible's most important truth, namely, justification by faith. It is said that "he believed in the Lord; and he [God] counted it to him for righteousness" (Gen. 15:6).

Abraham in his experience also proves the practical present benefits of godliness. If justification by faith may seem to some as an indefinite thing, holding only some future hope then let us remember that the beginning of that future is right now. Abraham began at once to reap the benefits of righteousness and godliness. It began in a law of life that brought him prosperity, peace, happiness and success.

His life is the living example of the Bible truth that "Godliness is profitable unto all things, having promise of the life that now is, and of that which is to come" (1 Tim. 4:8). People think of godliness as some kind of religious credit on which they will cash in when they die. The Bible says that godliness has "promise of the life that now is." It is for life as well as death. In fact, its most important phase is right now, for life is always the preparation for death.

Abraham proves to us that we do not need to scheme and lie and cheat and be selfish to get along in life. Remember what happened when a crisis arose between Abraham's herdsmen and those of his nephew Lot. There was difficulty because their respective herds were overrunning their grazing grounds whereupon Abraham said to Lot, "Let there be no strife, I pray thee, between me and thee, and between my herdmen and thy herdmen; for we be brethren. Is not the whole land before thee? Separate thyself, I pray thee, from me: if thou wilt take the left hand, then I will go to the right; or if thou depart to the right hand, then I will go to the left" (Gen. 13:8, 9). The end was that Lot chose the choicest land and left Abraham the poorest. But, Abraham did not lose by the result for far more than material results were involved. While "Lot pitched his tent toward Sodom" Abraham built an altar unto the Lord. Because of Lot's material concern we have two different results. Lot lost everything he had in the subsequent destruction of Sodom. But not Abraham, his treasures and pleasures were not linked with Sodom's sin; they were linked with God and Abraham proved that the Scriptures are right when they say, "Godliness with contentment is great gain."

Abraham's plea for peace, harmony and co-operation was based upon a single reason— "for we be brethren." It was not fitting that brethren should quarrel and compete with each other. Here is the basis for all disputes. Where brotherhood exists it should preclude all dissension. Brotherhood is not something which is created by our desires or imaginations. There is a sense in which the whole human race is a brotherhood and because of that fact we should live like a family. This is the brotherhood of the flesh and it has not as yet been able to establish peace and harmony. People and races take advantage of each other just as Lot did of Abraham. When we realize the new brotherhood of the Spirit, based on justification by faith, as Abraham did, then we will live like brethren. The formula "for we be brethren" will become the basis of all human relations in the home, in the church, in the bank, in the factory and in the world.

Abraham is the Bible's example of a man who conquers the unknown. He "went out, not knowing whither he went." How was it possible for Abraham to make a conquest of all the uncertain and unknown things of life?

In the first place, Abraham conquered the unknown by making sure of the known. Everything that concerned his life was considered. He was a man of honesty and industry. He was a man of sincerity and earnestness. Every known factor of life was dealt with. He left nothing undone.

Most important of all, Abraham took God into his calculations. He knew that God knew the unknown, the unseen and the future.

Abraham is known to us particularly as a man of faith. It is interesting to notice what faith meant to Abraham.

### 1. Faith Meant Obedience

"By faith Abraham, when he was called to go out into a place which he should after receive for an inheritance, obeyed" (Heb. 11:8).

Faith may either be a feeling or a force. As a feeling it is worthless. As a force it is the power of God released in life. On the other hand, the feeling of faith may be proper in the sense that it is a conviction. It is the conviction that God will perform what He has promised. However, the conviction is useless until we act on it. In Abraham's case he might have been convinced about the new land and its new life but until he got up and acted on his convictions and went into the new land it would do him little good. He must obey as well as trust.

### 2. Faith Meant a Future

"By faith he sojourned in the land of promise, as in a strange country, dwelling in tabernacles . . . for he looked for a city which hath foundations whose builder and maker is God" (Heb. 11:9-10).

The end of faith was not death for it reached to the other side of death. It gave life permanence and perpetuity.

Besides, the future was secured in the present for Abraham, at the time of God's promise, was without an heir and without an heir the future was meaningless. So "through faith Sarah herself received strength to conceive seed, and was delivered of a child when she was past age, because she judged him faithful who had promised. Therefore sprang there even of one, and him as good as dead, so many as the stars of the sky in multitude, and as the sand which is by the sea shore innumerable" (Heb. 11:11, 12).

Faith realized much in the present but it would realize more in the future. So far as Abraham's posterity was concerned they "all died in faith." They did not see all the promises fulfilled in their day but they did receive their benefits ultimately.

Christian experience is a present blessing. It offers much now but at its best and brightest it is even then incomplete as a present thing. It is God's downpayment which He will pay in full in the end. Much may be our share now, but more is coming. Abraham's faith took him into a new land, but that was only the beginning. Little did Abraham dream of the blessings which later came to that land in the days of the theocracy and which are still to come. Think of what Abraham would find now if he could pay a visit to Palestine. It is now a land of fine cities and great agricultural colonies. The cities produced $120,000,000 in products and the colonies 200,000 tons of grain and 200,000 tons of oranges in a recent year. More than most people realize or care to know, this land holds the hope of the world. The individual hope of the men and women of the world must go back to a cross on one of its hills where peace was made by the blood of that cross. The collective hope resides in the promises of things yet to be which center around this land.

### 3. Faith Meant God at Work

The moment Abraham exercised faith God began to work in his life. He did not always realize it, or perhaps see it, but the operation went on none the less. Eventually, however, the presence of God would become evident. We will see His footprints wherever He has been."

"Father," said Thomas, looking up from his studies; "how do you know that there is a God?"

"Why do you ask that question?" asked the father. "Do you doubt the existence of God?"

"Well," replied the boy, "I heard one of the professors say that we could not be sure there is a God. Is there any way really to know?"

"Do you remember, my boy, the other day that you were laughing about Robinson Crusoe's dismay at discovering that there were other persons on the island beside himself? How did he discover them? Did he see them? No; he saw one track of a bare foot in the sand, and he knew that it could not be his own. He knew that whoever made it could not be far off, for the tide had not reached it. All these things he knew to be true, although he had not seen the human being; and the knowledge was all gained from a mark in the sand.

"If one print of a bare foot in the sand is absolute proof of the existence and presence of a human being, what are we to suppose when we see the prints of the Master's shoes, as Bunyan calls it, covering the whole wide world? We see on mountain and valley the prints of the fingers of God. We see a million plants, and flowers, and trees, that only God could make grow. We see all the rivers and the springs of the world fed from the sky. We see a great universe, perfectly made and ordered, from the tiniest speck to the greatest of all the worlds. What do all these things mean— these millions upon millions of footprints on the clay of the world? They mean God, living, present, ruling and loving. They mean God, and nothing else."

To just what extent may one meet himself in this man Abraham? Perhaps not in all the details of experience. Perhaps not in the stature of his greatness and goodness, but I do think in this one thing that pertained to practically all his life. He was a pioneer. He went out "he knew not whither." Daily life is a constant pioneering.

Each morning of each day begins a brand new experience. We go out we know not whither. We begin something new. We enter a new land. We are like the Israelites to whom Joshua spoke as they prepared to enter their new land Canaan—"Ye have not passed this way heretofore." Every day of life is like that. We must walk a new road. Of course, there is a certain degree in which each day resembles every other day. It is the same house and the same duties and the same sickness, but with all this sameness there is a difference, for each day has the possibility of the greatest changes. We are pioneers every morning. Let us go forth as Abraham did, with faith, and we will find the way will open up before us.

> Listen to the exhortation of the dawn!
> Look to this day!
> For it is life, the very life of life.
> In its brief course lie all the verities
>     and realities of your existence:
> The bliss of growth,
> The glory of action,
> The splendor of beauty.
>
> For yesterday is but a dream,
> And tomorrow is only a vision;
> But today well lived makes every yesterday
>     a dream of happiness,
> And every tomorrow a vision of hope.
> Look well, therefore, to this day!
> Such is the salutation of the dawn.

Every time we undertake a new job or a new task we go forth we know not whither. Potential failure or success lies in each new mission. To anyone who really cares these things will be done with sincerity and conscience. The potential is always there—to fail or succeed. Abraham succeeded because he went forth in faith—a faith which set God working in his life. This will be the secret of our success.

Life itself in all its ramifications is a going forth we know not whither. It is long or short. It is here or there. It is children or no children. It is money or no money. It is health or sickness. Between these extremes there are all the variations of experience. With all these things it is a venture and we are pioneers of life. Yet we need not treat it as an experiment for as Christians we go forth each day and each year under the guidance of the One who said, "Lo I am with you always."

# 3
# *Jacob*
## *The Conquest of Self*

ANY PERSON'S GREATEST problem is himself. It is not his circumstances, disabilities or enemies. It lies within. Hence the conquest of self is the most important conquest of life. "He that is slow to anger is better than the mighty; and he that ruleth his spirit than he that taketh a city." This conquest of self reaches its most complete realization in that Christian who can say with the Apostle Paul, "I am crucified with Christ; nevertheless I live; yet not I, but Christ liveth in me: and the life which I now live in the flesh, I live by the faith of the Son of God, who loved me, and gave himself for me" (Gal. 2:20).

The story of the birth, life and death of Jacob deals with this conquest of self probably as no other story of the Bible does. Such a story is all the more valuable because it is a story of real life and not some artificial moral teaching. The man Jacob became was the result of coming to grips with life. His character was forged on the anvil of experience. He is not some synthetic religious person one reads about in books but never sees on the street. Jacob lived, breathed, fought and struggled in the flesh. It is possible to meet yourself in such a man as Jacob and through this meeting to find the way to the most important conquest of life—the conquest of self.

One meets many theories concerning this conquest of self. *We are told to express self* as some lovely thing of life. This is not the Bible's way, for its teaching is based on the fact that naturally we were born on the bias. The kernel of its idea of life is that man's nature is inherently wrong. This is proved by self-expression. Let any person express civilization, decency, culture and convention and it will be his normal and natural feelings without the restraints of evil. Law restrains us from acting and culture constrains us to act according to our normal selves. Wherever these are missing or ignored, man exhibits an abhorent and an evil self. Evil is born in us and when we express ourself we express what we are. This is why the world is a place of violence, unrest and evil. "From whence come wars and fightings among you? Come they not hence, even of your lusts that war in your members? Ye lust, and have not: ye kill, and desire to have, and cannot obtain: ye fight and war, . . ." (Jas. 4:1, 2).

A long time ago a great philosopher said, "The souls of emperors and cobblers are cast in the same molds. The same reason that makes us wrangle with a neighbor causes a war betwixt princes." War is just a quarrel on national or international dimensions. All these things spring from the same source—human nature.

J. Edgar Hoover, Chief of the Federal Bureau of Investigation said, "For years we have listened to some quack theorists and pseudo-psychologists who have preached that discipline and control were bad for children—that they should be left uninhibited to work out their own life patterns, their own self-discipline. But you do not acquire self-discipline if you never learn what discipline is. Neither can life's problems be worked out without experience, which can be secured only through hard knocks, or by guidance from the experience of others. Now we are reaping the harvest.

This is the result of the evil notion of self-expression. We have been sowing the wind and now we are reaping the whirlwind. We have not begun to feel the full fury of the blast, for ere the last restraints of World War II are lifted we shall undoubtedly come upon unprecedented days of evil.

The place where the correction of this should begin is in the home. Dr. Carl Yoder says:

> In a study of dominating and submissive parents' effect upon their children, it is interesting to tabulate the results as reported in first hand case studies. The children of dominating parents are reported as being courteous, obedient, interested in school, not boastful, generous, polite, self-conscious, do not talk back, have table manners, regular in school attendance, reliable, responsible and sensitive.
>
> The children of submissive parents are disobedient, irresponsible, have food fads, cannot express themselves effectively, have poor table manners, lack interest in school, are classroom nuisances, frequently late, lazy, selfish, stubborn, sulky and defy authority.
>
> Here is a revelation and a clear call for parents to accept the responsibility and exert authority for the proper training of the child.

All of this points to a single solution—the conquest of self.

*Then we are told to suppress self.* If self is essentially evil the thing to do is to keep it under. This is a sort of sit-on-the-lid philosophy. If there is something evil inside sit-on-the-lid and keep it from getting outside.

Jesus said something about what was wrong with self, "For out of the heart proceed evil thoughts, murders, adulteries, fornications, thefts, false witness, blasphemies; these are the things which defile a man" (Matt. 15:19, 20).

Paul said something about what was wrong with self, "Now the works of the flesh are manifest, which are these: Adultery, fornication, uncleanness, lasciviousness, idolatry, witchcraft, hatred, variance, emulations, wrath, strife, seditions, heresies, envyings, murders, drunkenness, revellings and such like . . ." (Gal. 5:19-21).

It is just as ineffectual as it is to express it. If you try to suppress steam in a boiler you will have a destructive explosion. In the same way people have tried to suppress their emotions and feelings; they have carried their grief and troubles within; they have brooded over wrongs with the result that there was a nervous collapse and a spiritual explosion and they went to pieces. Following this there was deep spiritual despondency and discouragement. They were tempted to no longer believe in Christ and the Bible's way of life.

The secret of the conquest of self is twofold. First, we must realize that there is an old self and a new self. The old self is what we were according to our first birth. It is evil and tends to wrong. The new self is what we are according to our second birth. It is righteous and holy and tends to good. The secret of conquering self is neither expressing nor suppressing self. It is in supplanting it. It is by supplanting the old with the new.

This is what the Scriptures say, "Knowing this, that our old man is crucified with him, that the body of sin might be destroyed, that henceforth we should not serve sin. For he that is dead is freed from sin. Now if we be dead with Christ, we believe that we shall also live with him: Knowing that Christ being raised from the dead dieth no more; death hath no more dominion over him. For in that he died, he died unto sin once: but in that he liveth, he liveth unto God. Likewise reckon ye also yourselves to be dead unto sin, but alive unto God through Jesus Christ our Lord. Let not sin therefore reign in your mortal body, that ye should obey it in the lusts thereof. Neither yield ye your members as instruments of unrighteousness unto sin; but yield yourselves unto God, as those that are alive from the dead, and your members as instruments of righteousness unto God" (Rom. 6:6-13).

The thing that is revealed here is that there can be two yieldings of self. We can either yield ourselves to unrighteousness or we can yield to righteousness. We can follow the lower nature or we can follow the higher nature. We can express self or we can express Christ. The way to keep from the expression of self is the supplanting of self-expression with Christ-expression.

How can this be done? Perhaps a very simple suggestion along this line can be the most effective thing we can do. It is this formula: In any given circumstance in which we are to act, let one's actions be decided on this basis—not what shall I do but what would Christ do. Decide and determine to express Him and not yourself.

It is true that something must be done about self. For almost two years the SS *Normandie*, later renamed the SS *Lafayette*, lay on her side in the water and mud of the Hudson river. While she was being refitted from a luxury liner to a troop transport fire broke out which resulted in her capsizing and sinking. Here she lay all those months utterly helpless and useless. Navy salvage experts went to work to raise her giant hulk from the water and refloat her for use. It was a stupendous task. Before she could float again they had to first get rid of the dead weight of water which filled the inside of her. To lift her by main force would have been impossible, but if they could remove the water within she would refloat herself in the water without. Hence every hole and opening in her giant frame was sealed tight. Everything above the main promenade deck had to be removed, including two masts, two complete decks and three funnels each big enough to accommodate both tubes of the Hudson tunnel. This meant that a total of 5000 tons of superstructure had to be taken off the ship along with 6000 tons of debris, 11,000 cubic yards of mud, 8000 pounds of broken glass and 100,000 tons of water. All of this dead weight had to be removed before the *Normandie* could float.

It is the same with us. There is the dead weight accumulated through self that so cumbers and clutters up our lives that we are actually sunk. We are so cluttered up with our petty activities and selfish motives that we are unfit for the bigger and better life that awaits us. This dead weight must be removed.

Jesus said, "If any man will come after me, let him deny himself, and take up his cross, and follow me" (Matt. 16:24). Self must be denied.

Paul said, "I am crucified with Christ: nevertheless I live, yet not I, but Christ liveth in me . . ." Self must be crucified.

However, denying and crucifying self is only part of the conquest. So far it is negative.

A recent book on World War II in the Mediterranean area gives the secret of the success of General Sir Bernard Montgomery as his determination not to be attacked, but to be himself the attacker. The author tells of the newly arrived general, in his swift survey of the field conditions, coming across a group of British soldiers busily digging trenches behind El Alamein, at the time when the British Eighth Army was on its knees. "What are you doing?" he brusquely asked. "Building defenses, sir," replied one of the men. "Then stop it," Montgomery ordered; "you'll never need them."

It is a secret of success also in Christian warfare. The person who keeps looking at his difficulties and his weaknesses, and examining his inner life's needs, will be kept doing so by the shrewd working of the crafty foes with whom we have to deal. The way of victory is to don the whole armor of God, and to realize that it is sufficient to keep the heart and being in the mind of conflict; then, using the shield of faith to ward off the enemy's accusations, and the sword of the Spirit to assail his positions, to move forward with praise and thanksgiving to the appropriation of the fullness and the holiness of Jesus. A positive Christian life based on the truth of the Word of God cannot be overthrown.

When Paul said, "I am crucified with Christ," he also said, "nevertheless I live." When he said that he was living he also said, "yet not I, but Christ liveth in me." When he said that he was living in the flesh he also said "by the faith of the Son of God." Here is the secret of the conquest of self. It is Christ's self instead of our own self. It is a new self instead of an old self.

This is not possible for us alone. Christianity is not merely a better human life; it is a new life. It depends on us to the extent that we follow and deny and yield and surrender. Paul said, "I can do all things through Christ which strengtheneth me." And He strengthens us through the Holy Spirit. When the Holy Spirit controls and commands there will be the fruit of the Spirit instead of the works of the flesh. The fruit of the Spirit is "love, joy, peace, longsuffering, gentleness, goodness, faith, meekness and temperance."

All of this is a rather lengthy introduction to an examination of Jacob the man who conquered self, but it is more than an introduction, it is the foundation of a new experience in life. It is the New Testament explanation of an Old Testament experience. It is the way we may live.

Jacob was born a twin. In that respect he may be unlike you, but it was around this twin brother of his that the drama of Jacob's life revolved. For instance, very early in life he gained an advantage over Esau through his purchase of Esau's birthright. This was not altogether because Jacob took advantage of his brother's misfortune, but because of Esau's deficient character and materialistic principles. While this is true it was not necessary for Jacob to employ any unworthy methods to obtain the birthright, for it was something which had already been granted him by God, even though Esau was the elder, for at their birth this prophecy was made concerning these twins: "And the Lord said unto her [Rebekah], Two nations are in thy womb, and two manner of people shall be separated from thy bowels; and the one people shall be stronger than the other people; and the elder shall serve the younger" (Gen. 25:23). This meant Jacob's ascendency over Esau. That which was given by divine right did not need to be achieved by human scheming.

Perhaps you will meet yourself in Jacob. The Christian is a child of God. This is so in a very definite sense. As such a child he is a member of a divine family and a heavenly kingdom. This means he has certain rights and privileges. They are God-given and are found in the promises of the Bible. As such a child with such promises the Christian has access to all the things he needs for life. The danger is that he may substitute a false kind of works for the right kind of faith. He may try to achieve these blessings by scheming like Jacob did when that which he seeks is his by divine grant.

Many times people make bargains with God to obtain God's favor. They try to buy their blessings when they have them already in the principle of faith. A common instance of this kind is the thought many people have when they go to church. This is supposed by them to be some virtue exchanged for God's blessing. If they go to church on Sunday, or perhaps on Easter, God will bless them through the week. But, going to church is not a religious bargain you make with God. Going to church is something which is primarily done for God and not for us. In the right sense worship is an act of reverence to God. We go to pay our vows. We go to commune with God. We go to honor Him. If we go because we think it will influence God to bless us then we have missed its meaning altogether. Here is the way the Psalmist put it, "One thing have I desired of the Lord, that will I seek after; that I may dwell in the house of the Lord all the days of my life, to behold the beauty of the Lord, and to inquire in his temple" (27:4).

Another form of this bargaining with God is found in some people who say to God that if He will answer their prayers they will not do or will do certain things. There may be a legitimate form of this when a person takes a definite step in life covenanting to do a certain thing, but generally speaking, it is bargaining. Prayer is never promised to be answered because we do certain things. It is true that "If ye abide in me and my words abide in you, ye shall ask what ye will, and it shall be done unto you." But, it is also true that prayer is to be based on God's will and God's will is the paramount consideration. You cannot imagine God placing Himself in the cheap place of a bargainer. We would want to do what He wants us to do regardless of the consideration. We should want goodness for the sake of goodness regardless of what bargain we make with God.

Another form of this bargaining is tithing. Many people give one tenth of their income, not so much from the principle which is involved as for the consideration which they expect to get. They do it because they expect God to bless them for it. On this basis it is a bargain.

We are to remember what Jacob forgot—that the blessings of life are on the basis of grace. They are ours by right of faith and because of birth and our membership in God's family and citizenship in God's kingdom. We do not need to scheme and bargain with God.

All this must not be construed in the wrong way. There are rights to respect and divine laws to observe. We are not so independent of obligations that we can do as we please and expect what we want. Remember Jacob and do not be a schemer.

An even more flagrant example of Jacob's scheming came a bit later in his dealings with Esau when he deceived his father into believing he was his brother and thus received Isaac's blessing. Once more his scheming was an unworthy effort to get by bargaining what God had already given him by promise.

This was immediately followed by experiences which gave Jacob the conquest of self. One was a *dream* and the other was a *struggle*. The dream was so beautiful that it has become immortal in literature. What the best men of the past had not seen this fraudulent youth beholds. Heaven is opened to his sight and the home of the Eternal is brought nigh. From earth to sky there stretches a great ladder and on its steps ascend and descend the angels of God. Now, the question we ask is this, Why did God give such a vision to such a man as Jacob? Are not our dreams the product of our past? Does Jacob the schemer become Jacob the dreamer in a moment? How can we account for this? The answer is that Jacob's dream was the great change in his life that began with his birthright. All of this lay dormant until now when it burst forth in his dream. It was a dream that was to be fulfilled by his patriarchal priesthood, but more still, it was a dream that was to be fulfilled finally and completely in Jesus Christ. Jacob's dream at Bethel was not an accident: it was the result of God's call to him. What Jacob saw under the stars he had seen in his own heart.

Life has various aspects and many mysteries but it also has its causes and effects. There is a place for dreams and visions— not the idle kind that we use as an escape from responsibility, nor the bad kind that comes from unwise eating. There is the dreaming of faith in place of Jacob's scheming of the flesh. The schemer had become the dreamer. He had now established communion with God and out of that deep personal spiritual experience came this vision of his life's place and labor. Anyone who proposes to take his place in life must have what Jacob had: not a fantastic vision but a well-founded revelation of God's will and plan. "Where there is no vision the people perish" and where there are no visions there is nothing done.

Before Jacob can materialize his dream and fulfill his vision he needs preparation. After Bethel comes Peniel. After the dream comes the struggle. Self must be conquered before life can be at its best. It takes more than a vision to make a great and useful life. It takes power and power requires preparation. The preparation of Jacob came at a place called Peniel. Peniel came because of a crisis. Jacob had to meet Esau on the morrow and he was afraid. Esau had a score to settle and Jacob, a debt to pay, and in preparation for what he feared was coming, he turned to God. The story reads like this:

"And Jacob was left alone; and there wrestled a man with him until the breaking of the day. And when he saw that he prevailed not against him, he touched the hollow of his thigh; and the hollow of Jacob's thigh was out of joint, as he wrestled with him. And he said, Let me go, for the day breaketh. And he said, I will not let thee go, except thou bless me. And he said unto him, What is thy name? And he said, Jacob. And he said, Thy name shall be called no more Jacob, but Israel: for as a prince hast thou power with God and with men, and hast prevailed. And Jacob asked him, and said, Tell me, I pray thee, thy name. And he said, Wherefore is it that thou dost ask after my name? And he blessed him there. And Jacob called the name of the place Peniel: for I have seen God face to face, and my life is preserved. And as he passed over Penuel the sun rose upon him, and he halted upon his thigh Therefore the children of Israel eat not of the sinew which shrank which is upon the honow of the thigh, unto this day: because he touched the hollow of Jacob's thigh in the sinew that shrank" (Gen. 32:24-32) .

Legend tells us that Jacob was a man of supernatural strength. God had caused the dew of the resurrection to drop upon him and his physical strength was so great that even in this combat with an angel he was victorious until touched in the thigh. However this may have been, there is considerable reason to believe it is true, for it is evident that Jacob was a determined and strong man. Up to this point his determination and strength were always self-centered. Jacob was ambitious for himself. He was not master of himself but was mastered by his desires, ambitions and plans. In these he employed unscrupulous and cunning methods. Now he faces himself and comes to the turning point of his career.

What happened to Jacob as he wrestled is a picture of God's dealings with His children today. Are we faced with some difficult problem? Are we opposed by some apparently insuperable obstacle? Are we at our wits' end in view of some terrible need? Jacob was, for on the morrow he must meet Esau. His method of meeting this crisis was appeasement. He tried to appease Esau with presents. This is what we read of Jacob's attempted appeasement of Esau:

"And he lodged there that same night; and took of that which came to his hand a present for Esau his brother; . . . and he delivered them into the hand of his servants, every drove by themselves; and said unto his servants, Pass over before me, and put a space betwixt drove and drove. And he commanded the foremost, saying, When Esau my brother meeteth thee, and asketh thee, saying, Whose art thou? and whither goest thou? and whose are these before thee? Then thou shalt say, They be thy servant Jacob's; it is a present sent unto my lord Esau; and, behold, also he is behind us . . . For he said, I will appease him with the present that goeth before me, and afterward I will see his face; peradventure he will accept of me . . . So went the present over before him; and himself lodged that night in the company" (Gen. 32:13-21).

This policy of appeasement failed; it always does. The League of Nations appeased Mussolini concerning Ethiopia and it was the beginning of the reign of terror by the dictators. Chamberlain appeased Hitler at Munich and it was the beginning, not of peace in our time, but of the world's bloodiest war. The United States appeased Japan by sending oil and scrap iron, thus permitting him to arm herself against us, to slaughter the Chinese and to perpetrate Pearl Harbor.

We appease our habits by a few indulgences and find that this appeasement leads to more complete slavery. We appease our enemies with various means only to find they grow stronger and more antagonistic. We appease self with pity and indulgence and find that we become more selfish. Self must be conquered, not appeased. It must be put under the control of God. Hence, before Jacob met Esau he needed first to meet God. At the end of that day we find him alone, yet not alone, for "there wrestled a man with him."

There comes a time in every life when it must be alone— alone only with God and away from the world. Here only can one find a correct judgment of his life and a true picture of his needs. Here one becomes conscious of the crisis and aware of the consequences. Here one sees, as Jacob must have seen, how futile is all his selfish planning, scheming, cunning and appeasing. Here one gets a true idea of how helpless he is without God.

In this aloneness "there wrestled a man with him." For once Jacob was not the aggressor, but the defender. Jacob did not wrestle with this man, the man wrestled with Jacob. Jacob was not seeking something from this antagonism, the antagonist was seeking something from Jacob. It was an endeavor upon God's part to bring Jacob to an end of himself. Before Jacob can become the great man God intended him to be, self must be conquered; the old nature must be put under the dominion of the new nature; God must be first and Jacob last; scheming and conniving must go out and the power of righteousness and faith must come in. This is the meaning of the wrestling; Jacob must be mastered.

Perhaps at first Jacob did not know just who his antagonist was. Perhaps he thought him to be an emissary of Esau. Perhaps even he thought he was Esau. At any rate he exerted all the resources of his great personal strength. Considering all that was involved he struggled with great tenacity so that hour after hour the contest lay in the balance. Here was no coward, no weakling no craven hypocrite. As much as we admire his courage we must recognize that it was misdirected. He was resisting God. He was preventing the conquest of self and the ascending of a new and greater strength in his life.

W. H. Griffith Thomas has recorded a similarity between Jacob and many of us today in *The Devotional Commentary on Genesis*.* He presents it in these words: "We do not realize that all these untoward circumstances, these perplexities, these sorrows, are part of the divine discipline and intended to bring us to the end of ourselves. Thus we struggle, strive, fight, and resist, all to no purpose. God had been trying to get Jacob to trust Him all these years. He met him at Bethel with vision and promises, yet how poor was the response. He met him again during those years in Haran, using disappointment and opposition to lead to trust, but with little or no effect. Now comes the

---

* Republished in 1988 as *Genesis: A Devotional Commentary* by Kregel Publications, Grand Rapids, MI.

crowning attempt to break down this man's self-confidence and to lead him to lean, to trust and to wait on his Covenant God."

What, you ask, is wrong with self-confidence? Must one always be depreciating himself? There is a right and a wrong kind of self-confidence. The wrong kind was Jacob's kind before Peniel It was his trust in his cunning, selfish, ambitious self. It was his trust and confidence in a self that was not conquered and mastered by God. The right kind of self-confidence says with Paul, "I can . . . through Christ." It is confidence in my self that comes when "I am crucified with Christ, nevertheless I live, yet not I but Christ liveth in me and the life that I now live in the flesh I live by the faith of the Son of God who loved me and gave himself for me." Jacob, whom God was endeavoring to prepare for a great and wonderful place, was endeavoring to do it on the basis of the old self within him and the old world without him.

At last Jacob became aware of what is taking place. He realizes the divine nature of his antagonist. Strong measures must be employed to make him realize this. God touches him in the secret of his strength. A wrestler's great strength is in the muscles of the thigh and touching the nerve that controls these muscles Jacob is made lame and incapable of further struggle. He has now come to the end of himself and when he does he seeks the beginning of God and a new self, for he says, "I will not let thee go, except thou bless me." Now a new day dawns for Jacob. All the scheming and conniving, all the seeking and striving of the past is over. He sees a new beginning. He sees a better way. He is conscious of the futility of all his own selfish efforts and he clings to God for His supreme and lasting blessing.

The cost of such an awakening was very great. Had Jacob learned it sooner he would have saved himself the tremendous price that his attempted appeasement of Esau cost him. He would have saved himself the handicap of being a cripple the rest of his life. "What he struggled for he lost; what he trusted for he gained."

With this experienced Jacob received God's blessing. That blessing meant more than an emotional delight. It lasted longer than one sweet moment. It touched his whole life for all his life.

*It meant a new self.* Henceforth there was a new identity for Jacob. Instead of Jacob the supplanter, it is Israel God's prince. "He became a mighty prince when he had been brought to know himself as a weak man." Instead of merely being Isaac's son he was now linked with God's purpose. Instead of flight from the consequences of his own deeds it was progress and blessing in the will of God. All of this and more is what Jacob's new name meant.

*It also meant a new power,* "for as a prince hast thou power with God and with men and hast prevailed" which means that since he has power with God he shall now prevail with men. God's power was for Jacob's new life. Instead of dependence upon his own cunning to advance himself he was now supported by the mighty power of God. All of the resources of heaven were behind him. How like this is its New Testament counterpart "Ye shall receive power after that the Holy Spirit is come upon you" (Acts 1:8). It means God in the life.

*It likewise meant a new name.* "And Jacob called the name of the place Peniel; for I have seen God face to face, and my life is preserved" (Gen. 32:30).

*All this meant a new fellowship.* It was fellowship on the basis of a transformed character. Now face answered to face and heart beat with heart as Israel walked with God through life. Now there is insight and foresight, calm courage, patience and power. Now he is more than conqueror over every foe.

## SHOW ME THY FACE—

> Show me thy face—
> One transient gleam
> Of loveliness divine
> And I shall never think or dream
> Of other love save thine.
> All lesser light will darken quite,
> All lower glories wane;
> The beautiful of earth will scarce
> Seem beautiful again.
>
> Show me thy face—
> My faith and love
> Shall henceforth fixed be,
> And nothing here have power to move
> My soul's serenity.
> My life shall seem a trance, a dream,
> And all I feel and see
> Illusive, visionary—thou
> The one reality.
>
> Show me thy face—
> I shall forget
> The weary days of yore;
> The fretting ghosts of vain regret
> Shall haunt my soul no more;
> All doubts and fears for future years
> In quiet rest subside,
> And naught but blest content and calm
> Within my breast reside.
>
> Show me thy face—
> The heaviest cross
> Will then seem light to bear;
> There win be gain in every loss,
> And peace with every care.

With such light feet
The years will fleet,
Life seem as brief as blest,
Till I have laid my burden down
And entered into rest.

Show me thy face—
And I shall be
In heart and mind renewed;
With wisdom, grace, and energy
To work thy work endued.
Shine clear, though pale,
Behind the veil
Until, the veil removed,
In perfect glory I behold
The Face that I have loved.

—Selected

One more thing remains to be said about this remarkable incident of the conquest of self. Jacob came to Peniel alone; he went away with God. Jacob came to Peniel in the night; he went away with the sunshine upon him for it reads, "And as he passed over Peniel the sun rose upon him" (Gen. 32:31). Surrender brought sunrise and sunrise meant a new day. No longer was it to be struggling in the dark, but rather walking, working, singing in the light.

One of the strangest and perhaps most puzzling things about this incident is said almost at the end of it— "And he halted upon his thigh." Jacob went away from Peniel a lifelong cripple. Paul's thorn and Jacob's lameness are akin. Both meant God's power. Both men were greater with their liabilities than without them.

Peniel preaches to each of us. We can be greater than our difficulties. We can be greater than our handicaps. We can be greater than our limitations. We can be greater than our circumstances. Let self be conquered and God enthroned and this greatness will be ours.

# 4

# *Joseph*
## *The Conquest of Temptation*

JOSEPH APPEARS BEFORE us in a most normal manner. We see him in the midst of family life as one of a group of many brothers. His conquest of life is not drawn in the unnatural colors of some sort of impractical piety, but instead it begins in the most common of places, the home.

The story of Joseph's conquest of life has many profitable lessons. Among them is the outstanding fact of the unseen operation of God's providence which brings complete victory for truth and righteousness. In spite of family jealousy and imperial revenge Joseph is vindicated and his life completely justified. The providence of God overruled the evil designs and deeds of those who plotted against Joseph. This perhaps is the greatest lesson of Joseph's life and should serve to encourage us to pursue righteousness, truth, honesty and godliness as the best policy for our lives.

It seems that all through Joseph's life he was followed by the plotters of evil. It began in his own family at an early age. Here his brothers, growing jealous of their father's favorite son, planned to dispose of him so they could have their own evil way. The excuse for this was their father's favoritism, but the reason for it was their own wickedness. It seems that early in life Joseph took a stand for righteousness and refused to join his brothers in doing things they knew their father would condemn. This, of course, angered the brothers and turned them against Joseph. Naturally it made it difficult for him as it will today for anyone who will live for principle. Joseph might have appeased his brothers and remained quiet, but he was a man of high principle. This brought him into conflict with his family. This also set his brethren against him, but the deeds they designed for evil, God purposed for good. God permitted them to carry out these evil things but used them to bring Joseph to the place of mighty power. Let us believe that if we do what Joseph did God will do for us what He did for Joseph.

It is very unpopular to oppose evil. We must expect opposition instead of applause. Our rectitude makes evildoers uncomfortable. We are a constant reminder of their evil doings and therefore engender their hatred toward us.

What Joseph did, he did as a young man. We assume that folly lies with youth and virtue lies with age and experience, but that is not universally true. Here is a young man of great personal character and strength. He was willing to stand alone in the hardest place in all the world—in the midst of his own family.

Everyone of us reveals in youth what we are going to be in maturity. What we are is what we will be. There is a certain mellowing by age and maturity by experience but youth is always an accurate gauge of how high we will climb and how far we will go. It was so in Joseph's case. The prime minister of Egypt can be seen in the young man who was willing to stand against evil in his family.

There was a reason for it, of course. His family was a big factor. We must remember that this alone was not enough, for Joseph's brothers had the same training. As the same care brings one field into fruitfulness and another field into withering death so we find the opposites of life resulting from the same advantages. In Joseph's case we find faith. He yielded and surrendered to the moulding influence of God. When he dreamed the prophetic dreams of family supremacy it was a fulfillment of what had already happened in Joseph's character as well as what would happen in family history. God was at work in the young man. That is the most glorious thing that can be said of any person. Think of what might have happened in Nazareth if the people knew that God was working in the carpenter Joseph's shop! Well, He works today in human lives. The happiest discovery you can ever make is God at work in your life. What an honor? What a thrill! What a prospect!

Joseph had a dream and he had the courage to tell it to his brothers—"For, behold, we were binding sheaves in the field, and lo, my sheaf arose, and also stood upright; and behold, your sheaves stood round about and made obeisance to my sheaf" (Gen. 37:7). This could mean but one thing—Joseph's place above his brothers. They hated him for it.

Joseph had yet another dream—"For, behold, I have dreamed a dream more; and, behold, the sun and moon and the eleven stars made obeisance to me" (v. 9). The meaning was very plain. It meant Joseph's place even above his father and mother. It was too much for his jealous brethren. They hated him the more and no doubt they resolved then to do away with him.

Notice how circumstances played into the hands of Joseph's plotting brothers. Circumstances turn out for the advantage of bad men as well as good and it is not right to believe that circumstances in themselves are always right. In this instance Jacob sent Joseph to visit his brethren and report their progress. Sent on a good mission it turns out for evil, for his brothers take advantage of him and sell him into slavery.

This was the first turn of events against Joseph, but, as we shall see, Providence was quietly working for Joseph even though evil was working against him. For while his brothers thought this was Joseph's end it proved to be the beginning of his illustrious career. His captivity brought him at last to Egypt where God had designed he should go. Thus, even our enemies and their plotting can bring us to our goal. This in itself is not enough. Joseph must at all times be what God wanted in him. God was counting on Joseph just as Joseph must count on God. God needed Joseph just as Joseph needed God. This reveals the reciprocal relation which exists between God and us. Life is a partnership with God. It is a companionship. It is both privilege and responsibility.

When Joseph found himself in this adversity he suffered the greatest test of his career. The perfidious and nefarious act of his brothers in selling Joseph into slavery was an evil deed indeed. How would Joseph take it? Later when tried in Potiphar's house and sorely tempted his righteousness is seemingly rewarded with evil and he is thrown into prison because he would not sin, how did he take it?

So far as cause and effect were concerned there was no cause for this effect. Joseph had done nothing to deserve this treatment. We often find ourselves saying, what have I done to deserve this treatment? What kind of justice is it that brings sickness, suffering, betrayal, sorrow and a host of life's disappointments? That is an eternal question in life and we seem, on so many pages of the ledger of life, to be unable to balance the budget of experience.

In Joseph's case he had done nothing to deserve this kind of justice. But, it was not justice. It was not even cause and effect. It was in fact, the working of divine providence, for God was working to bring Joseph into the place of destiny, the place of his greatest usefulness.

Of course Joseph did not know this. How could he have known that he was at that moment the child of destiny being moved by the hand of God? All he could see were his captors and the evil deed of his brothers. He did not fail, however. He was true to God. His faith did not waver.

It would have been very easy for Joseph to have endured this ill treatment and this foul fate had he known it would end in the chair of the prime minister. But he did not know. He suffered as if this very experience was the end itself. It would have been easy had Job known that at the end of all his suffering he would be vindicated and his possessions would be restored twice as much as at the beginning. It would have been easy had Paul known that his thorn in the flesh was an advantage rather than a disability. It would be easy for you if you knew now that the thing you are suffering is God's means to something greater. There is no glory and no greatness in that kind of endurance. To endure and to persevere because we know what we are going to get out of our trials is not praiseworthy. Then the motive of our conduct is reward, but in the greatest of souls, like Joseph, Job and Paul, the motive was God and the experience was an evidence of pure faith and real character. And so, today, you cannot know what lies, ahead of you any more than Joseph knew that the road the slave traders of Midian were taking would lead him to the house of Potiphar and then to prison but at last to the chair of the prime minister. But, he trusted God, and you must do the same. If you cannot know whither the road of your sickness, your frustration, your disappointment or your sorrow is leading you, you can travel in trust and you can say, "I know whom I have believed, and am persuaded that he is able to keep that which I have committed unto him . . ." (2 Tim. 1:12).

Adversity, for Joseph, was not a penalty for wrongdoing or a consequence of mistakes or a trial for discipline. It was the way of Providence for the triumph of life. Faith, for Joseph, was not the belief that all will come out all right in the end; it was the knowledge that all is right now: that the very experience itself is right. In the light of this, Romans 8:28 has a new meaning. It does not mean that good is merely the end of the working together of all things; it means that the present working is good. Intrinsically it may be bad, but providentially it is good. Slavery and imprisonment are not good in themselves but in the hands of Providence they work out a good purpose and therefore are good now because the end of the purpose is for good.

In Joseph's case God did not lift him out of the valley; He exalted the valley itself. He did not remove the suffering but transformed it. In Job's case God did not stop the tornado or dry up the boils: He gave Job a faith greater than this trial and at the end a vindication and restoration worthy of that faith. In Paul's case God did not remove the thorn: He gave him grace sufficient for its pain and in the process a usefulness and greatness otherwise impossible. In your case—what? It will be no different. Life is life and God is God and faith is faith always and everywhere. Believe God and trust Him and follow the formula used by Moses of whom it is said that "he endured as seeing him who is invisible."

## HIS PLAN FOR ME

When I stand at the judgment seat of Christ,
And He shows me His plan for me,
The plan of my life as it might have been
Had He had His way, and I see

How I blocked Him here, and I checked Him there
And I would not yield my will—
Will there be grief in my Savior's eyes,
Grief though He loves me still?

He would have me rich, and I stand there poor,
Stripped of all but His grace,
While memory runs like a hunted thing,
Down the paths I cannot retrace.

Then my desolate heart will well-nigh break
With the tears that I cannot shed;
I shall cover my face with my empty hands,
I shall bow my uncrowned head.

Lord of the years that are left to me,
I give them to Thy hand;
Take me and break me, mold me to
The pattern Thou hast planned!
                              —Martha Snell Nicholson

Among the many practical lessons for life which Joseph's career teaches us is the lesson that the good way is not an easy way; the way of conspicuous success and usefulness is the way of the Cross.

The greatest of the enemies of Christianity today are not to be found in the forces opposing the church from without, but those within its ranks. The greatest threat of Christianity today is to be found in our softness, lack of discipline and our identification with the world about us. In our easy, soft, comfortable, crossless existence we are no different from the modern pagans about us. When the church fails to take up its cross it has miserably failed.

In this story of Joseph we are also reminded of the uncertainties of human life. How true it is that we know not what a day may bring forth. Joseph sent on an errand by his father, does not return to his father's home. How often there are similar occurrances amongst us. A loved one goes off in the morning and by evening he is no more. It was sudden death by a stroke or a street accident or a railroad collision or a mysterious disappearance. What of those who are left to suffer the catastrophe? Are they to live forever in the shadow that has come upon them. They must not, for their life would be continuously miserable. Nor should we borrow trouble on the strength of life's uncertainty and live each day in the dread of what may happen. "Sufficient unto the day is the evil thereof."

We are also reminded that in "seeking to defeat God's purposes we are all the while unconsciously helping in their fulfillment. These brothers of Joseph were bent on making the realization of his dream impossible, and yet by their actions they moved one step nearer the elevation of their brother" (W. M. Taylor). They were seeking their own ends and yet they were all the time contributing to bring about the purpose of God concerning their hated brother. They meant evil but God brought good. They were inspired by hatred and selfishness but divine love overruled.

The scene now shifts to Egypt. Evil was doing its worst but God was doing His best. The people change whose deeds affect Joseph but the purposes of God do not change. Good fortune follows bad fortune and then bad fortune follows good fortune, but Joseph's faith is the same in all kinds of fortune. Exalted or debased, accused or acquitted, it is all the same. Here is a stalwart stedfastness that reveals the greatness of the man and it should inspire us.

Joseph now faces the greatest test of his life. Temptation of the most enticing kind is dangled before him; but he conquers. His conquest is not because he mustered supreme faith and courage and strength in that immediate moment of temptation, but because he learned and suffered and trusted in the days before. Conquest in anything is not the triumph of the moment of battle. Its secret is in the preparation that precedes the battle.

Upon arrival in Egypt Joseph is taken to the slave market of the Capitol City by his Ismaelitish captors and put up for sale. It was no mere chance fortune or coincidence that Potiphar, captain of Pharaoh's guard came looking for a servant. To say that Potiphar was "the captain of the guards" meant that he was chief-marshal or chief of the royal police. Perhaps he was the head of the Egyptian Gestapo, a sort of Heinrich Himmler. What fate awaited Joseph in such hands? We shall see.

Upon being bought by Potiphar, Joseph began his story-book experiences in a manner that rivals the most fantastic fiction, but it was neither fiction nor fantastic. It continues on the solid base of Joseph's previous life of honesty, righteousness and faith. What Joseph was in Jacob's house, he is in Potiphar's house. What he did in Canaan, he does in Egypt. As a result we read that "the Lord was with Joseph, and he was a prosperous man" (Gen. 39:2).

These blessings and favors were not forced upon Joseph by God. Joseph was not some kind of experimental guinea pig whom God was working on. He was a rational, spiritual individual who was walking with God. Whatever blessing and prosperity or even adversity came into his life came because Joseph was willing to go all the way with God.

When Joseph saw what awaited him in Egypt; when he suffered the humiliation of being a slave and now a servant he still believed he was in the hands of Jehovah and he remained faithful and submissive. He did not squirm and complain or rebel and impugn God. He determined to accept his situation. Consequently he adjusted himself to his restricted life; he worked willingly at his tasks; he did everything that was required of him with his best skill. He soon had the confidence of his master who "left all that he had in Joseph's hands; and he knew not aught he had, save the bread which he did eat."

The almost incredible thing about this is the fact that it was happening to a man who was in adversity; he being unjustifiably wronged. God was turning his captivity into a great triumph.

We all have our captivities of one sort or another at one time or

another. Joseph's captivity was one thing, ours may be another so far
as geography and time is concerned, but the fact is that he was taken
whither he had no wish to go, and was prevented from going back
where he wanted to be. Restrictions like that are often laid upon us
by bodily illness which puts us where we do not want to be and
prevents us from being where we want to go. We become captives.
In such situations we can either surrender or struggle. We must never
submit abjectly to anything that is not honorable. Neither must we
struggle against God. Many people's struggles are not the efforts to
get well so much as the strivings of rebellion against God.

In Joseph's case he knew rebellion and struggling was useless, for
escape was impossible. He recognized something far greater—that
God was with him and that He had a purpose in this adversity.

When Paul suffered with a thorn in the flesh he did not supinely
and abjectly submit to it like a fatalist. He prayed and sought
deliverance in healing. He was persistent to the full limit of his faith
but when he reached a given point in his faith he recognized the will
of God. Even then he did not surrender to hurt feelings and begin to
complain about the injustice of a God who would permit him to be
thus afflicted. Instead, he surrendered to the will of God and said,
"Most gladly therefore will I rather glory in my infirmities, that the
power of Christ may rest upon me. Therefore I take pleasure in
infirmities, in reproaches, necessities, in persecutions, in distresses
for Christ's sake; for when I am weak, then am I strong" (2 Cor.
12:10).

If Paul was to be handicapped with bad eyes he was determined
to make that hindrance a help. With his bad eyes he wrote more
portions of the sacred scriptures than any other person whom the
Holy Spirit was pleased to use.

And so it was with Joseph. If he was to be a slave he determined
to be the best of slaves. Hence, whatever he was required to do he
did both willingly and well.

Whatever restrictions and limitations we are under let us determine
to make the best of the opportunities we have. Complaining about
what we have lost or what we are suffering never improves any
situation. Fretting only tightens the bonds that bind us.

What Joseph did was a thing of character. He acted in faith,
recognizing God's hand in his life.

Prosperity in captivity is a paradoxical expectation but that is
exactly what happened to Joseph, for it says that "he was a prosperous
man." The reason, of course, was not Joseph's circumstances, but
Joseph's character and that character was not the cultivation of a
moment's resolution. It went back to God, back to Canaan, back to
Jacob and back to the days of Joseph's youth.

Once again the scriptural principle had been fulfilled—"them that
honor me I will honor" (1 Sam. 2:30). God was remembering Joseph
because Joseph remembered God. God was making much of Joseph
because Joseph had made much of God.

Moreover, God's blessing upon Joseph came upon others for "the Lord blessed the Egyptian's house for Joseph's sake." God's blessing upon godly parents overflows to their children. His blessing upon Christian leaders extends to those who follow. There is an accumulating and overspreading compensation in godliness that we must not fail to recognize.

In Wycliffe's version of the Scriptures he translates the phrase "He was a prosperous man" to read, "He was a lucky fellow;" not lucky in the sense of being the child of blind good fortune, of course, for that kind of good fortune has no place in the life of God's children. It was not good fortune, but God's fortune. The lucky fellow is not the rich man or the free man or the healthy man, but the man of character who can say, the Lord is with me. Prosperity does not spring out of our circumstances but comes when we put life on the basis of God's presence with us.

Storms can rise upon the sea of life of even such a one whose prosperity is from God. However lucky we may presume him to be, it does not preclude the possibility of what men call ill winds and bad fortune. And so, Joseph is plunged into an embarrassing situation. All has been going well. He had arisen to be the steward of his master's house. He is a trusted and honored servant. He was young, manly and personable but these very attributes proved to be a handicap. It led to the evil desires and design of his master's wife who tried to deceive her husband and demean Joseph by enticing him into evil and sin.

Joseph's manhood was not skin deep. His character was more than a reputation. His strength was more than physical. It went back to God in his life, just as did his prosperity and peacefulness. It was more than an expedient. It was the quality of godliness in his character, therefore when tempted he answered on this wise, "But he refused, and said unto his master's wife, Behold, my master wotteth not what is with me in the house, and he hath committed all that he hath to my hand; there is none greater in this house than I; neither hath he kept back any thing from me but thee, because thou art his wife, how then can I do this great wickedness, and sin against God?" (Gen. 39:8, 9).

Thus does it describe Joseph's conquest of temptation and in it lies the hope of ours, for the lessons which it teaches belong to us for our temptations which, while not the same, are none-the-less real and important.

Temptation may be both a test and a trial. It may result from our own foolishness and realized vigilance of life or it may be providentially permitted. In Joseph's case, it was the latter, for the prison experience that followed was the springboard that landed Joseph in the prime minister's seat. The ladder that led down into the dungeon also led up to the throne.

Joseph's refusal to sin was both rational and spiritual. He refused on the ground that to do so would have been wrong in a twofold sense. First, it would have been disloyal to Potiphar who trusted Joseph. Second, it would have been unfaithful to Jehovah who also trusted Joseph. The perfect faith of the master called for the perfect faithfullness of the servant. Gratitude, trust, honor, devotion to such a master demanded, and should have, the uttermost integrity of which he was capable. Above and beyond all this, duty to God reigned supreme. Joseph "could not, and therefore would not commit this great wickedness and sin against God. To him God was first. The lessons of the home had not been forgotten in spite of all the mistreatment he had received. On the contrary, the way in which the Lord God of his father had been with him and prospered him in his servitude was an additional reason for loyalty and integrity. Thus, on the highest ground of his relation to God, he faced this temptation and won the victory" (Griffith Thomas, *Genesis*, p. 372).

Joseph conquered temptation not only because he said "No," but because he also fled from its presence. Being negative must be followed by being positive. We must not only answer; we must act. Joseph fled and found safety in putting distance between himself and his foe. It will be good for us to do the same thing. It can be conquered not only by saying "No," but also by fleeing its presence. It was such counsel that Paul gave young Timothy, "flee also youthful lusts." If we are going to get on in righteousness we must get away from the presence of unrighteousness.

Among the wholesome lessons we moderns may learn from Joseph's experience is the one that reminds us that there is peril in prosperity. It is oft-times suggested that affliction and adversity are the only experiences that have danger. This is not so, because prosperity has greater danger to our character. Many can stand the tests of adversity who cannot bear prosperity. In Joseph's prosperity lurked the peril of temptation. He was now in a favored place where he had access to much treasure and where Potiphar's evil wife had access to him. Let us treat prosperity with caution and beware of its dangers.

Another fact is this, severe temptation in one form or another may follow unusual blessing. Joseph enjoyed the unusual blessing of being lifted from a slave block to a high place in Potiphar's house, but out of his exaltation came his temptation. Privilege always brings responsibility. The greater our advantages, the greater our dangers. The valley is always at the bottom of the mountaintop. Spiritual exaltation may bring the normal reaction of emotional depression. Do not be discouraged by this depressive feeling; recognize it as the thing that often follows moments of great exaltation and in its understanding you will be sustained. Another lesson stands out. Do not temporize with temptation. Deal with it firmly. Be positive. It may be costly but it pays, for "it is better to lose a good coat than a good conscience" (Matthew Henry).

Being right does not always mean you are going to be treated right. Righteousness is not always rewarded immediately with righteousness. One may find himself suffering unjustly for having been just. What must Joseph have thought when he found himself in prison after withstanding temptation. Had God forgotten him? Did he wonder whether there was any God at all? How could such a fate be reconciled with his faith? First betrayed by his brethren and now imprisoned because he preferred honor more than evil.

Perhaps at this point Joseph wondered whether it would not have been been better had he compromised as an expedient and taken the short cut to ease and affluence. Surely, there was no immediate justice in what happened. Here he, an innocent man, was in prison while the evil temptress remained in luxury.

To be tempted to distrust God is the very height of all temptation. We see the wicked person spreading himself like a green bay tree and we ask ourselves, does it pay to be righteous. We see, so often, the innocent suffering for the guilty and the guilty one prospering in his way. Often we see the good lying in the chains of bitterness while the wicked live in peace and plenty. Seeing without believing may make us bitter and cynical but God forbid!

The answer for a situation like that is Psalm 37 which deals specifically with such a problem. It tells us, "trust in the Lord and do good." Faith and faithfulness must continue no matter what happens and regardless of who prospers. We must not judge God by what happens today; there is a tomorrow. We must not do right just because it is profitable, but because it is right.

Life is not worth living only when there is some material gain involved. "There is no profit like a good conscience, and no reward equal to the approbation of God." We must never forget that "the wages of sin is death." Speaking of this, one who had lived in sin said, "The wages of sin is death and I am glad I quit before payday."

Be not too much concerned about reputation and success. Let them look out for themselves even though they should sometimes be under a cloud. Look well to character. It is the most cherished possession of life and any life that retains integrity of character is worth living.

Just rewards do not always come in fun and at the time we think they are due, but as God is God, come they will.

Perhaps, for the moment, right may be on the scaffold and wrong may be on the throne, but God surely stands in the shadows keeping watch over His own. "Delight thyself also in the Lord; and he shall give thee the desires of thine heart. Commit thy way unto the Lord; trust also in him; and he shall bring it to pass. And he shall bring forth thy righteousness as the light, and thy judgment as the noonday. Rest in the Lord and wait patiently for him; fret not thyself because of him who prospereth in his way, because of the man who bringeth wicked devices to pass. Cease from anger, and forsake wrath; fret not thyself in any wise to do evil. For evildoers shall be cut off; but those that wait upon the Lord, they shall inherit the earth" (Ps. 37:4-9). That is the character of both a good and a great life. It is God's challenge to us.

However we may feel about the justice of Joseph's sentence to prison we can see the unerring hand of Providence in permitting this adversity. Joseph was never nearer to glory and greatness than when he was in Pharaoh's prison. Time must have languished on his mind but Joseph went more quickly to God's place for him by way of the dungeon than he could have through any other passage. According to God's method down meant up. Although Joseph might have roamed the plains and valleys of Canaan a free man for a hundred thousand years he would never have found such an opportunity of promotion as came to him in the dungeon. Yes, God's way will always prove to be the best way, the quickest and the surest way.

The circumstances that put Joseph in prison had none of the elements of justice in them. He was a victim of false accusation. He was innocent but innocence is not always recognized when slander is abroad. Potiphar's wife slandered Joseph and deliberately lied about him to save her own face and to gain revenge. Hearing what was said about Joseph it was easy to say, "Well, there must be something to it or she would not dare to say it." It is like that well-known saying one hears today, "Where there is smoke there must be fire." That is not necessarily true. Jesus was the subject of false accusation. So was Paul. In both instances there was much smoke but no fire. The smoke was created by enemies who profited when others were discredited. So it was with Joseph. Life is full of such things. It is full of injustice, full of false report and full of slander. In any case, the loser is never the one who is taken advantage of but rather the one who does the evil deed. Wickedness is its own reward both here and hereafter. Injustice may put a penalty upon the innocent. Injustice and slander may mar a reputation but it cannot touch a character. Let reputation suffer so long as character keeps its integrity.

This is precisely what Joseph did. He suffered demotion and imprisonment. His body was put under the limitations of a dungeon but his spirit was never shackled. He still retained his integrity. He still kept faith with God. He still believed that whatever this imprisonment meant it was all right, for God knew what He was doing.

This sort of attitude and spirit was promptly and justly rewarded. it was no accident that "the keeper of the prison, committed to Joseph's hand all the prisoners that were in the prison, and whatever they did there, he was the doer of it." What Joseph had been in Canaan he was in Egypt. What he had been in Jacob's house he was in Potiphar's house. What he had been as a steward he was as a prisoner. What he had done under prosperity he did under adversity. Thus in prison his faithfuless resulted in his position of responsibility. He was faithfully loyal to God under all circumstances. He was true to his convictions wherever he found himself. He never compromised. He never sacrificed a principle to gain an advantage. His spiritual vitality was amazing. His spiritual stature was magnificent.

God honored Joseph according to his worth and work. It is written, that "the Lord was with him, and that which he did, the Lord made it to prosper" (Gen. 39:23). To believe the Bible is to believe a very practical truth, namely, that God will bless and honor those who bless and honor Him.

Nothing will reveal more completely what our Christianity is worth than the way we meet our difficulties. Joseph met many difficulties. He might have sulked and soured. He might have been unbelieving and bitter. Instead, he revealed an unconquerable spirit because he trusted God. He refused to demean God by attributing any unworthiness to Him.

In prison Joseph finds himself once more in the center of providential circumstances. Among the prisoners are two former officials of Pharaoh's Court. They are troubled and disturbed about dreams which they have separately dreamed. Joseph, who practices his religion in prison as well as outside, suggests a means by which their dreams might be interpreted. He says to these dreamers of dreams, "Do not interpretations belong to God?" Forthwith the dreams are told Joseph and he tells the interpretations. They are fulfilled to the letter. One man is released and the other is executed.

What of Joseph? Are there any dreams that tell his fate? Is there any hope for his release? Humanly speaking, it rests on a very slender thread. That thread is the remembrance one has of a kindness and for a long time (for two years) it is forgotten. When the chief butler was released according to Joseph's dream interpretation he charged him thus, "But think on me when it shall be well with thee, and show kindness I pray thee, unto me, and make mention of me unto Pharaoh, and bring me out of this house; for indeed I was stolen away out of the land of the Hebrews; and here also have I done nothing that they should put me into the dungeon" (Gen. 40:14, 15).

How true it is that those whom we help often have a very poor remembrance of our kindness. We remember our grudge easily but soon forget others' favors. Done an injury we can keep it fresh for years in the vase of memory but done a benefit we let it slip through our minds with scarcely a trace of notice. Many have been the people who were like this chief butler who, enjoying the return of prosperity soon forgot the benefactor of his adversity.

There is a continuing consolation in all such treatment, namely, that there is One who does neither forget nor fail for "Jesus Christ is the same yesterday, today, and forever. He has not forgotten thee, friend, no matter in what kind of a prison you may languish. Thy friends may have forgotten. Those who have benefited by thy kindness may have forgotten. Thy family may have forgotten, but not He. Believe it and count on it.

Proof of this is found in the fact that although the butler forgot Joseph and allowed him to remain in anonymity in that dungeon, God ultimately forced circumstances upon him that brought Joseph to the notice of Pharaoh. It was a royal dream. It affected the whole nation. Nay more, it affected the people of Israel up in Canaan and what affected them affected the course of world affairs. The unerring hand of Providence reached down into the prison and brought Joseph out to sit upon a seat immediately next to Pharaoh himself, for Joseph became Prime Minister of Egypt.

What happens in the course of the years is a well-known story and does not immediately concern the object and purpose of this discussion, for our purpose is to see how Joseph conquered temptation and the results.

The results are interesting, not only as they affected the life of one man but the course of a whole nation and the destiny of a whole world, and, for us, our everyday lives for the practical lessons are priceless.

The thread of the entire story is Joseph's later interpretation of all the evil acts of others directed at him, "Ye thought evil against me, but God meant it unto good." Every evil act was providentially employed for good. That is precisely what Romans 8:28 means, "And we know that all things work together for good to them that love God, to them who are the called according to his purpose."

A coincidence is what happens. A providence is what is intended. God's intentions are revealed in the providences that surround Joseph's life. Think of the providence which brought the Ishmaelites to the spot at which his brothers were feasting at the very moment Joseph was in a pit near by. Think of the providence which brought Potiphar to the slave market at the very time Joseph was put up for sale. Think of the providence that permitted Joseph to suffer imprisonment and the presence there of two officials of Pharaoh's Court. Notice at how many crucial points Joseph's life touches the lives of others and is carried forward to the place God has prepared for him and the purpose he is to fulfill.

Every providence is like the junction point on a railroad. Here trains come from east and west, north and south, just in time to join others. The place of arrival is also the place of departure. This is no coincidence; it is an intention. It was planned that way. Thus the Divine Dispatcher of human lives on the great railroad of life directs the movement of events so that they shall come to the junction points of His will. Here contacts are made and directions are changed and life goes on to fit the pattern He has chosen. Only the "fool hath said in his heart, there is no God" (Ps. 14:1).

Here, take note, the providences of God are not the whole story. He is not directing men and events as if the world was some great plaything of the gods. We are not moved by His will against ours. The character of the individual has as much to do with these movements as the providence of God. Providence is not fatalism. Things do not happen because they have to be. Behold in Joseph how this works out.

Had Joseph chosen to act otherwise than he did at the various junction points of his life he would have thrown away all the opportunities which they afforded. For instance, had he violently resisted his brothers when they put him in the pit it might conceivably have led to his death. His patient sufferance led Reuben to seek to save his life, which he did. Joseph was sold to the Ishmaelites and brought to Egypt. If, again, in the house of Potiphar he had not determined to live and work honorably and faithfully, he would never have risen to eminence. Again, had this not been true, he would never have come to the notice of his master's wife. If, when tempted, he had not remained honorable and righteous he would never have been put in prison, all of which would have prevented him from coming to Pharaoh's notice and he would have missed the means of preparation for the great tasks of his life. Joseph's character and God's providences were joined in unity. Opportunities given to us at the crucial junctions of life must be matched by character. When we fail it is not because we have had many adversities, but because we have failed God at the time of adversity. Those who live with God and have their characters shaped by His hand will find that prisons of many kinds and adversities of every sort are but the junction points of destiny to greater and higher service.

The last lesson to be read in Joseph's life with its conquest of temptation is one already considered with more or less attention but one which bears our final consideration.

"The secret of Joseph's power was the consciousness of the presence of God. God had not forgotten him though it might seem to have been the case. The very incident that was apparently the most injurious was the link used by God to bring about his exaltation. . . . To the man who is sure that he is in the pathway of God's will there will come the consciousness of the Divine presence and blessing which will be an unspeakable comfort as he 'rests in the Lord and waits patiently for him.' God will bring forth His righteousness as the light and His dealing as the noonday! The very troubles that seem to overwhelm will prove blessings in disguise, and before long the Divine justification of His servant's faithfulness will be seen and be manifested to all men. Evil may have its temporary victories, but they are only temporary. God and right and truth must prevail and it is for the servants of God to wait quietly, to go forward humbly, to live faithfully and to trust boldly until God shall justify them by His Divine interposition, and glorify His grace in their lives" (Griffith Thomas, *Genesis*, p. 376).

# 5
# *Moses*
## *The Conquest of Inferiority*

MOSES PRESENTS THE remarkable example of a man who overcame national and personal handicaps to become his people's emancipator and the father of a great nation. There are, of course, many lessons in Moses' life but none are more striking and illuminating and helpful than this one which concerns the conquest of inferiority.

It will be found that more people suffer from inferiority than from pride and arrogance. For every one of the latter there are ten or a hundred of the former. Moreover, it is often a weak defense and refuge for people who wish to escape their legitimate duties. They cannot because they will not.

People who retire within themselves and brood over their own thoughts and seldom have counsel with others are more apt to suffer from this handicap of inferiority. They are too much in their own company. Fellowship and companionship with others are necessary. Above all, the sense of God's presence in their lives is important.

So far as Moses is concerned, he was born into an inferior race. That is, according to the judgment of the Egyptians. The Egyptian Pharaoh had deterniined to give him no chance. Along with other Hebrew slave children he was declared to be unfit to live. He was rejected by the culture of that day and with the rest of the infants consigned to death.

Pharaoh's plans were neutralized and nullified by faith. Moses' mother arrayed herself against Pharaoh's order. Faith overcame fear, even the fear of a royal edict and we read, "By faith Moses, when he was born, was hid three months of his parents, because they saw he was a proper child; and they were not afraid of the king's commandment" (Heb. 11:23).

This apparent inferiority of race was overcome through the fact that God was with them. There is no doubt that Egypt was a great nation, but the Hebrews with God were greater. Bear in mind, these Hebrews were hostages in Egypt; they were slaves and vassals; they were a conscript people; they had no subject rights and no political or social privileges. Yet God was among them and He began His movement of liberation with this man Moses—the man with the inferiority handicap. God needed someone who would trust Him and work for Him. That one was provided in a little woman by the name of Jochebed. Except for her faith in defying the king's commandment, Moses would have been an unremembered sacrifice to a nation's brutality. He lived because she believed. He lived because she dared.

Jochebed dared all this by the simple, yet sufficient instrument of faith. She was only a slave, lost in the mass of slaves in a foreign country, but she knew God. God was not handicapped for "if God be for us who can be against us?" This meant a working majority and with that in mind Jochebed hid her baby in the river.

While faith recognized the supremacy of God it must at the same time suffer the presence of the enemy. Here a mother must surrender her child. She must give him up to the principle of death for in committiag him to the river it was surrendering him to the principle of death. Faith means crucifixion but crucifixion also means resurrection. Faith means surrender but surrender also means acquisition. Faith means giving up, but giving up also means fullness once more. And so, with Jochebed's faith for Moses began the human chain of circumstances which Providence forged on the anvil of experience for one of the greatest epics of life ever recorded.

The pendulum next swings to the opposite extreme for at the climax of the succeeding course of events we see Moses the victim of overconfidence and unwise zeal. Following his rescue from the river by one of the daughters of Pharaoh he spends the years of his youth in the royal palace. Here circumstances conspire, at the hands of evil intelligence, to make him forget the inferiority of his Hebrew origin. He is educated in Egypt's culture so he may forget the traditions of his race. Wealth, advantage, position, comfort, prestige and a host of other things are all put in his way but that peculiar quality of Hebrew nationality refused to be disowned. Moses could not be made an Egyptian by assimilating him into Egyptian culture and educating him in Egyptian wisdom or initiating him into Egyptians traditions. It is impossible to gentilize the Jew. Even though he tries to change himself, he cannot. Even though he tries to forget, he cannot.

All the anti-Semitic hatred and barbarity of the present evil world with its slaughter of millions of Jews has not served its evil and diabolical purpose, for the Jew still lives. If he is fewer in number he is greater in the will to live. This is not a natural phenomenon. It goes back of humanity to deity. It goes back of the modern Jew to the Old Testament Jew. It goes back to Moses and back of Moses to Abraham to whom God said, "And I will bless them that bless thee, and curse him that curseth thee; and in thee shall all the families of the earth be blessed" (Gen. 12:3).

Through centuries of adversity, slaughter, wandering persecution, bitterness and conspiracy the Jew has survived. No matter what the method employed he has refused to become anything except a Jew. The first illustration of this we see in Moses, whose entire youth and formative years were spent under foreign care. Everything is done to make him forget who he is, whence he came and whither he is going; but it failed.

What he is, Moses reveals by what he does. Dressed in the garments of an Egyptian prince, speaking with the accent of Egyptian culture, walking with the bearing of royal training Moses sees a Hebrew being abused and beaten by an Egyptian. With the apparent loss of his identity, without perhaps, any knowledge of who he was or where he came from he rebels against this injustice and slays the Egyptian in order to save the Hebrew. This is his great awakening. However the knowledge comes to him, he is now aware of his identity, but he sees himself in the wrong light. He is the victim of an unwise zeal. He tries to do by revolution what God will do by revelation. He hopes, it is said, to start an armed resurrection and to rebel by force and to institute civil war to obtain the liberation of his people. Of course he fails because he has not chosen the right weapons with which to fight and without them he is doomed and his is a lost cause.

He has chosen force rather than faith and independence of God rather than dependence upon God. Moses must play his part; but not Moses alone. This is too big an order for this man. It takes God at the head of the column and in front of the battle.

Out of this failure comes Moses' first great lesson. From an inferior race in the Egyptian's eyes Moses makes the mistake of thinking that human supremacy will succeed. He fails and he flees. When he flees it is not the flight of a coward. He sees the futility of his deed and the folly of his plans. He also sees the whole past in retrospect and the future in prospect. If he is to succeed in his life mission he must have help and he now understands that it must be God's help. And so we read, "By faith Moses, when he was come to years, refused to be called the son of Pharaoh's daughter, choosing rather to suffer affliction with the people of God, than to enjoy the pleasures of sin for a season; esteeming the reproach of Christ greater riches than the treasures in Egypt: for he had respect unto the recompence of the reward. By faith he forsook Egypt, not fearing the wrath of the king; for he endured, as seeing him who is invisible" (Heb. 11:24-27).

This remarkable and revealing portion of Scripture tells us that Moses did three things which underline the success of any life.

## 1. He Refused

A man is said to have good common horse sense when he can say "nay." A person must learn to decline. There are elements and conditions in the world with which he dare not ally himself. Refusal is as noble as espousal when it is the rejection of that which is contrary to God's will. The time had come now for Moses to refuse any longer to have any identity with the Egypt which was enslaving and oppressing his people. Every form of injustice is being practiced upon them, including extortion, violence, insult, contempt, treachery and scorn. If Moses is to save his people he cannot save himself. He must sacrifice himself, his future, his comfort, his benefactors and his royal prestige. Was this not also necessary for Jesus Christ who was challenged to come down from the cross and save Himself? "He saved others himself he cannot save," He was mocked. He must sacrifice Himself to save us. "For ye know the grace of our Lord Jesus Christ, that, though he was rich, yet for your sakes he became poor that ye through his poverty might be right" (2 Cor. 8:9). It was in this spirit that Moses "refused to be called the son of Pharaoh's daughter."

The crossroads of decision face all at some time in life. Moses must choose between two destinies—as the son of Pharaoh's daughter or as a son of God; as a member of the royal family or as a member of the despised Hebrews; as a leader in a growing national concern or as a leader in an apparently lost cause. He must make his choice between the glitter of Egypt and the gloom of Israel. He chose and he chose well. We will see how well.

## 2. He Chose

His refusal to be "called the son of Pharaoh's daughter" was good but it was not enough. To turn his back on his past was not enough. He must be positive as well as negative. We find him "choosing rather to suffer afflictions with the people of God than to enjoy the pleasures of sin for a season; esteeming the reproach of Christ greater riches than the treasures in Egypt."

No amount of negatives will make us either good or great. No one ever became a Christian by virtue of what he did not do. No personal holiness is attained by merely saying "no" to evil. It is what we do, added to what we do not do, that makes life a living, holy, happy experience. It is "no" to the lowest and "yes" to the highest. It is "no" to sin and "yes" to righteousness. It is "no" to the bypath and "yes" to the highway. It is "no" to the low road and "yes" to the high road. It is "no" to the devil and "yes" to the Lord.

Moses' choice of faith led him contrary to the ordinary course of desire and nature. "It led him to despise all the pleasures, attractions and the honors of Pharaoh's Court. Not only that, but also to relinquish an apparently wide sphere of usefulness. Human expediency would have conducted him along quite an opposite path. It would have led him to use his influence on behalf of the people of God—to act for them instead of suffering with them. According to man's judgment, Providence would seem to have opened for Moses a wide and most important sphere of labor; and surely, if ever the hand of God was manifest in placing a man in a distinct position, it was in his case. . . . With all these circumstances in his view, to abandon his high, honorable and influential position could only be regarded as the result of a misguided zeal which no sound judgment could approve" (C. H. M.).

This is the way natural reason would look at Moses' choice when he chose affliction rather than pleasure and reproach rather than treasure. It meant giving up the highest social position in all the land. It meant giving up Egypt's pleasures. The Egypt of that day was comparable to the New York of modern life. It was the playground of the world. It meant giving up the treasures of Egypt. To say that Egypt was a land of treasure was no trite saying. It was among other things, the granary of the world. Upon it converged the sea lanes and land roads of the civilized world. Ships and caravans brought the world's commerce to its cities. It was a treasure house indeed. To all of this potential wealth, comfort, pleasure and prestige Moses said "No." In their stead he said "Yes" to affliction and reproach which meant hardship, suffering, obscurity and scorn. Did he lose or did he gain? Was it foolish or was it wise? You know the answer.

This is a good time to ask oneself what he has said "No" to and what he has said "Yes" to. Am I trying to win by only saying "No"? Am I just negative without being positive? We must be able to say "No" before we can be able to say "Yes."

### 3. He Forsook

Moses forsook Egypt. For what? A desert hideout? A shepherd's lonesome job? Forty years of stagnant life? This is what it appeared to be, but it was all a part of God's plan. You see, Moses was not ready as yet for his life's task. He must be schooled and prepared. While forty years seems like a long time, it was not the length of time that mattered but what Moses did later. Jesus spent thirty years in obscurity and only three years in ministry, but the thirty were necessary for the three, even for the Son of God. We become impatient for want of opportunity and activity not realizing that it may be our Horeb or our Nazareth. Silence does not necessarily mean the absence of God. Obscurity does not necessarily mean rejection by God. Look at Moses and encourage yourself.

Moses was well trained but he was not trained well enough. A person "might have taken out his degree in the school of man, and yet have to learn his alphabet in the school of God." The person whom God will use must be equipped with widely different qualifications than those acquired by the mind alone. These can come only from God's presence hence we find Moses at Horeb, Elijah at Cherith, Ezekiel at Chebar, Paul in Arabia and John on Patmos. Jesus was no exception, for we find Him at Nazareth for thirty years. Where have you been?

Faith was behind this refusing and choosing and forsaking of Moses. It was "by faith" that he refused and "by faith" that he chose and "by faith" that he forsook. It is interesting to notice what faith overcame. It overcame fear. It was so with Moses' mother Jochebed whose faith made her unafraid of "the king's commandment." It was so with Moses whose faith made him unafraid of "the wrath of the king." Faith gives wisdom for it is "through faith we understand." Faith gives vision for it enables us to see what the mind can neither conceive nor perceive. "But as it is written, Eye hath not seen, nor ear heard, neither have entered into the heart of man, the things which God hath prepared for them that love him. But God hath revealed them unto us by his Spirit" (1 Cor. 2:9, 10). Faith gives courage and enables us to defy human edicts and custom and wisdom. Faith gives strength, for Moses "endured as seeing him who is invisible." Faith puts true value on the things of life and makes affliction worth more than pleasure and reproach worth more than treasure.

Moses is not done with Egypt even though he forsook it. There is a task yet to perform in it but before he is ready to perform that task he must forsake it. The final readiness comes out of a notable experience at Horeb, the sight of a bush that "burned with fire" and yet was not consumed. That bush experience was the call to his great task. It was a symbol of his people, who, while in a furnace of affliction, were not consumed and destroyed by their predicament, for God was in their midst.

What Moses had failed to do by revolution, he would be able to do by revelation. What he could not accomplish by force could be done by faith.

The heart of the revelation of the burning bush was the present nature of God. He was and is the great I AM. This made faith practical. Here was a common bush uncommonly on fire. It could mean but one thing—that every common duty of every common day can claim the uncommon help and blessing of the great I AM. Moses discovered that God was not in the sanctuary alone: but in the desert as well. He discovered that God was not forever drawing a line between secular and sacred so that He would only stay in the realm of the sacred and never come over into the secular. Here was God in a bush on a desert revealing Himself to a shepherd. This was something new in divine relations. If God could make a bush blaze He could do the same with a home or a shop or a hospital or a sickroom.

The greatest test of Moses' life came now. God said, "Go, and gather the elders of Israel together, and say unto them, The Lord God of your fathers, the God of Abraham, of Isaac, and of Jacob, appeared unto me, saying, I have surely visited you, and seen that which is done to you in Egypt; and I have said, I will bring you up out of the affliction of Egypt unto the land of the Canaanites, . . . unto a land flowing with milk and honey" (Ex. 3:16, 17).

The hardest thing anyone had to do was to go back where he had failed. It was required of Moses. He had thought once to deliver his people by force and by his own hand. He is sent back now by the hand of God, but Moses is fearful. Inferiority and inability loom large and he is afraid he will fail. Fearing that he is unable and incapable of persuading the people, God provides a simple proof of ample power. He asks of Moses, "What is that in thine hand?" Moses replies, "A rod" (see Ex. 4:2). Moses under the training of God and the discipline of the desert was now at the opposite extreme of personal opinion.

The first time he tried to liberate his brethren it was in overconfidence; now he sees himself with no confidence. He is timid and diffident. He does not realize that the symbol of personal power lies in his own hand. It is a rod; a common shepherd's rod. It is the rod he used as he herded his sheep. God was prepared to take Moses as he was and to use what he had. He had a rod. What he had was what God needed and it would be enough. He can take the weakest instruments to accomplish the greatest ends. It might be, as in this case, a rod; or, as in other cases a ram's horn, a cake of barley meal, an earthen pitcher, a shepherd's sling or a needle. It is not the excellence of the instrument but the significance of its investiture. When invested with the presence and the power of God it can do wonders. Its value is in its surrender. In Moses' hand it is but a shepherd's rod; in God's hand it is a symbol of omnipotence. In Moses' hand it made him a leader of sheep; in God's hand it made him a leader of men. It is the surrender-value of little things that makes them great things. Our surrendered weakness becomes sufficient power.

One more deficiency deters Moses. He complains of not being a man of words. How like human nature these two things are; I cannot do anything and I cannot say anything. I suppose they are the most common complaints men make and the most frequent excuses men offer.

Inferiority comes from two fears:

The first is *fear of failure*. It is fear that one cannot do the things required of him. This arises from a false humility. It appears at first as if the inferior-minded person may be deeply thoughtful of his own shortcomings, but the opposite is so. It is his fear of losing self-respect. This is a false humility and springs out of unbelief. Fear of failure is taking a wrong estimate of God's promises and provisions.

Paul learned the great secret of personal success and accomplishment when he said, "I can do all things through Christ which strengtheneth me." The secret is in the strengthening Christ. This will turn diffidence to confidence, weakness to power, self-consciousness to Christ-consciousness.

The other fear which causes inferiority is *fear of man*. We are afraid of what others may say. We can be sure of one thing: there will be both praise and blame; some will approve and others disapprove. Criticism must not deter us from doing. That kind of fear is unworthy of one who walks and talks with God.

The conquest of inferiority while perhaps not a simple thing is certainly not complicated or difficult. Moses conquered his diffidence by faith and will. He believed God and acted on what he believed. One thing is certain, you will never conquer inferiority by doing nothing. You must act, not in a falsely assumed self-confidence, but in the strength and the power of Christ.

"What is in thine hand?" It matters not how simple, unattractive or insignificant it may appear. Its value is in its surrender. There was no magic in the wood fibres of Moses' rod. Cast down at the command of God it became a serpent; retrieved it became a rod once more. With it Moses parted the waters of a sea and brought water from a rock, but power does not lie in wood. There was no power in wood to provide dry land in the midst of water and water in the midst of dry land, but there was power in the God who commanded it so and when the man of the rod yielded to God and the rod yielded to the man it accomplished what otherwise could not have been done.

# 6
# Joshua
## The Conquest of Foes

JOSHUA'S PLACE IN the gallery of characters of the Bible is not won because of the great and unusual genius of the man. He is indeed a man of great achievement for it was he who, by God's hand, led the people of Israel into the promised land and conquered its foes. It was he who enabled the people to settle in their appointed places and have rest round about. However, he achieved this not so much by the genius of a brilliant strategy as by obedience. He is an example of the man who obeys orders. He became a great leader of his people because he was a faithful follower.

The Bible, like life, is full of those who aspire to be great. They want to be at the top. It is fitting that some should, but life cannot be top-heavy with leaders. Some must give orders and some must take orders. Some must lead and some must follow. Some must command and some must obey. Some must invent and some must execute. There is a place always for hewers of wood and drawers of water. Even Jesus said of Himself, "The Son of man came not to be ministered unto, but to minister, and to give his life a ransom for many" (Matt. 28:20).

Joshua appears in the long procession of Bible people as the man who glorifies duty and obedience. He represents the working man, but in a very distinctive way, for as such a man he is entrusted with great responsibility and became the conqueror of the traditional foes of his people. This would tell us that we too may meet our common life-foes; things that threaten our happiness and property and peace should be conquered by us, not as leaders or great men or geniuses, but as common men and women who have learned one supreme lesson—obedience.

Joshua is met for the first time on the pages of the Bible under significant circumstances. We meet him at a place called Rephidim. A battle is going on. Joshua is the leader of the forces of Israel. Its fortunes fluctuate. There is advance and then retreat and not until the day is ended does victory come for the Israelites. Joshua is the field commander but the secret of victory does not lie alone with him. In the leadership of this battle he is a subordinate. A battle is going on behind this battle. A spiritual conflict directs the physical combat for on the top of a hill overlooking the battlefield stands Moses before God. His hands are lifted in prayer and when they weaken Israel's forces weaken. When they are strengthened by the support of Aaron and Hur, Israel's forces triumph. Thus does Joshua learn his first great lesson at the beginning of his long and useful life. It is the lesson of obedience and submission. He recognizes the priority of the spiritual over the physical. He is taught the value of prevailing prayer. Prevailing prayer is availing prayer. It availed on the field because Moses prevailed on the mount.

Behind every one of us must be the invisible. The Amalekites saw Joshua but they did not see Moses. It was this unseen force which Moses represented and this unheard voice of prayer that swayed the battle. Moses had learned the value of the invisible for "he endured as seeing Him who is invisible."

The invisible presence brings visible results. It means that God is at work. What would otherwise require a work at great length can be done in far less time when God undertakes.

Charles Darwin, who first gave to the world the theory of evolution, was a deist. He taught that the Creator started the universe and then left it to work out its salvation through an endless process of development from lower to higher forms of life. He called it "natural selection" and "the survival of the fittest."

In his study of the development of man he went to South America where he found a race of men so low in the scale that they were little more than animals. With all the interest and thoroughness of his scientific mind, he studied these people. Their minds were those of undeveloped children; their bodies were diseased; their surroundings were beastly. According to his theory ages must pass before they could rise to the level of civilization.

Years after Darwin went again to South America to visit the aborigines in whom he had been so much interested. To his amazement he found them transformed. They were clothed and could read and write. They had schools and churches and were taking their places among the civilized peoples of the southern hemisphere.

In his journal Darwin confesses that there is something he had omitted from his calculation. *It was God.* The missionary had been there. God had touched those degraded men and women and they had been born again. What natural selection could not have done in a thousand years God had accomplished in two decades.

The next notice we have of Joshua is in connection with an important mission. He had been sent in a company of twelve men to investigate the new land upon whose borders they had come and which they were intending to occupy. The purpose of his mission was not altogether proper for it was not so much one of investigation and information as it was verification. They wanted to verify what God had said, as if His instructions could not be relied upon. If it had been for reconnaissance, to ascertain where the country had best be entered and how it could best be taken, it would have been a different matter.

The return of the mission brought conflicting reports. All admitted that it was a lush land; that it was fertile and beautiful, but a majority was against occupation because they considered the hazards and difficulties too great. They looked at God through their difficulties rather than at their difficulties through God.

However a minority which included Joshua and a companion named Caleb was sure that occupation should be attempted because it could be accomplished. They said, "Let us go up at once, and possess it; for we are well able to overcome it." They were well aware of the difficulties and had taken a full and complete estimate of the obstacles, but they believed the occupation could be and should be made. The basis of their convictions was faith for they said, "the Lord is with us; fear them not."

This report and these convictions reveal the trait in Joshua which made him such a successful campaigner against his foes. No other character in the Bible had so many battles to fight and so many foes to overcome as Joshua. He was able to do it because he had learned to obey.

Only once in Joshua's career is it recorded that he used his own judgment. That was when he made a league with the Gibeonites. They employed craft and deceit and took Joshua in and he became involved in a league that brought liim no end of grief.

This does not mean that Joshua was some kind of puppet who responded when God pulled certain strings. Joshua was a perfectly normal man. He had a mind and he used it but he did not use it independent of God. He was obedient. The reason for the Gibeonite deceit is stated in these words, "And the men [Israel] took of their [Gibeonites] victuals, and asked not counsel at the mouth of the Lord" (Jos. 9:14). Their minds were not in tune with God's mind because they acted independently of God.

When it is stated that Joshua did not use his own judgment, except in this one case, it is meant that he did not use his judgement independently of God. He was in the habit of taking counsel with the Lord. He brought himself into such harmony with God's mind that he thought God's thoughts after Him. He set His thinking according to the mind of God just as we set our watches according to the sun. If anyone became so independent as to say his watch was the only one that was right he would soon find himself out of time and out of step with everyone else. Even if he depended on other watches this would be so. He must have an authoritative source of time.

On the way to the office every day we pass at least five different clocks. We check the time with each one as a force of habit and invariably there is a difference in time between the several clocks. To trust anyone of them would bring confusion and so we trust none of them. We know they are relatively correct but not absolutely so. When we enter a radio broadcasting studio it is different. A broadcast operates by radio time, not by the clocks on the street. So we check our watch after radio time which is sun time and we are correct. Like Joshua, whoever will respect this rule for life will find himself on the right side. This world is being timed by God's central timepiece and the world is being run by God's mind, laws, principles and purposes. Find out what time it is, yes, find out what truth it is and you will be safe.

Joshua campaigned against many foes but not all were conquered in the same way. Some were taken by divine help as at Jericho, when, after marching around that city's walls, they were shaken to earth by a mighty earthquake. Some were taken only because "the Lord fought for Israel" as at Gibeon when "the sun stood still in the midst of heaven, and hasted not to go down about a whole day" (Jos. 10:13).

Some of the foes represent the foes of our flesh and some the foes of our spirit. Some represent the internal foe, some the external foe and some the infernal foe. Some we must master and some only God can master for us. Some can be defeated only by prayer and fasting and some only by bold conflict.

As with Joshua's conquest of the foe we find that the land was not conquered in a day or in a year. At the death of Joshua it is recorded that "there remaineth yet very much land to be possessed" and so it will be with our lives. The conquest is not made in a day or a year. Life is a constant battle and a never ceasing warfare, but victory will come, as it came to Joshua, by obedience.

## 1. Obedience of Faith

Once again we see the importance of faith in life; not faith as some kind of daring and adventuresome feeling but faith as the link between man and God. The two words, "by faith" and their equivalent, which are found times in the eleventh chapter of Hebrews, are the two most important words in a Christian's vocabulary. They represent the difference between omnipotence and impotence, power and weakness, success and failure.

## 2. Obedience to Conviction

A man may have faith in one sense but lack the conviction to carry it out. Conviction is assurance such as the Apostle Paul had when he said, "I know whom I have believed, and am persuaded that he is able to keep that which I have committed unto him against that day." To act in the light of that kind of conviction is to live a life of great adventure. One is not limited to the present day or the present circumstances or the present condition.

3. *Obedience to the Laws of God*

There can be no doubt of the reasonableness and importance of this obedience. All life, whether physical or spiritual, is regulated by law. The world exists because of law. Law does not mean something written in the cosmic statute books. Behind the decree is deity. Behind the law is the Lord. Behind the principle is a Person. It is the person of Christ who "is before all things, and by him all things consist."

Likewise, there are laws for the spiritual life. There is the law of faith, the law of retribution, the law of justice, the law of reward, the law of prayer, and so on. To respect and obey these is to conquer our foes and possess the land.

One last thought lingers to be gathered up for use. Joshua achieved a greatness which is within the reach of everyone who reads these words. It is the greatness of obedience in life's routine. Joshua was unlike Moses and Joseph and Abraham in that he did not possess what we call outstanding genius. None of us would presume to think we could become like them but all of us can be like Joshua. Ha glorified duty, detail and routine. He carried out a higher will and plan.

Routine comprises nine-tenths of life. It describes most of the things we do. Without routine, society would cease to exist. It is what we call common work. It is what we do mechanically. Few men survey life from the mount. Most of them are on the plain or in the valley. Few women look at life from the couch of leisure. Most of them must be in the kitchen. There is only one Madame Chiang but there are many Mrs. Smith's. What is there to do about it? Lament one's fate and sour on life? Never! Make your valley the loveliest spot in the world. Make the common things uncommonly beautiful. Make the routine a thing of glory. It can be done by obedience.

# 7
# *Gideon*
## *The Conquest of Futility*

PERSONAL WEAKNESS AND futility is often the result of genuine humility carried too far. It is personal depreciation in the extreme. There is a fitting place for this when one faces God but there is also to be a legitimate recognition and reckoning of strength, ability and power when we face what God means in an individual's experience. Just about the first thing we read of Gideon is the depreciation of his life; this feeling of weakness, of futility. We hear him say, "Oh my Lord, wherewith shall I save Israel? behold, my family is poor in Manasseh, and I am the least in my father's house" (Judg. 6:13). This is often the case with us. Why I cannot possibly matter in this world. I am nobody. Look where I came from. Look where I live. My family is not prominent and I am the weakest of them all. A feeling of this kind can defeat anybody, but if we will reckon with God in our lives we will have the balance of power that can conquer any foe.

Futility is the result of doubt. Here is Gideon beating out his wheat. His country is in a deplorable condition. Almost 200 years previously his nation had come to this land to make it their homeland. God was with them. He had blessed them and when Joshua, their new land leader died, the land was practically occupied. There were few exceptions of unconquered people, but these few became a curse to Israel just as any unconquered habit, disposition, feeling or passion will in us. These few became the source of Israel's future enslavement. When Gideon beat out his wheat under an oak it was in fear of the Midianites, one of these unconquered peoples. They and the Amalekites were constant threats to the people of Israel. Because of their raids and depredations they had to build hideouts in caves and dens in the mountains to keep from being exterminated. Here now was Gideon, an obscure farmer beating out his wheat beside a winepress to escape detection. He is visited by a messenger from God with an unbelievable message. "The angel of the Lord appeared unto him, and said unto him, The Lord is with thee, thou mighty man of valor" (Judg. 6:12). When had Gideon ever known that he was a mighty man of valor? Why he was only a farmer. It did not take much valor to be a farmer. This was unbelievable. Furthermore, how could it be possible that God was with him. Why, God was not even in the nation, let alone with him. God, according to Gideon's view, was synonymous with victory, liberty, prosperity, freedom and miracles of manifestation. Gideon seemed to be quite sure God was not among Israel. His reply is given in these words, "Oh my Lord, if the Lord be with us, why then is all this befallen us? and where be all his miracles which our fathers told us of, saying, Did not the Lord bring us up from Egypt? but now, the Lord has forsaken us, and delivered us into the hands of the Midianites" (Judg. 6:13).

Perhaps it is natural and understandable that Gideon should think this way, but it was not right. It was true, of course, that the past had been filled with conquest while the present was filled with defeat, but it was not right to attribute this defeat to God. It was not God's fault, but the nation's. The fault goes back to an apostasy in the nation. In a previous chapter in Judges it is written, "And the people served the Lord all the days of Joshua, and all the days of the elders that outlived Joshua, who had seen all the great works of the Lord, that he did for Israel . . . And also all that generation were gathered unto their fathers: and there arose another generation after them, which knew not the Lord, . . . And they forsook the Lord God of their fathers, and followed other gods, of the gods of the people that were round about them . . . And the anger of the Lord was hot against Israel, and he delivered them into the hands of spoilers that spoiled them, and he sold them into the hands of their enemies round about . . ." (Judg. 2).

Behold what sad irony is in this situation. It was exactly as God had said, for years before as the nation was preparing to enter this land God gave this instruction, "Then ye shall drive out all the inhabitants of the land from before you, . . . But if ye will not drive out the inhabitants of the land from before you; then it shall come to pass, that those which ye let remain of them shall be pricks in your eyes, and thorns in your sides, and shall vex you in the land wherein ye shall dwell" (Num. 33:52-55). And here it was, exactly as had been said. The present masters were the previous foes that were not dealt with. They were appeased and compromised.

It is exactly so in life today. Habits and dispositions and associations that are not dealt with remain to be "pricks in our eyes and thorns in our sides." The Midianites and Amalekites were exactly that to Israel.

Gideon was complaining and blaming God for their predicament. So do we, both nationally and individually. We are saying, "If the Lord be with us, why then is all this befallen us?" What has befallen us does not proclaim the failure of God, as we charge. It proclaims our failure. This is certainly so nationally. We have failed God as a nation. We maintain a mock piety. We exhibit a sham Christianity. We have certainly forsaken and forgotten the God of our fathers.

We must never be allowed to forget our origin. That origin is found in that broad term religion. Let us warm it up and say "Christianity," for our founding fathers had very definite Christian convictions.

Our government was the result of revolution. As one reads history he is reminded that our national government was born out of the same revolutionary movement which engulfed France. The French Revolution and the American Revolution were part of the same tidal wave of liberty. In France men turned from the church and inaugurated what they called the Age of Reason. What happened? Liberty deteriorated into license; there followed a Reign of Terror wherein the streets of Paris ran with blood: and after that came a dictator named Napoleon. But on this side of the Atlantic, where the soil was cultivated by the Puritans of New England, the Quakers of Pennsylvania, the Huguenots of the Carolinas; here where the churches maintained their freedom of conscience and their habits of prayer, America brought forth from her revolution, a Constitution, a Washington and an enduring Republic.

Our schools were born in the Christian faith. "Excepting only the state universities, which themselves are the product of a civilization fashioned by the church, almost every institution of higher learning in America had a religious origin. Harvard was named for a preacher and was founded by the Puritans. Yale was founded to 'propagate in this wilderness the blessed reformed Protestant religion.' Dartmouth was founded by the Congregationalists for the propagation of the Christian faith, and Amherst was established for the purpose of educating for the gospel ministry young men in indigent circumstances, but of hopeful piety and promising talents.' Many other institutions of higher learning were established by the Baptists, the Presbyterians and the Methodists."

We have sacrificed those sacred Christian convictions and manner of life to a false kind of progress and a wrong kind of knowledge. It is fashionable with us to be religious; but we are afraid and ashamed to be Christian.

Once again our boys have died on battlefields, our nation has gone through another bloody period; and as war has ravaged our homes we say, "If the Lord be with us, why then is all this befallen us?"

The laws of God apply to nations as well as to individuals and one of the laws of God says, "Be not deceived; God is not mocked: for whatsoever a man soweth, that shall he also reap" (Gal. 6:7). It is not difficult nor farfetched to see this retribution in our nation today.

Gideon's perplexity is ours in many ways. We see the forces of evil prevailing. We see the church faltering and quarreling and divided. We see the world unable to compose its troubles. We say, "If the Lord be with us, why then is all this befallen us?"

The same perplexity meets us when we consider our own lives. We find a total absence of glory. There are no glorious pages of life. We feel the surge of enemy armies in our soul. We cringe and crouch beneath the sword of oppressive feelings, habits and sins. We are no longer masters of life. We are driven, like Israel, into the dens and caves of our own depressions and discouragements. We do nothing but retreat. Victory and conquest are just a memory, something other people had long before us. We cannot remember that we ever had them. It is the same old story—"If the Lord be with us, why then is all this befallen us?" Our minds are filled with interrogations and not a single affirmation. We complain about God but never praise Him. We have God on the judgment seat and not on the throne. We hold Him at arm's length but never walk with Him through the day. It has never occurred to us that we might be at fault. A little introspection instead of accusation would be very revealing. Find out where you are wrong and you can find where you can be right. Find out where you left God and you can find out where you can begin again with Him.

It will not be wise to abuse and accuse ourselves unnecessarily. There is a difference between retribution for sin and chastening for child-training. It is well in any case to take a very humble attitude and to inspect life carefully and prayerfully.

Notice here how Gideon reacted to the great challenge which the Angel gave him. At first he gave in to the feeling of futility. What could he do? How could he matter? By what means could he save Israel? He was reckoning with himself in all this but he failed to reckon with God. In that moment of failure and weakness God revealed Himself to Gideon. God's revelation became Gideon's confidence, assurance and strength. God's revelation was at a place of sacrifice—an altar. This was Gideon's new beginning. It will be ours too. An altar means renewal, dependence, dedication, surrender and consecration. Gideon found it and he went from that altar to do one of the most daring deeds of his life. He went out and tore down and desecrated and destroyed the altars of Baal that belonged to his own family. There must be no false gods while he serves the true God. There must be no divided loyalties. In doing this he flaunted death; he defied the prevailing custom of the day. Gideon was now a new man. He had met God. He had exchanged inferiority for superiority.

The secret lay in a new concept of life, God's presence in the human person. It is later recorded at a great crisis that "the Spirit of the Lord came upon Gideon." This means that God clothed Himself with Gideon. Gideon became God's clothing. Gideon became God's instrument. The New Testament counterpart of this is found in the truth of the Holy Spirit and His presence in the believer whose body is declared to be the temple of God. He clothes Himself with His people. They become His eyes and hands and feet. They give expression to His truth. They take His bodily place in life.

The recognition of this great fact will bring a mighty awakening to every Christian. The residence of the Holy Spirit in the redeemed person will mean an entirely new concept of life. It will make life sacred. It will make it useful, happy, contented and holy. It will be vastly different than the religious conception that life is a struggle to find God. Here God finds us and dwells within us.

Look at the difference it made when God clothed Himself with Gideon. He was able, with only 300 men, to meet a Midianitish army which is described "like grasshoppers for multitude" and to defeat them in utter rout and confusion. Here was a man who had complained of his incompetence and who was convinced of the futility of life, now being able with 300 men to rout an army. The secret lay in God's presence in his life. He climbed a height beyond his natural powers. He performed a task beyond his natural ability. He revealed an intelligence beyond his natural gift. He reached a place beyond the prospects of his natural birth. He did it because God chose to clothe Himself with Gideon.

There is a challenge here for us. This is the ace of the Spirit's manifestation. He is the Trinity's present representative to man. He is God's gift to the church. He is a historical and spiritual fact and can become a personal experience. When we awake to this and our life is filled with the Spirit we too will arise out of obscurity, futility and weakness.

Just how can we be clothed with the Spirit of God today? This is a troubling and perplexing question to many. Around it gathers many vagaries and much confusion. It is the case of most of the fanaticism that prevails in the church. It does not come because people are not earnest or sincere, but rather because they are ignorant of the simple principles upon which the Holy Spirit manifests Himself today.

To begin with we must recognize that the Holy Spirit is an accomplished fact in history. He was given and He has come and therefore is now present among the people of God. It is not necessary to tarry, wait, plead, agonize and suffer for His coming. He has come and is here. The experience that the child of God is to seek in connection with the Holy Spirit is not His baptism nor His indwelling, but His infilling. This comes by the recognition of faith and the surrender of faith. First we recognize that these things are so on the basis of the Word. Then we surrender our lives to His dominion so that it may be so in us. It may be accompanied by a great emotional experience or it may not. It will not be the result of what we do either by law or works. This will continue to be the secret of our power and blessing as long as we recognize that we are His temple.

# 8
# *Ruth*
## *The Conquest of Sorrow*

THE STORY OF Ruth is one of the most tender and touching in all the Bible. It is one of the most helpful too, because it is so true to life and so practical. It deals with the fortunes of a home; the struggles of a family and the inevitable sorrow which comes to all. Moreover it has a very significant setting for its climax, since it centers in Bethlehem. The sorrow of a world finds surcease in Bethlehem too, just as the sorrow of a family found its solution there long ago. The significance of the place is not greater than the significance of the persons because the two principals of the story, Ruth and Boaz, are in the ancestral line of the Savior, thus linking this ancient story to every modern home and family and individual.

The sorrow of the story begins in an alien setting to remind us that the sorrow of the world is alien to the plan and purposes of God. He did not plan a world of sin, sickness, death, war, evil and crime. He planned and produced a world of perfection of which He could give this estimate, "And God saw everything that he had made, and, behold, it was very good." To it in the course of events came an alien principle, sin. From Him man was driven in alienation and the world suffered in all its parts. Like Moab, into which Naomi and Elimelech fled, this world is an alien place to us.

Both joy and sorrow occur in life. Ruth, the Moabitess, found joy when she married one of the sons of the Israelites, Naomi and Elimelech. She also found sorrow when death came and took her youthful husband from her arms. Three times death struck its indiscriminating blows in Moab. Three times it left widows. Three times it brought the tears of grief and sorrow. Three women must make decisions.

One of the bereft women, Naomi, made her decision to go back. She would go back to her native soil and to her father's God. There is something very comforting about that. In Moab Naomi was out of the land of the covenant. She was like a backslidden soul. She and her husband had chosen the land of alien gods. Now she realized the mistake and must return to the God of her fathers. Life is much like that. The pastures of life always seem greener somewhere else. The other man's job always appears easier and more lucrative. Faith in God seems too static and unprogressive and we rise up to do something about it. So we go to Moab. In Moab we realize that green fields and full pantries are not everything in life for "man doth not live by bread alone." Life is better in a land of famine with God than in a land of plenty without Him. Faith that suffers is better than a faith that is surfeited, for a faith that is willing to suffer means a character that is prepared for anything.

The second woman of the trinity of widows, Orpah, made her decision to stay. She decided to stay in Moab; to cast her lot with her own people and her own gods. We do not know with what reluctance or with what relief Orpah left her mother-in-law but we do know by her act that her decision was to stay. From that moment she slips into an oblivion from which she never emerges. Her name is never meationed again. She becomes lost from our view forever. This was the consequence of her choice. It was unwisely made but we do not believe ignorantly so. Orpah had seen through the successive sorrows of Naomi's household what faith meant. She saw the difference between this Israelitish home and Moab's homes. To many people the best choice is the easiest. It was easier to leave Naomi than to go with her. It was easier to stay in Moab than to go to the land of Israel. It was easier to say "no" than "yes."

Orpah's choice became her destiny. It is so in life. The fortunes of life are bound up in our choices. We choose and we become. We choose and it is done. We choose and life changes. We choose and we are forgotten or we choose and we are remembered. We choose and we stay where we are or we choose and go on to something bigger, better and greater. Our lives are in our hands for better or for worse, for greater or for lesser.

The third woman, Ruth, made her decision to go on. Here was the choice of a new faith. She had seen how sorrow was conquered in Moab and she concluded that such a faith was worth any sacrifice. Her mother-in-law had urged her to stay with her people and find her future there. She had seen in Naomi what she wanted for herself. In this hour a new faith was born and it was the turning point of Ruth's life.

Naomi, the mother-in-law pointed out to Ruth that her sister-in-law Orpah had gone back to her people and to her gods and suggested that Ruth should do likewise. In this hour Ruth's faith was born. It had been a-borning through the years of life in Naomi's home; now it came to full life. It was not born out of theoretical considerations. She did not weigh in a careful mind the respective and competitive claims of Moab's Chermosh as against Israel's Jehovah. She did not decide on the basis of doctrines but on the evidence of results. She saw the results of a faith in God in Naomi's life. That was enough.

Ruth's decision is expressed in words which have never been matched for their beauty, courage or devotion, "Entreat me not to leave thee, or to return from following after thee; for whither thou goest, I will go; and where thou lodgest, I will lodge; thy people shall be my people, and thy God my God; where thou diest I will die, and there will I be buried; the Lord do so to me, and more also, if aught but death part thee and me" (Ruth 1:16, 17). Ruth went on to Israel, on to Naomi's God, on to glory and immortality.

Here are three decisions and three destinies. Here are three choices and three characters. Here are three ways of life and three destinations. Here are three faiths and three futures.

The conquest of sorrow began with Naomi in Moab. She did not allow herself to become embittered or discouraged. It is true that when she returned to Israel she said, "Call me not Naomi, call me Mara: for the Almighty hath dealt bitterly with me." But a bitter experience did not give her a bitter spirit. She was only expressing her attitude of regret and showing her contriteness. Out of *bitterness* she learned *betterness*. Instead of losing faith she found a strengthened faith. There was a recognition of the hand of God in her life and while it meant sorrow and pain she did not rebel. Moreover, she did not succumb to her sorrow. She saw the mistake of her earlier years and determined to go back to the covenant land of her fathers.

Sorrow often brings an awakening which nothing else can affect. Through tears we can see better and farther than otherwise. Sorrow had a winnowing effect by separating the grain from the straw. It did with Naomi, for she saw how vacant Moab was and how even the best there was not worth anything compared to the land of her fathers and the faith of her fathers.

Have you had sorrow? You know then the sting of hot tears and the tear of a broken heart and the vacantness of an empty room and the lonesomeness of an absent loved one. How did it leave you? Were you bitter or mellow? Did you bless or curse? Did you blame or praise? Job's wife said, "Curse God and die." Job said, "What? Shall we receive good at the hand of God, and shall we not receive evil? In all this did not Job sin with his lips" (Job 2:9, 10).

Sorrow can be conquered by faith. It is by far the greatest weapon we have. Faith gives one the sight of "a city which hath foundations, whose builder and maker is God." Faith gives one the hope of resurrection, "For this corruptible must put on incorruption, and this mortal must put on immortality. So when this corruptible shall have put on incorruption an this mortal shall have put on immortality, then shall be brought to pass the saying that is written, Death is swallowed up in victory. O death, where is thy sting? O grave, where is thy victory? The sting of death is sin; and the strength of sin is the law. But thanks be to God, which giveth us the victory through our Lord Jesus Christ" (1 Cor. 15:53-58).

The conquest of sorrow comes because of redemption so beautifully illustrated and set forth in the story of Ruth. Redemption reverses the effect of the curse which came upon life and the world through sin. Redemption brings in eternal life and makes its possessor the kin of God instead of an alien away from God. Redemption means the ultimate end of death therefore all who share in its blessings hold the key to the conquest of sorrow. Redemption leads us from a Garden with its sin to a City with its sinlessness for there shall in no wise enter into that eternal City "anything that defileth, neither whatsoever worketh abomination, or maketh a lie; but they which are written in the Lamb's book of life" (Rev. 21:27).

Death among many other things, means extinction. This is what Ruth and Naomi faced in returning to Bethlehem. They faced the extinction and end of their family life. They faced the alienation of their inheritance. In the course of events the hand of God brought a beautiful redemptive experience into their lives and Ruth found herself one of the links in the ancestry of the Savior of the world.

The story of this redemption begins in a barley field where Ruth is following the reapers, gleaning stray stalks of grain that she and her mother-in-law may live. Into that field comes its owner and the master of the reapers. Upon sight of Ruth the gleaner, his eyes light with a new gleam and his heart leaps with a new throb. He is a new kind of master for as he walks through his fields among his workers he says to them, "The Lord be with you" and from a hundred throats the response comes in unison, "The Lord bless thee." Here is a new employee-employer relationship. It is not subordination but equality. Upon inquiry concerning the gleaner in his fields Boaz finds out that she is Naomi's daughter-in-law. He already knows the story of her noble decision to follow Naomi back to Bethlehem and to know her God. Love awakens and he gives tokens of his care by instructing his reapers to scatter handsful of grain on purpose for her.

The story of redemption reaches its climax when Boaz agrees to become Ruth's kinsman-redeemer. Ruth had married into the family of Elimelech, Naomi's late husband. As such she would share its future, but Naomi finds herself impoverished. She is the owner of land which had belonged to her dead husband and which, under the pressure of circumstances, she must now sell in order to support herself. There was a law in the land known as the law of kinsman redemption which provided that when an Israelite was unable to redeem his property a near-of-kin could do it for him. Likewise this law provided not only for the redemption of jeopardized property but also for the raising up of a seed in case there were no children and the family line faced extinction. In the case of Ruth, Boaz was found to be a near kin and was therefore the redemptive hope of this family. As events reveal, he agreed to perform the part of a kinsman-redeemer and redeem the inheritance and marry Ruth. From this union came the immediate ancestors of King David and the ultimate ancestors of the Redeemer Himself.

Thus in an old custom and by an old law came a foreshadowing of the redemption of the world and the conquest of sorrow. Jesus Christ, because He became bone of our bone and flesh of our flesh, was our near kin and in position to be the Kinsman-Redeemer for the entire human race. He found us with our inheritance of life in jeopardy. It was mortgaged by sin. We were morally and spiritually bankrupt and physically corrupt. The sentence of death was upon us. Into this crisis He steps to become our Redeemer. He had already identified Himself with our life by incarnation. He now identifies Himself with our sin by crucifixion and conquers our death by resurrection. He redeems the lost inheritance and gives to the dying human race the gift of eternal life, thus saving it from eternal death. This is redemption by Christ, the world's Kinsman-Redeemer.

Redemption is God's answer to human sin and sorrow. It is the basis upon which we can conquer it. It is the transmission of God's life to us, for it is written, "And I give unto them eternal life; and they shall never perish" (John 10:28).

It is good to notice that Christians never meet for the last time, although the next time may be in the morning. There is always the next time, either here or there, earth or heaven.

We must also not forget that only those are heaven bound who are heaven born. A new life means a new birth. Eternal life means a birth in kind. Let us be sure of the birth and we can be certain of the life.

"If asked the remedy for the heart's deepest sorrow, I must point to the old, old story, told in an old, old book, and taught with an old, old teaching, which is the greatest and best gift ever given to mankind" (William E. Gladstone).

This old, old story is found in Ruth's conquest of sorrow wrapped up in one of the most beautiaul love stories ever written.

# 9
# *David*
## *The Conquest of Greatness*

FEW MEN CAN stand to be great even as few men can stand to be rich. It is easier to bear poverty than riches and easier to bear mediocrity than magnificence.

Few of us hope to be great in big things but all of us can be great in little things. We may never expect to be a great leader of the world in any field of endeavor but such greatness is not the only kind of greatness to be found or achieved in life. Greatness is the stature of a man's character in his own little world. It is the strength of a woman's life in her own little sphere. It can be achieved by everyone, everywhere. I know many great people whose names have never appeared in print in any newspaper and perhaps the only time they ever will, will be the morning the newspaper carries the notice of their deaths in the column of vital statistics. They are like Paul who said, "as unknown and yet well known." They are unknown in a world that worships at the shrine of a god named BIG. They are well-known in the eyes of a God who honors faith, righteousness, truth and faithfulness.

David was a man who was great in everything. David carried his greatness without pride. It is true that he had his moments of unworthiness but these were not the result of his greatness. It was when he slipped back into the lower elements of his human nature that we find David in sin. These blemishes only reveal how honest is the record of Scripture for the Bible is truthful. It does not picture its great men without flaws or faults, else they would be fictitious and unreal.

David's greatness began in smallness. It began at a time when he was overshadowed by seven brothers, all bigger than he. He was a pigmy among giants. He was a boy among men. He was small among the strong and stalwart. On the basis of human assumption he did not have a chance. The brothers were the ones who would serve their king and country. They were the hope of Israel. They were the ones who would do things. As for David, he was so inconsequential that when the prophet Samuel came to his father's house to anoint a king he was not even considered. He was given the monotonous and distasteful task of tending the sheep.

When the prophet Samuel came to Jesse's house to anoint a king he called the seven sons before him in order of their age. He was tremendously impressed with the oldest son and said, "Surely the Lord's anointed is before him. . . . But the Lord said unto Samuel, Look not on his countenance, or on the height of his stature; because I have refused him; for the Lord seeth not as man seeth; for man looketh on the outward appearance, but the Lord looketh on the heart" (1 Sam. 16:6, 7). All seven of Jesse's most eligible sons were rejected. Human calculations had been wrong. There was only one hope left, the lad who had never been given a chance. It was the shepherd boy who did not count. He was sent for and immediately the Lord said to Samuel, "Arise, anoint him: for this is he."

David had his qualifications of eye value. Anyone looking on Michelangelo's magnificent statue of "The Boy David" can appreciate this for the artist seems to have sensed the extraordinary charm and handsomeness of the lad. It says in the Scripture that he "was ruddy, and withal of a beautiful countenance and goodly to look to" (1 Sam. 16:12). However, David had more than eye value. Samuel had been warned not to choose a king by appearance only "for man looketh on the outward appearance, but the Lord looketh on the heart." What was in David's heart that won him the anointing? God looked where man could not and saw what man could not— "a man after God's own heart." He saw a man who would do His will. He saw a man who would follow in the light that he had. He saw a man obedient and faithful. It was what He had looked for in seven men and could not find. Now he found it in a shepherd boy; a boy who was considered so unimportant that he was sent to do the family's most menial task. Whom man rejected God accepted. Whom man overlooked God looked upon.

It is a paradox of this life that David's greatness began in smallness. This is the way of life with God. The first shall be last and the last shall be first. The mighty shall be forgotten and the meek shall inherit the earth. The proud shall be brought low and the humble shall be exalted. The chief apostle and the greatest human force in Christianity said, "I take pleasure in infirmities in reproaches, in necessities, in persecutions, in distresses for Christ's sake: for when I am weak, then am I strong." This is the paradox of power.

*David was great as the champion of his people.* In this, the first great test of his life, he had to overcome smallness in order to achieve greatness. The shepherd-lad must throw aside his meekness and be bold and brave, but being bold and brave was not enough. There must be something to back up these qualities. David had it, for what he learned as a shepherd in taking care of the flock he would use now in championing the nation. David had qualifications, for he said to King Saul, "Thy servant kept his father's sheep, and there came a lion, and a bear, and took a lamb out of the flock. And I went after him, and smote him, and delivered it out of his mouth: and when he arose against me, I caught him by his beard, and smote him, and slew him. Thy servant slew both the lion and the bear; and this uncircumcised Philistine shall be as one of them, seeing he hath defied the armies of the living God. David said moreover, The Lord hath delivered me out of the paw of the lion and out of the paw of the bear, he will deliver me out of the hand of this Philistine" (1 Sam. 17:34-37).

David recognized his moral right as well as his physical might. He counted both as being necessary. He did not expect to walk across the valley to the Philistine's camp and see their roaring giant topple over in a faint of fright. He did not expect to conquer him by some miracle of divine intervention. He expected to win by the prowess which he learned while tending sheep and by the power of the living God. His was a righteous cause. His was a just contest. God would be with him and that was enough.

The result is well-known. With carefully chosen stones and inerrantly aimed sling, David felled the giant Goliath.

Suppose the shepherd-lad had chosen to remain a shepherd. He could have. He did not have to volunteer to champion the armies of Israel. He might have argued truly that he was only a lad, experienced only in the crude arts of the field, who had never worn armor, unsheathed a sword or hurled a spear. Had he done this the first test of his career would not have materialized. David would have lost greatness in smallness. The king would have been obscured in the shepherd and the man would never have emerged out of the boy.

There is a place where faith must take the reins of life. It must sense the hour, the time and the place. It must venture everything. It must be bold but not brazen. It must be daring but not foolish. It must be venturesome but not reckless. That moment came to David in the valley of Elah. He seized it and succeeded.

*David was great as a poet-musician.* Few, if any, and we can be safe in saying none at all, ever achieved the poetic greatness of David. Think of the Psalms and you will realize how true this is. These are more than words in poetic splendor; they are revelations.

Where did David gather the material for his poems? Did it come from dreams and visions of fancy? Not his poems. They came from the material of life. They were born out of both faith and fact. They were experiences he had lived.

David tuned the strings of his harp on the tunes of his heart. He had learned the music of solitude tending the sheep. He was a musician in heart before he became one of lips and hands. His ability had none of the arrogance and temperment normally found in artists. It was simple, artless and captivating. Due to all these factors, as well as the hand of God, David found himself in the palace soothing the king with his music.

It was amidst such scenes as this and in so exalted a place as the king's presence that David went through some of the most disappointing experiences of his life. Here began what later followed him all through his life—the evils of jealousy and the deeds of injustice. When King Saul saw the mounting popularity of David he tried to kill him and for years David was pursued like an animal hunted by the hounds.

Out of these experiences and others that followed, came the thirty-seventh Psalm which begins by saying, "Fret not thyself because of evildoers, neither be thou envious against the workers of iniquity." One can easily become disturbed over the apparent prosperity of evil and dishonest people. Justice does not always become apparent in this world. What is there to do about it? Grow bitter, become cynical and sour? Not at all! David, by inspiration says, "Trust in the Lord, and do good; so shalt thou dwell in the land, and verily thou shalt be fed. Delight thyself also in the Lord; and he shall give thee the desires of thine heart. Commit thy way unto the Lord; trust also in him; and he shall bring it to pass. And he shall bring forth thy righteousness as the light, and thy judgment as the noonday" (Ps. 37:3-6).

Here is a plan and a promise. It is a plan for life and a promise that righteousness will have its certain reward. Injustice is one of the most difficult of all things to bear. Particularly so when one has received it at the hands of those who go on in prosperity in spite of their evil. We react variously. One type of reaction is to retaliate, but this is both unwise and unchristian. Retaliation only increases aggravation—

> Doing an injury puts you below your enemy;
> Revenging one makes you but even with him;
> Forgiving it sets you above him.
>                                              —Benjamin Franklin

Another type of reaction is to become discouraged with righteous living and to think that it does not pay and then to engage in unworthy activities.

Two words prescribe the Christian's attitude in meeting injustice in any form. They are, "Fret not"—"Fret not thyself." The dictionary gives an illuminating definition of the word "fret." It means to eat away; gnaw; to wear away; rub; chafe; agitate; disturb and to irritate. When one frets he is chafing himself; he is wearing away his patience; he is gnawing at his peace of mind. He is only hurting himself. Fretting hurts the one wronged and does not touch the wrongdoer. It is not a remedy, but a worse aggravation.

Nor should we be fretted and goaded into a state of desperation where we will do evil to try to counteract the evil done us. "Fret not thyself in any wise to do evil." Do not allow injustice to goad or aggravate you to evil acts. Evil is one of the devil's tools and righteousness can never come from it. No good can ever come out of it.

The antidote for fretting is resting. Rest in the Lord rather than fret over evil. We are to "trust in the Lord;" "delight . . . in the Lord;" "commit . . . unto the Lord;" and "rest in the Lord."

It is suggested that we may not immediately see the results of this policy so we should not be disappointed but rather "wait patiently for Him." We must not demand our time for redress and justification. It will only come in God's time. In the meantime, it is essential and necessary that we "trust in the Lord, and do good." This policy pays; it works; it is bound to win. It did for David. Once when he might have retaliated he showed mercy and it gained him far more than hatred and vengeance could ever have gained. Circumstances put Saul in his hands. The king took refuge in the very cave where David and his hunted men were hiding. David's men urged him to take vengeance and to slay Saul but instead David cut off a part of Saul's garment as an evidence of his mercy and said, "The Lord forbid that I should do this thing unto my master, the Lord's anointed, to stretch forth mine hand against him, seeing he is the anointed of the Lord." He then pleaded with Saul for reconciliation which was effected only because he had shown mercy when he might have taken vengeance.

Injustice, injury, ill-treatment and suffering is bound to come in life, either justly, deservedly or innocently. It is good to have some policy to deal with it. The suggested one of Psalm 37 is the wisest and the best. It was written by one who tried and proved it. He undoubtedly wrote it at the very time he was experiencing undeserved persecution, or at least at a time when he had had opportunity to know its reality. The Psalm is a masterpiece of graciousness, common sense and pure Christianity. It offers us the best means of self-defense and self-vindication. It is both defensive and offensive. It gives both a course of action for life and a prospect for the future. At its conclusion David writes, "I have seen the wicked in great power, and spreading himself like a green bay tree. Yet he passed away, . . . and he was not: yea, I sought him, but he could not be found. Mark the perfect man, and behold the upright; for the end of that man is peace."

The thirty-seventh Psalm is only one of 150 such songs but it is one of the most representative and practical since it was forged on the anvil of experience and deals with a problem and condition which is just as modern as it is ancient.

It was possible for David to ascend to a place of greatness because he mastered injustice. It was a part of his schooling and preparation. Not only that, it is a part of life. It reflects the imperfection of human character and reveals the need of Christian character.

*David was great as a king.* It was to this place that he was anointed as a very young man. He was chosen over the heads of his seven elder brothers. There was something prophetic and typical and symbolic about that. Seven has in Scripture a numerical value. In mathematics it has the value of seven units but in Scripture it has the value of perfection. It denotes something complete, full and final. The choice of seven days in a week was not an accident. It was a chosen measurement of time because it denoted perfection. It marks, in consequence, something finished hence the number eight always denotes the beginning of something new. The first day of the week after the seventh day is the eighth day but we do not call it the eighth day. It is the first day and the begiuning of a new week. In the case of David he was the eighth, or, in other words, with the rejection of his seven brothers, he was the first. He was the beginning of a new era, a new dynasty and a new destiny. David began the Davidic kingdom which Scripture tells us will never end. The throne of David will never lack a king. It will be occupied by none other than the Son of God. Thus in being chosen king over the heads of seven brothers David's symbolic significance carries him to a throne that is greater than any on earth.

All of this points to a natural conclusion. Such a throne requires a king in keeping with its place and power. David was not a small man in a large place. A giant throne did not seat a pigmy king. Some modern kings reveal their pigmy natures but not David. For 40 years he reigned in splendor and power, establishing the nation in great influence.

David's life, however, was not all conquest, glory, success and goodness. He had his weak moments and his dark days. Although king of a nation he was not always kinglike in his own heart. But David felt his weakness and this was his strength. He would do nothing without God. He must hear His voice before he led an army or built a temple. When he sinned he would cry out, "Against thee, thee only have I sinned." There was nothing impersonal about his confessions. When modern kings and presidents issue proclamations calling for prayer, sin is only implied. It is always "we," never "I." David's confessions were personal— "Have mercy upon me, O God, according to thy loving kindness: according to the multitude of thy tender mercies blot out my transgressions. Wash me throughly from mine iniquity, and cleanse me from my sin" (Ps. 51:1, 2).

David's life is a reminder of the state of life. Every child of God has two natures, an old and a new one. One is generated by the first Adam; the other by the last Adam. One is of death; the other of life. One leads to sin; the other to righteousness. As Abel had his Cain and Abraham his Lot and Isaac his Ishmael and Jacob his Esau and Joseph his brethren and Moses his Amalek and Joshua his Achen, so David had his Saul. In a correct and distinct sense there were within David the conflicting elements of a king and a slave. At times the greatness of David stands out and at other times the weakness. At times he is the conqueror and at other times the conquered. At times he cries out to say, "Oh that I had wings like a dove! for then would I fly away, and be at rest. Lo, then would I wander far off, and remain in the wilderness. I would hasten my escape from the windy storm and tempest" (Ps. 55:6-8). At other times he rejoices to say, "He that dwelleth in the secret place of the most High shall abide under the shadow of the Almighty" (Ps. 91:1).

David failed when he relied on himself; he conquered when he remembered the Lord. His conquest of life was not because he was some person of celestial gifts. Born a shepherd, handicapped because he was overshadowed by seven attractive brothers, David came out of obscurity because of that one great quality which has marked every conqueror who ever walked across the pages of the Bible-faith. He is found in the galaxy of stars for whom faith was not only a way to life but also a way of life, for in Hebrews 11:32-34 it says, "And what shall I more say? for the time would fail me to tell of Gideon, and of Barak, and of Samson, and of Jephthah: of David also, and Samuel, and of the prophets: who through faith subdued kingdoms, wrought righteousness, obtained promises, stopped the mouths of lions, quenched the violence of fire, escaped the edge of the sword, out of weakness were made strong, waxed valiant in fight, turned to flight the armies of the aliens." In this galaxy David is the brightest star, whose life shines with a radiance and brilliance that will bring hope and inspiration to all who see it.

# 10
# Solomon
## *The Conquest of Privilege*

THERE IS A SENSE in which Solomon does not belong in the Bible's great procession of conquerors because there appears much to indicate that he suffered many personal defeats. His life is marred by religious apostasy and a marriage standard which we could not condone. On the other band there are evidences of greatness in Solomon that require his place in any list of Bible conquerors.

To begin with, Solomon is a second generation son. It calls attention to the fact that children born into families of good circumstances must face, by that fact, a handicap not generally recorded. We can call it the peril of privilege. Privilege becomes a peril when that privilege is so common as to be taken for granted. The obscure is more perilous than the obvious. Obviously sickness is a peril but because health is more obscure it is more perilous than sickness. When we are sick we are careful to take means to recover, but when we are well we are careless. By the same tokens life is more perilous than death. Wealth is more perilous than poverty; understanding is more perilous than ignorance; privilege is more perilous than under privilege. Reduce any condition to a state of familiarity and it becomes a peril. A gun handled for the first time is not nearly so dangerous as one with which we have become familiar. The first time one drives an automobile he is very cautious at intersections, but familiarity takes away that caution.

The privileged classes are the greatest menaces to the world because they may become so accustomed to their privileges as to misuse them. It has been so with privileged-wealth, privileged-royalty, privileged-aristocracy, privileged-nationality and even privileged-religion. Jesus said, "A rich man shall hardly enter into the kingdom of heaven." This is not because riches in themselves are a bar to heaven, but because they are trusted in to the exclusion of God. Paul said, in this same connection, "For ye see your calling, brethren, how that not many wise men after the flesh, not many mighty, not many noble are called [all because these people of privilege allowed their privileges to be either so common as not to be important or else to be so important as to take God's place in their lives]: But God hath chosen the foolish things of the world to confound the wise; and God hath chosen the weak things of the world to confound the things that are mighty: And base things of the world, and things which are despised, hath God chosen, yea, and things which are not, to bring to nought things that are" (1 Cor. 1:26-28).

The greatest enemies Jesus had were in what was then the equivalent of the church. His greatest foes were not Pilate, Herod or Caesar but the Scribes and Pharisees, the leaders of the religious thought and life of that day. They had succumbed to the peril of privilege. They took advantage of their position to exploit the people. They enjoyed the status quo more than the Messiah's anticipated coming. When the modern crucifixion of Jesus comes it will not come from atheists or communists but from the modern version of the Scribes and Pharisees.

When Jesus Christ came, the first thing and the last thing he did at the beginning and ending of His career was to cleanse the temple. It was not the brothels or the gambling houses or the courts, but the House of God. It had become the victim of the peril of privilege.

One of the most striking examples of this is to be found in the church of Laodicea, the church prophetic. It was "rich and increased with goods" yet it knew not that it was "wretched, and miserable, and poor, and blind and naked" and because it was lukewarm and neither cold nor hot Jesus promises to spue it out of His mouth.

How different from this church of privilege is the church of persecution at Sardis. Persecution has always been a great purifier. It has always been an agency for appreciation.

Second generation Christians face this peril of privilege today. They receive home benefits and blessings they did not provide. They worship in church buildings they did not sacrifice, sweat, work and pray to build. They inherit organizations they did not conceive. They affirm a faith they did not have to travail for. Because of this there is indifference and decline.

This is graphically illustrated in second generation mission fields, Uganda in Africa, particularly. Here where native savages were saved and built great churches, where they had to pay a high price for their faith, second generation Christians are now in the places of leadership. The old fire, enthusiasm, power and zeal are gone and Christianity has become conventional and accepted. There is no more persecution. Becoming and being a Christian does not involve the separation and sacrifice of former days. It is the old story of the peril of privilege.

The greatest peril of privilege is in the pride that privilege so often produces. This comes in the face of the fact that most of the privileges we enjoy are unearned. The home we live in, the family we were born into, the clothes we wear, the food we eat, the advantages we

have, the education we receive, the church in which we worship and
the salvation we possess are all unearned. They are gifts of others to
us. Life is a gift of God. So is the new life a gift of God's grace. These
should make us humble and understanding. They should produce
appreciation and generate devotion instead of that unwholesome pride
and ungodly complacency which is so often true.

Solomon is an example of one who conquered the perils of
privilege. He is a second generation son. "David is dead, and a man
of different mould has mounted the rostrum. Will Solomon sway the
masses as David did? By natural gifts, no. The new preacher has not
the elements of the old. In every respect they are contrasts. David is
extemporaneous; Solomon is elaborately prepared. David spoke in
outbursts; Solomon deals in rounded periods. David was
unconventional; Solomon is steeped in culture. David appealed to
human experience; Solomon expounds abstract principles. David
revealed the man; Solomon exhibits the scholar. David was the
sermon; Solomon gives the sermon" (George Matheson, *Portraits of
Bible Men*, First Series, p. 298). Overshadowed as he was, Solomon
nevertheless took his place in God's plan.

*Solomon conquered the privilege of birth.* Birth may put us in a
fortunate position. The advantage which our birth may give can be a
peril—the peril of what we do not do. Often the child with few
advantages goes farther than the child with many. Born again children
from non-Christian homes are often more earnest and devoted
Christians than those from Christian homes.

Solomon overcame these perils. He inherited a throne which
dominated an undivided empire. He presided over this empire with
great success. His was a reign of peace for there is no period of
protracted peace in all the Jewish annals like the reign of Solomon.

The unity of the kingdom under Solomon might have been
achieved in two ways. It could have been done by seeking a common
danger from without and engaging in war, or by the suggestion of a
common interest, from within and engaging in cooperative efforts.
Many times rulers "have sought to purchase domestic peace by the
incurring of a foreign war. A nation divided by factions has often
been driven into unity by the call to arms against another nation . . .
but this was not the policy of King Solomon. . . . He felt . . . that to
heal domestic discord by outdoor discord was a superficial gain. He
wanted peace all around—peace not only in the inner parts, but on
the borders and at the gates. Accordingly, he chose another way—
what seemed to him a more excellent way. Rejecting the idea of a
common danger, he turned to the plan of a common interest" (George
Matheson, *Portraits of Bible Men*, First Series, p. 305).

Peace in personal life is often sought by people from the outside
rather than from the inside. People think that by many preoccupations
and much external activity they can unite the disunited factions of
mind and emotions and thus gain peace. Such a peace is only a

superficial gain. Peace must come from within. It must be God's gift to the life. When it is within it will be without, on the borders and at the gates "and the peace of God, which passeth all understanding, shall keep your hearts and minds through Christ Jesus."

*Solomon conquered the privilege of wealth.* "His ships travelled the seas in search of merchandise; they touched at every port where the spirit of commerce dwelt. His caravans range the land in the service of the trader; they go forth with native produce and return with foreign treasure. It visits Tyre. It reaches Arabia. It treats with Egypt. It has intercourse with Babylon. It possibly touches the shores of India" (George Matheson). This wealth offers Solomon access to every kind of pleasure known to man, but pleasure and treasure finally found a subordinate place in Solomon's esteem. This is what he says:

"I said in mine heart, Go to now, I will prove thee with mirth, therefore enjoy pleasure: and, behold, this also is vanity. I said of laughter, It is mad: and of mirth, What doeth it? I sought in mine heart to give myself unto wine, yet acquainting mine heart with wisdom; and to lay hold on folly, till I might see what was that good for the sons of men, which they should do under the heaven all the days of their life. I made me great works; I builded me houses; I planted me vineyards: I made me gardens and orchards, and I planted trees in them of all kind of fruits: I made me pools of water, to water therewith the wood that bringeth forth trees: I got me servants and maidens, and had servants born in my house; also I had great possessions of great and small cattle above all that were in Jerusalem before me: I gathered also silver and gold, and the peculiar treasure of kings and of the provinces: I gat me men singers and women singers, and the delights of the sons of men, as musical instruments, and that of all sorts. So I was great, and increased more than all that were before me in Jerusalem: also my wisdom remained with me. And whatsoever mine eyes desired I kept not from them, I withheld my heart from any joy; for my heart rejoiced in all my labor: and this was my portion of all my labor. Then I looked on all the works that my hands had wrought, and on the labor that I had labored to do: and, behold, all was vanity and vexation of spirit, and there was no profit under the sun" (Eccl. 2:1-11).

One does not need to be born into economic affluence to be subject to this peril of wealth. All that is necessary is to be born out of need. It is to never know what hunger is or what an empty pantry is, or to always have clothes or to always have a sufficient income or allowance. There is peril in this and the danger that we may forget the prayer of dependence "give us this day our daily bread."

Solomon conquered his peril in a very forthright and proper manner.

First of all we find him seeking wisdom. When asked what God should give him he responded by saying, "Give therefore thy servant an understanding heart." His desire became his possession and much more, for God said, "Behold, I have done according to thy words: lo, I have given thee a wise and understanding heart: so that there was none like thee before thee, neither after thee shall arise like unto thee. And I have also given thee that which thou hast not asked, both riches, and honor" (1 Kings 3:12, 13). He does not choose to be rich, but he became rich. He does not choose to be famous, but he became famous. He does not choose to be powerful, but he became powerful. All of this because be chooses to be wise. This is more, upon Solomon's part, than a desire to know many things. He has many things to say in later days about what true wisdom means. He found in purely intellectual wisdom a source of grief and said, "For in much wisdom is much grief: and he that increaseth knowledge increaseth sorrow" (Eccl. 1:18). True wisdom meant a true regard and reverence for God for "The fear of the Lord is the beginning of wisdom" (Ps. 111:10).

This fact, coupled with Solomon's faith, reveals the secret of his life and success. The crowning achievement of his life is in connection with his faith in God, the building of the temple. It represents not only that God was in Solomon's heart but that the heart of the nation was to revolve around God. It meant stability and strength as well as hope and prospect. Solomon could say, "But the path of the just is as the shining light, that shineth more and more unto the perfect day" (Prov. 4:18).

# 11
# *Elijah*
## *The Conquest of Discouragement*

ONE OF THE most dramatic, bold, venturesome, fearless and brave characters of all times suddenly bursts into our presence as we reach the seventeenth chapter of 1 Kings. The first thing we see or hear of him is in Samaria where he is calling the judgment of a drought and famine upon the land of Israel. Elijah comes without introduction and leaves without warning. He has neither beginning nor ending. He appears abruptly and disappears in like manner. There is no mention of father and mother and no word of childhood or youth. He suddenly bursts upon the scene to denounce idolatry and to pronounce judgment. There is a solitary magnificence about Elijah that puts awe upon us as we see him appearing abruptly in the king's court to pronounce the vengeance of God or to defy Queen Jezebel and her evil retinue of false gods and lackey priests.

Despite this meteoric nature of Elijah's life he is not so much unlike other human beings that we have no hope of finding something helpful in the study of his life. Elijah reminds us of the impulsiveness of human nature. Elijah acted from the heart explosively and impulsively. He did not calculate or meditate over his deeds. He acted first and meditated afterwards. This is why we find him in the wilderness. Many of us have often sat beneath the juniper tree of discouragement.

Elijah's name is linked with two other names of the Old Testament in a very significant way. It is in connection with death. Elijah, Enoch and Moses are united in one common bond, the bond of death. Death to them was unlike death to all others because they stand typical of its conquest and its defeat. All three escaped both its process and its consequences.

Enoch had no deathbed. Moses had no burial. Elijah had no corruption.

There is no record of Enoch's death—he simply walked with God and God took him.

There is no record of Moses' burial except the fact that God "buried him in a valley in the land of Moab." Where, no one has ever discovered. There is no tombstone, or marker, no evidence of his entombment.

There is no record of Elijah's corruption in death. He was suddenly gathered up by a chariot of fire and whisked into heaven.

Here the three stages of death are reversed and set aside indicating the triumph of the Christian faith over death which the Bible describes as man's last enemy. Here the deathbed is conquered by Enoch who does not die but enjoys translation. Here the burial is conquered by Moses who leaves no recorded word or knowledge of the place of his entombment for human veneration as if to say that there is no tomb, there is no grave anticipating the cry of triumph: "O death where is thy sting and grave where is thy victory?" Here also the physical corruption of death is conquered by Elijah who escapes death's corrupting hand by being gathered full of life, full of strength and full of activity by heavenly charioteers.

There can be no greater test of any faith than the test that death puts upon it. Does faith end in a grave? Does it end in some vague immortality? Is faith, as it is for the Christian, a certainty of life in the presence of a personal God? The Bible teaches us the latter kind of faith. It calls for either a translation out of life or a resurrection out of death. Some must suffer the tomb and experience the corruption and some will go without dying, but all will know the presence of God.

Elijah's conquest of life goes back to both his nature and his acts. He was an impulsive man, capable of the extremes of emotion. He was capable of great exaltation and great depression. He was capable of great aggressiveness and great discouragement. Perhaps he is like you in a greater or lesser degree. Have you ever cried, "Oh that I had wings like a dove, for then would I fly away, and be at rest. Lo, then would I wander far off, and remain in the wilderness"? (Ps. 55:6, 7).

Elijah's acts and circumstances had as much to do with his condition as his nature. He was a man of great responsibility. He was entrusted with the dangerous duty of shaking his finger of accusation beneath the nose of a weak and conscienceless king and a brutal and evil queen. He had to threaten and judge. It was his obligation to denounce personal sin and national idolatry. Elijah must call the nation back to its primitive faith—the worship of an invisible God without visible objects and means. He was the first great Protestant. He opposed images and representations of deity. He opposed the worship of God by means of the sense of sight, touch and smell. He calls the people back to the worship of God in the heart rather than in the hand. He demands the abolition of idolatry. He asked for a spiritual worship rather than a sensual worship.

This meant danger and it brought the threat of death. It meant danger in many ways, not only from the revenge of Ahab and Jezebel, but from the consequences of his own pronouncements. He must suffer from the sins of the nation. Whatever judgment the evil receive, the righteous must experience. Since Elijah pronounced the judgment of a famine he must experience the perils of that famine, but God took care of him. He sent Elijah to Cherith where water came from the brook and food came by ravens.

Here Elijah is taught the difference between false religion and true religion. The false religion demands, the true religion gives. The false gods must be ministered unto, the true God ministers. The false gods were impotent to help in trouble, the true God could help when there was no human hope. It was one thing to destroy an idol by force and another thing to discredit that idol by revealing something better. Hence Cherith with its brook and its ravens.

The employment of ravens is not so much a mystery as it appears. The raven was an unclean bird because among other things it was a carrion feeder. Because of its flesh eating habit it was the only means to be providentially employed in ministering to Elijah. It was both natural and supernatural. It is both common sense and beyond explanation. The supernatural element lies in the fact of God's providential use of these birds. The natural element lies in the fact that God employed the kind of bird that fitted the need. The ravens were omnivorous which means they ate all kinds of food. Unable to find grain in a time of famine they preyed on animals and deposited them where Elijah could find them. This they did unconsciously but providentially. Thus did God care for His servant.

Being ministered unto, Elijah is now called upon to minister. Being ministered unto by an unholy and unclean bird Elijah is called upon to minister to one whom the Jews considered unholy, a woman from the alien land of Zidon. She was a widow in great need. She was beyond the borders of Israel. She was out of the pale of Israel's faith. She belonged to a heathen people, yet she worshiped God even though it was not after the same pattern as Elijah. She was, of course, the exception. She, among all the rest of her people, had seen the light and found the truth. She, among all the rest, would obey God.

We must not be so sure in our classification of who are and who are not Christians, that we do not make mistakes. This widow of Zidon would have been left out but God brought her in. Men put her down as an infidel but God classified her as a believer. We, with our dogmatic shortsightedness do much the same. It may be one of our greatest surprises in heaven to find those there whom we never considered eligible. The standards of God are righteous and eternal but the judgments we make are often bigoted and erring.

At Zidon Elijah ministers to the widow and she to him. Her venture of faith becomes the never failing source of supply. The barrel never wasted and the cruse never failed. The God of Israel reveals Himself as the God of the people. He is interested in their well-being. He can help them in their need, but not so the idols of Baal. They are helpless and impotent. They are a mockery and a sham. In this manner Elijah's denunciation of idolatry is backed and supported by a demonstration of Jehovah's practical presence among His people. It must ever be so with us. To denounce a false system is not enough. We must demonstrate the truth by its own power. Setting up a doctrinal standard to which we demand all men to repair is not enough. There must be, with that standard, the evidence of divine presence and power. Christianity is not a lot of abstract religious rules. It is a life which professes and claims to have God at its very heart. It is therefore required that the evidence of God should accompany the standard of truth.

This was the very thing which followed Elijah's experience at Zidon. From there he went to Carmel where were gathered 450 idolatrous priests of Baal who came in response to a challenge laid down by Elijah to King Ahab. The 450 priests were supported by 400 prophets of Baal. The purpose was a final and conclusive test of truth by the power of prayer. Elijah did not gather to have a debate. Religious debates are futile and senseless gatherings. They settle nothing and secure less. Elijah was not interested in establishing the truth of Christianity by argument. It was not to compare word for word, sentence for sentence, paragraph for paragraph of the respective creeds of Baal and Israel, it was for a far more practical and important purpose. Elijah was the one who proposed it. He did not stand on the defensive side but on the offensive. He proposed that the truth of Baal and the truth of Israel be established by its most practical evidence—the evidence of the power of prayer. An altar is set up and a sacrifice arranged. The Baalites were to pray to Baal and Elijah was to pray to Jehovah and the God who answered by fire which consumed the sacrifice would be God indeed.

The results of this test are classic. The Baalites prayed, pleaded and cajoled their god and tortured themselves with knives and lancets until they were smeared with blood, but no answer from their god. Then Elijah goaded them into frenzied fury by suggesting that they were not praying loud enough for their god might be talking and could not hear them or on a hunt or journey, or perhaps sleeping. The knives and lancets were plied with reckless abandon and the prayers poured from their lips in religious fury, but still no answer.

Then Elijah did a singular thing. He drenched the sacrifice upon his altar with water so there could be no accusation or excuse of fortunate circumstances. At the exact hour that the evening sacrifice would be offered in the temple he offered a quiet, simple, rational prayer of faith. He said, "Lord God of Abraham, Isaac, and of Israel, let it be known this day that thou art God in Israel, and that I am thy servant, and that I have done all these things at thy word. Hear me, O Lord, hear me, that this people may know that thou art the Lord God, and that thou hast turned their heart back again" (1 Kings 18:36, 37). The result of that prayer was an answer. The answer was a demonstration of God's practical presence among His people.

There are some things that should be carefully observed in this connection. Not all prayer is to be offered as a test. When one once tests the quality of metal it is conclusive and final. He does not test it again and again. This test and others in the Scripture have resulted in this report in the Bible which should be conclusive and final, "He that cometh to God must believe that he is, and that he is the rewarder of them that diligently seek him" (Heb. 11:6).

Prayer is not an elaborate ceremony and ritual. It is a recognition of God's existence and presence and a simple expression of need and statement of request. It is based solely upon faith on the human side and the will of God on the divine side. It is not to be valued because of its words, or its emotions or its frantic appeals. The responsibility of its answer rests entirely with God. Elijah put the test upon the basis of God's reality—"let it be known this day that thou art God in Israel." It was God's reputation which was at stake and not Elijah's. The priests of Baal were defending their reputations while Elijah was expressing confidence in God. The result was highly satisfactory.

As a consequence of what happened on Mt. Carmel Elijah was put in jeopardy of his life by Queen Jezebel's threat to exterminate him. He had removed her religious hold upon the people by destroying the priests she sponsored. She determined that Elijah must go. He fled for his life, not so much from Jezebel as from himself. Surely there could be no real fear in his heart of this evil woman after the complete victory of Carmel. He knew God well enough to know that the queen could hold no terrors for him. Like him, many of us expect the exaltation of success to continue always. We expect God to sweep, not only the priests of Baal from the face of the earth, but also their sponsors and we awake to find that like Jezebel the devil is still here. He has not been destroyed. He still lives to threaten us. He still exists to destroy us. We allow the devil to obscure the Lord as Elijah allowed Samaria, where Jezebel lived, to obscure Carmel where he had destroyed the idolatrous priests.

Discouragement is a terrible thing. It results from many causes and brings various reactions. It results in the obscuration of faith and the prostitution of strength. It leads us into the blind alley of despair and drives us into the wilderness of depression. We see nothing of God and everything of an evil and foreboding surrounding.

Elijah found a juniper tree and prayed to die but God gave him strength to live. From the wilderness he went to Horeb. He left the juniper tree for a cave. At the depth of his depression he met God. Under the juniper tree Elijah met the angel of encouragement. In the cave Elijah met the God who encourages. In the strength of the angel's ministrations Elijah traveled forty days and forty nights. Reaching the cave Elijah forgot all about dying, but here he was full of complaining.

The Word of the Lord came to Elijah, "What doest thou here, Elijah?" He had no business in that cave. His business and his place was among his people. Here he was pitying himself and lamenting his lonesomeness. "I have been very jealous for the Lord God of hosts: for the children of Israel have forsaken thy covenant, thrown down thine altars, and slain thy prophets with the sword: and I, even I only, am left; and they seek my life, to take it away" (1 Kings 19:10).

What a place for a prophet—in a cave! What a place for any child of God! Yet many of us have been in caves: the caves of despondency, worry, hopelessness and fretfulness. If any are there now God is saying. "What doest thou here, Elijah?" A cave of despair is no place for any child of God. He belongs on the mount. He belongs in the surging stream of life, not in a cave.

We can draw particular strength from this old story of the prophet who went and hid himself from God, and when God asked him why he was not working he said, somewhat sulkily, that there was none to help him, and what was the use of just one man trying to change the world? You remember God said in effect, "Get right back to work. You are not the only one. There are good men to this number in that city and there are more of them elsewhere." And so God shamed that soul back to its duty.

Often it has seemed that we were fools to speak when others were silent. Yet when we did speak we found many others ready to speak also and the solitary voice became instantly a chorus and things were done that in the silence people had whispered were impossible.

Do you remember the story of King Robert Bruce of Scotland? He took refuge out of sheer necessity in a cabin and there God sent a little spider and spun a powerful lesson for the king. His wife had been taken captive. His brother had just been executed. Robert Bruce was in despair. As he lay one morning on his wretched bed considering whether to go on or give up, his eye was suddenly attracted to a spider which was hanging at the end of a long thread from one of the beams above him and endeavoring to swing itself to another beam for the purpose of fixing the line on which it meant to stretch its web. The insect made the attempt again and again with no success. Six times Robert Bruce counted that it tried and failed and it occurred to him that just six times he had fought in battles against the British and had failed. Said he, I will be guided by this spider. If it makes another attempt and is successful I will venture a seventh time, but if it fails I will give up my cause. He watched the spider carefully as it swung itself with all its strength toward the beam. This time it was successful and Robert Bruce's course was cast. He went on to glorious success.

Not unlike this are some of the lessons God teaches us by one means or another as we lie in our caves of despair. Elijah, whose ally was none less than the God of Mt. Carmel, was now asked to account for his despair on Mt. Horeb.

Elijah is directed to "go forth and stand upon the mount before the Lord. And behold the Lord passed by." None will ever see the

Lord pass by so long as he remains in his cave of despondency. He must get out. He must leave. He must "stand upon the mount." Our God is not a God of the caves but of the mount. Caves belong to the devils of despair and mounts belong to the God of hope and vision.

Elijah views a majestic spectacle on the mount. It was a parade of the elements—the wind, the earthquake and the fire.

There came a great wind but it is written that, as the Lord passed by He "was not in the wind." Wind is the emblem of force. God does not generally work by force in this age of Grace. He does not stop wars, crime waves, blasphemers or any kind of evil by force.

Then there came an earthquake but it is written that as the Lord passed by He "was not in the earthquake." Earthquakes are the symbol of fear. God does not use fear as a weapon to coerce men. He does not drive them in frightened, maddened, stampeding herds into the kingdom of heaven. God does not have a hell for the purpose of scaring men into a heaven. He tells us of its existence and warns us of its reality but never uses it as the urge to get us into heaven.

After this there came a fire but it is written that as the Lord passed by He "was not in the fire." Fire is the emblem of destruction. God's way is not a way of destruction. There have been instances of necessary judgments but in this age of Grace He does not destroy in order to build. He does not destroy in order to construct. When the disciples of Jesus wanted to call down fire upon a village of rejectors in Samaria He said, "Ye know not what manner of spirit ye are of. For the Son of Man is not come to destroy men's lives but to save them" (Luke 9:56).

The cyclonic wind uprooted trees about the awe-struck Elijah: the earthquake tore down the cliffs about him: the fire melted the rocks around his feet, but God was not in any of them. Yet it says "the Lord passed by." Where was God if he was not in the wind, the earthquake and the fire? He was manifest in a voice, for after the wind, the earthquake and the fire there came "a still small voice."

The voice of God said, "What doest thou here, Elijah?" His complaint was characteristic of a man in despair. He had lost his perspective. The juniper tree and the cave had shriveled his soul. He saw nought save his difficulties and himself. He saw himself as the only one left whom God could trust. Now his life was threatened. God reminded Elijah that there were still 7000 pairs of knees unbowed to Baal. After all he was not alone. He was not the last line of defense. He was not God's last hope. Nor are we.

Perhaps the panorama of mighty power that swept past Elijah was but God's answer to Elijah's thought. Perhaps he (Elijah) wanted to use force and miraculous powers, fear and destruction to scatter the evildoers. We too would like to reform the world by a show of force and fear, but these are not God's weapons. When God came in Christ He was the God of the "still small voice." He walked through the land and called men and women to follow Him. By those who followed Him he proposed to work His works. It would not be reformation by force but regeneration by grace.

Change the scene from Mt. Horeb to Mt. Calvary. Instead of the Tishbite see the Galilean. Instead of the silent fastness see a surging mob. Instead of wind, earthquake and fire see darkness, black as hell, covering the earth at midnight. Instead of a cave see a cross and on that cross hear a man say, "It is finished." Then remember that "God who at sundry times and in divers manner spake in times past unto the fathers by the prophets, hath in these last days spoken unto us by his Son." Christ is the voice of God for these days. His is the only authentic voice.

He has spoken:

## 1. With the Voice of Prophecy

Great men can tell us about today but only Jesus Christ can tell us about tomorrow. He has told us of a tomorrow, already almost two thousand years long, filled with wars and rumors of war, strife and trouble. He spoke truly and accurately.

## 2. With the Voice of Lament

Twice Jesus wept: once over death and once over sin. Once at Lazarus' tomb and once over Jerusalem's sin. His lament over Jerusalem was not that it was filled with murderers, adulterers and thieves so much as for a greater sin—the sin of unbelief. It was not the sin of what they did, but what they would not do. They would not allow Him to gather them into the embrace of His love and forgiveness.

## 3. With the Voice of Authority

The people once passed this judgment after Jesus spoke: "He taught as one having authority and not as the Scribes and Pharisees." His authority extended to the elements, the dead, the sick, the demons, the angels and to men. He still speaks with authority and it is folly to deny it.

## 4. With the Voice of Forgiveness

Any man can expose sin but only Jesus Christ can forgive sin. The religious leaders exposed the sin of the woman in the temple but it was Jesus who said, "Go and sin no more."

What the world needs is not so many to tell it what is wrong with it but a Christ who can forgive and heal its sins and wounds. We need forgiveness with its subtraction more than prosperity with its addition.

With whatever voice Jesus spoke, His words were the words of light. He among all men could say, "I am the light of the world." His word is the word of enlightenment. It is the word that illuminates life and makes it worth living.

One of the characters of "Beside the Bonnie Briar Bush" tells of a time in his life when he had no ear for the voice of God. Then sickness came upon him and death came near and his soul awoke within him and he began to cry like a child for its mother. His wife went to the local Scotch minister. He was very kind and came to see the dying man and talked of many things, including his farm, but the sufferer said nothing to this. "I was hoping he would tell me what I was to do for my soul but he began upon the sheep market and I knew he was also in the dark. After he left I turned my face to the wall and wept." Then he said to his wife, "Wrap me in a plaid and put me in a cart and take me to Alberfeldy for there," said he, "is a man who knows the way of the Lord and it is better to die with my face to the light." He did not need merely to die with his face to the Light. He found the Light and died in it. For us, it is possible to live in the Light and walk in it and our dying will be but the coming to the end of a road which has been lit by that Light that "shineth more and more unto the perfect day."

Elijah had been taught and had learned a tremendous lesson on Mt. Horeb. He knew now whence his strength came. He saw God in the proper light. Never again does Elijah seek a juniper tree or a cave in which to nurse his feelings. He goes from Horeb to Samaria to denounce King Ahab for his sins. He divides the Jordan by the power of God and at last is swept up into heaven in a chariot of fire. He left the world a conqueror.

# 12

# Nehemiah
## The Conquest of Opposition

NEHEMIAH WAS A builder. Blessed are the builders for theirs shall be the joy of construction. There are so many wreckers and destroyers. So much of life is consumed with tearing down. War is a great destroyer. It destroys substance, society and human life. War is the result of a greater destruction—the destruction of trust and love.

We are to be builders. Building requires a vision, a plan and materials. The plan and materials are provided for a noble Christian life. What is needed is the vision to complete the plan. It is written thus, "For other foundation can no man lay than that is laid, which is Jesus Christ. Now if any man build upon this foundation gold, silver, precious stones, wood, hay, stubble; every man's work shall be made manifest: for the day shall declare it, because it shall be revealed by fire: and the fire shall try every man's work of what sort it is" (1 Cor. 3:11-13). In this manner the results of life will be tested and judged on the basis of workmanship and materials. It is necessary to remember that we are to be the builders.

Building is not a simple task of putting materials into building form. It requires concentration and determination. There are often countless obstacles and hindrances. There are lessons of this kind found in the life of Nehemiah.

Nehemiah was a Hebrew captive living in Persia at the time of the reign of King Artaxerxes. It was brought to his attention by certain fellow captives that a remnant of Jews who returned to Jerusalem were in a pitiful plight. Moreover, the city was lying in ruins. This news distressed Nehemiah and he set himself to fast and pray. He confessed his sins and the sins of his people before God. He plead His ancient promises to His people and reiterated the prophecies of restoration. God, in response to His servant's prayer, began to work. In course of time Artaxerxes the king, was moved by the plea of Nehemiah, to send him to Jerusalem to rebuild the city. Here Nehemiah and his companions viewed the ruins. Its walls were broken down and its gates were burned. Determination came to the builders and they said, "Let us rise up and build." And Nehemiah answered them, "The God of heaven, he will prosper us; therefore we, his servants will arise and build" (Neh. 2:20).

Those intrepid men repaired the walls and rebuilt the gates. It was not their comfort which they sought first, but their security and defense. All builders should consider essential things first. There needs to be walls of defense and security about our lives, yet, consider how few are wise builders. So few people live with any constructive plan of life. They never plan and build the defenses against the future. They never set up any walls of faith and prayer against the approach of the inevitable enemies of life. All they are concerned about are the material comforts of today.

It seems that Nehemiah and his fellow builders had little trouble with materials and labor. The ruins offered the former and their own unquenchable zeal the latter. Nevertheless they had their difficulties. Two formidable enemies watched their labors with growing jealousy and hatred. They were Sanballat and Tobiah. They hated the Hebrews and viewed their rehabilitation with evil concern and were determined to oppose them in every possible way, not only to hinder, but to halt altogether this work of rebuilding the city.

Opposition takes many forms, but it usually begins with ridicule. When that fails then more drastic measures are employed. Ridicule was the first weapon Sanballat and Tobiah used against Nehemiah and his helpers. It is said that he "mocked the Jews and he spake before his brethren and the army of Samaria, and said, What do these feeble Jews? will they fortify themselves? will they sacrifice? will they make an end in a day? will they revive the stones out of the heaps of rubbish which are burned?" (Neh. 4:1, 2). They not only ridiculed their intentions of rebuilding the city but laughed at their work already done and said, "Even that which they build, if a fox go up, he shall even break down their stone wall" (v. 3).

Just how did Nehemiah meet this opposition of ridicule. First of all, he prayed and sought strength and encouragement from the Lord. He prayed and said, "Hear, O our God: for we are despised: and turn their reproach upon their own head, and give them for a prey in the land of captivity: And cover not their iniquity, and let not their sins be blotted out from before thee: for they have provoked thee to anger before the builders" (v. 4). Like the Apostle Paul, they, "thanked God and took courage."

Prayer is a great encourager. It serves to clear the air and to drive off the fogs and storms that obscure our sight of God. It gives an inner strength and joy that helps us endure what otherwise would be intolerable.

When Nehemiah prayed he saw his enemies in their true light. He accepted their ridicule for what it was worth. He considered its source. What is more, he saw God in His place. He was persuaded that with God on his side no opposition would be effective and need be feared.

Nehemiah did more than resort to prayer. One cannot do more than pray until he has prayed, but he can do more than pray after he has prayed. This was Nehemiah's policy. He prayed and worked. Perhaps he prayed as he worked but at any rate we read, "So built we the wall: and all the wall was joined together unto the half thereof: for the people had a mind to work" (v. 6). They not only had a heart to pray and believe, but they had a mind to work. Meditation and determination are necessary qualities in life. Prayer and labor, faith and works all have their part. One is out of balance without the other.

The strategy of the enemy of our souls is to get us to stop praying and to stop working. If he can get us to use our time answering ridicule and false accusation he has then accomplished his purpose. If Nehemiah had stopped his work and used his time in replying to his critics the main objective of his life would have been thwarted.

It is well to remember this today. Ridicule by the belittling of our efforts, the smallness of our numbers and the hopelessness of our cause will gain its purpose if we stop our work to answer our critics. The proper procedure is to pray and work. Two boys were on their way to school when they noticed the clock. Time had slipped by and they were in danger of being late. One boy said, "Let us stop and pray that we will not be late." The other one said, "No, let's run like sixty and pray as we run." He had the right idea and we will too, if we will tend to our business and not be diverted from the main objective of life.

If ridicule does not succeed, opposition will take the form of threatenings. That is what Nehemiah's enemies did. When they "heard that the walls of Jerusalem were made up, and that the breaches began to be stopped, then they were wroth, And conspired all of them together to come and to fight against Jerusalem, and to hinder it" (vv. 7, 8).

Nehemiah's defense against this form of opposition was to pray and watch. He did not idly disregard the threats of his enemies. Nor did he foolishly answer threatenings with threatenings. His first defense was prayer and his second defense was watchfulness. It is written, "Nevertheless we made our prayer unto our God and set a watch against them day and night." This was a wise strategy. It was the advice Jesus gave His disciples, "Watch and pray." It is what we must follow.

While they watched and prayed they continued to work. The work was not halted for a moment. Nehemiah delegated some to carry the sword and others to carry the trowel. Some would defend while the others carried on the construction of the wall. Besides this, those that worked on the outermost ramparts carried the sword at their side while they wielded the trowel in their hand. They recognized that they must defend themselves when the occasion arose and it proved that their defense was the very thing that discouraged their enemies.

Opposition will never be conquered by closing our eyes to its reality and existence or by ignoring it. We must have weapons of defense. These weapons are numerous. They can be an answer to every accusation, a good conscience, a strong character, positive convictions and a bold and courageous manner, all of which are supported by prayer and faith in God. If our enemies see that we ignore their threats they will overrun us with their abuse and opposition.

The sword and the trowel are the weapons of a persevering life. The sword is defensive and offensive while the trowel is an implement of construction. It would have been a completely lost cause if Nehemiah had directed his workers to lay down their trowels to take up the sword. Had they done this the purpose of their mission in Jerusalem would have been abandoned. Never stop work to fight. Be ready to fight and repel the invader but always keep up the work. A man's greatest defense is the work he is doing. If he constantly answers the attacks made on him he cannot work and if he does not work, he will not be able to fulfill the purpose of his life. During all the time Nehemiah was at his task he was the subject of ridicule and threatenings but not once did he lose the vision of his mission and cease his work in order to answer his critics.

If neither ridicule nor threats succeed, opposition may take the form of deceit and craft. By this time the walls had been so thoroughly restored that there was not a single breach anywhere. Even the gates had been rebuilt, save for the hanging of their doors. When Sanballat and Tobiah heard this they tried craft and deceit. They tried to inveigle Nehemiah to a village away from the city where they intended to do him harm. Nehemiah was wise to their ways and sent this reply, "I am doing a great work so that I cannot come down: why should the work cease, whilst I leave it and come down to you?" (Neh. 6:4).

The enemy's strategy of deceit will seek to get us to be diverted from our work. It may be by curiosity or by compromise or by many other means, but the one thing it seeks is to get us so preoccupied with other matters that we are no longer employed with the one important thing God gave us to do. If churches can be kept busy doing church work they will have no time for the work of the church. If Christians can be kept busy in diversionary enterprises they will have neither time nor strength for the primary enterprise of building.

We may be deceived in thinking that we can appease our enemies. Nehemiah might have thought this and gone to the suggested rendezvous. Europe learned that it did not pay to do business with Hitler just as the fly learned it did not pay to do business with the spider. The parlor was very beautiful but the end was bad. Being agreeable and acquiescent to the suggestions of associations from our enemies will result in disaster. Nehemiah was wise enough to refuse and his refusal was based on the one constantly remembered policy of keeping his work going. The work is the important consideration. It must go on.

If ridicule, threats and deceit fail, opposition may take the form of misrepresentation and false accusation. Sanballat and Tobiah failing of their purpose to stop the work of the Jews by all previous methods, now stoop to the lowest form of skulduggery, misrepresentation and false accusation. They accuse Nehemiah of plotting revolt and of preparing defenses to establish a rival kingdom. It was a form of blackmail for they offered to withdraw their accusations if Nehemiah would stop his work.

God gave this builder great wisdom. He saw through the purposes of his adversaries. He knew what was behind their propaganda and said, "For they all made us afraid, saying, Their hands shall be weakened from the work, that it be not done. Now therefore, O God, strengthen my hands" (v. 9).

Nehemiah denied all that was said but with that denial he refused to enter debate. To debate with his enemies on the merits of their accusations was what they wanted. Walls cannot be built with words. A man put on the defensive is taken off the offensive. Progress ceases when we stop to chase the dogs that bark at our heels. A lie will have its day and we must admit that it has quite a day, but even the worst lie has limitations. A good life is our best defense and a good conscience is our best meat.

Nehemiah took refuge in God and kept on with his work for he knew that these accusations were false. Truth is the only thing that hurts. If an accusation is true, correct it; if it is false give it a dignified denial and keep on working, keep on living, keep on trusting, keep on keeping on.

When all of these weapons of opposition fail there is yet one more to be pulled out of the arsenal of evil. It is fear. Nehemiah's enemies hired a man among the Jews to prophecy his death, who suggested that he go into the temple and stay there in hiding for his enemies were determined to kill him. The answer of noble Nehemiah is a classic. "And I said, Should such a man as I flee? and who is there, that, being as I am, would go into the temple to save his life? I will not go in" (v. 11).

Nehemiah had nothing to fear either inside or outside, from God or from man, consequently he took no craven refuge in God's house. To have done so would have been a tacit admission of guilt. It would have indicated his fear instead of faith. Nehemiah knew what he stood for and refused to move. His best and most invincible protection was his faith in God and his personal integrity.

Let a very simple secret establish your life in both peace and security. It is this, "If God be for us, who can be against us?" If you are on God's side you are on the winning side. It makes no difference what you see when you look inside or outside at the moment. God is not to be judged by appearance or by time. Listen to this answer.

"He that spared not his own Son, but delivered him up for us all, how shall he not with him also freely give us all things? Who shall lay any thing to the charge of God's elect? It is God that justifieth. Who is he that condemneth? It is Christ that died, yea rather, that is risen again, who is even at the right hand of God, who also maketh intercession for us. Who shall separate us from the love of Christ? Shall tribulation, or distress, or persecution, or famine, or nakedness, or peril, or sword? As it is written, For thy sake we are killed all the day long; we are accounted as sheep for the slaughter. Nay, in all these things we are more than conquerors through him that loved us. For I am persuaded, that neither death, nor life, nor angels, nor principalities, nor powers, nor things present, nor things to come, nor height, nor depth, nor any other creature, shall be able to separate us from the love of God, which is in Christ Jesus our Lord" (Rom. 8:32-39).

While opposition took the numerous forms of ridicule, threats, deceit, misrepresentation and fear, Nehemiah met and conquered every one. He never lost sight of the goal. He never diverted his efforts. He kept right on. What were the results? Success. It is written in these words, "So the wall was finished in the twenty and fifth day of the month Elul, in fifty and two days" (Neh. 6:15). It was incredible but true, and the reason for this phenomenal success lay perhaps in the statement of a single sentence, "For the people had a mind to work." They stayed with their purpose and they conquered opposition.

The crowning token of success came in the justification that Nehemiah's enemies were forced to pay this noble man, "And it came to pass, that when all our enemies heard thereof, and all the heathen that were about us saw these things, they were much cast down in their own eyes: for they perceived that this work was wrought of our God" (v. 16). Here was justification and vindication for Nehemiah. It will surely come to all who will follow his plan of life. It may not come as quickly but it will come as certainly. The secret of Nehemiah's conquest of opposition can be summed up in a single sentence. He kept his eye on the goal. While he recognized the reality of the opposition which threatened him he refused to stop his work and to engage in dispute. He had work to do and he did it. He saw the goal and he kept on toward it. He was persuaded of the presence of God and he considered all else in its lesser importance.

Nehemiah finished what he started. He succeeded in what he set out to accomplish. This shall always be the crowning accomplishment of his life. He will be remembered as a stedfast man who obeyed God and persevered in his work. His life should be a great incentive to all who regard It.

# 13
# *Job*
## *The Conquest of Adversity*

SCARCELY ANY CHARACTER of the Bible reaches the stature and magnificence of Job. Although the book that bears his name and tells of his adversities is forty-two chapters in length, less is known of Job than most any other primary character in the Bible.

The eminence of Job is reached in a field of human experience rather than human endeavor. It is not because he was a great prophet or a great leader or a great ruler, but because he was a great sufferer.

While Job was a man of the world in the sense that he was a successful businessman, it is the delineation of his character that stands out. His character is more precious and valuable than all the prestige of his position and all the accumulation of his treasure. It is shown to be the most valuable possession that any person can have. Its value in the case of Job is revealed against a background of tragedy and adversity. It is not set forth, as most of us would like it to be in our experience, in relation to ease and comfort and unbroken prosperity.

To begin with, Job is revealed as a perfect, upright and God-fearing man. Because he fears God he flees evil. His reverence of God is revealed in his rejection of evil. This righteousness of Job is established at the very beginning of the account of his life to contradict and counteract the idea that his afflictions are the result of his sin. It is often said of those who suffer adversity' that it is the result of sin, but in the lives of the two greatest sufferers in the Bible, one the Old Testament Job and the other the New Testament Paul, it is true of neither.

In fact, the book of Job is a refutation of speculative theories on the problem of suffering. It reveals the despair of old theories. Their explanation of the evils of the universe have been incapable of accounting for these evils. None of them are capable of furnishing a solution for the adversities and sufferings of earth. When its end is reached the book of Job sees the inglorious retreat and exit of a group of proud philosophers and the ascendency and vindication of Job. The philosophers tried to give an answer for suffering in an explanation: Job gave an answer for it in an experience.

When Job met with adversity he had something to lose. He was a man of means, with much property, a large family and a high place in the world. It is said of him that "this man was the greatest of all the men of the East." What he lost was worth losing and what he gained through his loss was worth gaining.

Job's conquest of adversity was not achieved by the sheer power of his will. No amount of will power can retrieve a fortune and a family loss in a series of physical calamities or a health loss by a total affliction of body-boils. It was achieved by what he retained in the midst of all his losses: he retained God. This retention is very dim and very slim at times. The thread of faith is stretched very tenuously but it holds. At one time all Job sees of God is divine omnipotence but he faithfully holds to the thread of light until it becomes a glare.

Job's conquest of adversity is achieved because he considers the forces of two worlds. He considers an invisible world and a visible world. That is why the book of Job differs from all other attempts to explain the problem of suffering. It takes us behind the scenes of suffering and shows us that there is an unseen world of evil to reckon with. Unless we reckon with this world we will flounder in a bog of speculation and confusion.

Job becomes the object of physical assault. The means is natural calamity. The source is a satanic desire to prove that whenever and wherever a man is religious and righteous it is solely because he finds it profitable to be so. When Jehovah asked Satan to consider Job "that there is none like him in the earth, a perfect and an upright man, one that feareth God, and escheweth evil" Satan answers by saying that Job does not fear God for nought. The reason for his fear is his reward. He says that Job found out that it pays to be pious for has not Jehovah put "an hedge about him, and about his house, and about all that he hath on every side? thou hast blessed the work of his hands, and his substance is increased in the land" (Job 1:10). It is suggested by Satan that a fair test of Job's integrity would be to remove this protecting hedge and take away Job's possessions and see the result. According to Satan the result will be Job's capitulation. He will surrender his faith. He will turn upon God for his only interest in God is his personal prosperity in material things.

Satan's contentions are false for when a series of physical calamities sweep from Job all his possessions and every one of his children he does not turn against God. He proves that his righteousness is not for material gain. His reaction to his adversity is described in these words, "Then Job arose, and rent his mantle, and shaved his head, and fell down upon the ground, and worshiped, and said, naked came I out of my mother's womb, and naked shall I return thither: the Lord gave and the Lord hath taken away: blessed be the name of the Lord. In all this Job sinned not, nor charged God foolishly" (1:20-22).

Failing in this test to prove his contention that men are righteous for the profit it pays, Satan suggests another test, "Skin for skin, yea, all that a man hath will he give for his life. But put forth thine hand now, and touch his bone and his flesh, and he will curse thee to thy face" (2:4, 5). What follows is the loss of Job's health in an affliction of boils from head to feet.

It is one thing to lose one's means of support and even to lose one's family, but when the body is touched and strength is depleted by the weakness of sickness, that is another thing. It is hard to fight on a bed, paralyzed or fevered. Job found this out upon an ash-pile seeking antiseptic relief for the total pollution of his body by running abscesses.

Here he was met with another calamity, the betrayal of his wife. In this hour of adversity when a man needed the moral and spiritual strength of a wife's faithful counsel and comfort she reveals her perfidious character by suggesting, what Satan had always contended, that under trial Job would make his denial. She was what Satan said Job was, a turncoat and a hypocrite.

Job's answer is a classic of courage and character, "He said unto her, Thou speakest as one of the foolish women speaketh. What? Shall we receive good at the hand of God, and shall we not receive evil? In all this did not Job sin with his lips" (2:10).

Where Satan stops, man takes up. Job had refuted the satanic contention that piety was a pretense, religion was a sham and righteousness was a racket. Satan makes his exit with his figurative tail between his legs. He is thoroughly discredited by Job's integrity. The worst he can do is not bad enough to move Job from his purity and sincerity. Entrance is now made by some of Job's friends. They are called such anyway. They take up where Satan leaves off. They are not seeking to establish that Job's righteousness is for material gain but rather that Job's adversities are because of moral and spiritual wrong and sin.

Under the repeated impacts of adversity Job is greatly shaken. He rues the day he was born. He desires the day of death. In this state of physical and spiritual weakness his three friends pounce upon him and accuse him of personal sin because of his unusual adversities. At first he refutes their arguments by the evidences of his righteous life. He denies that he is a special sinner because his life was pure and true. That argument is borne out by God's estimate of Job which said that he was "perfect and upright, and one that feared God, and eschewed evil."

Job finds it is quite impossible to achieve vindication in the eyes of men by argument alone. Men will not to be convinced. Argument is with them only a device of maintaining a controversy. They must have their own opinions no matter what it costs another in suffering or sorrow. Job turns to God and in the dire need of his life he finds a faith which can not only face calamity and adversity but which can survive the severest onslaughts of evil. In the succeeding cycles of conversations Job makes a remarkable confession of faith; he reveals a most exact kinship to all men and women who pass through sorrow and suffering.

Job conquers adversity by his faith in God. At one time we hear his cry from the antiseptic ash-pile, "Though he slay me, yet will I trust him." At this time his faith may have been somewhat blind and God may have been some where distant, but Job believed with what faith he had. Again we hear his cry, "For I know that my redeemer liveth, and that he shall stand at the latter day upon the earth: and though after my skin worms destroy this body, yet in my flesh shall I see God" (19:25, 26). Here his faith may have placed his hopes off into the future but it was such faith as would ultimately help him. Again we hear his cry, "But he knoweth the way that I take: when he hath tried me, I shall come forth as gold" (23:10). Here his faith sees a purpose in his present experiences. He is convinced of the justice of God's dealings. He is sure God knows and cares. This sustains him as he bears his great adversities.

Yet Job needs more than a faith that looks only to the future: he needs more than a faith that embraces a God who is afar off. He needs a God who is near: a God who is present. Yes, Job needs a God on his ash-pile; with him as well as on the throne in heaven. This is the need of all men and women. There may be a certain religious peace in paying respects to a God who "sitteth on the circle of the earth" but it is better to know a God who can be touched by the feelings of our infirmaties. It is neccessary to have a God who can be company for us beside our bed of sickness and comfort to us beside our graves of sorrow. It is equally needful to have a God who will multiply strength, increase ability and be our counsel in all the ways of life.

Such a comfort as this, which all men need, Job found. He found it in a faith that could face all the stern facts of life. He found it in a faith which gave him a personal experience with a personal God. God was no indefinite force. He was an intimate friend. God was no longer an avenger. He was an advocate. God was no longer afar off. He was heart-near.

Job found such a faith in humility. He did not find it in a laboratory, a classroom or a law court, but on an ash-pile. He found it amidst adversity. He was not roaming the pleasure haunts of men. He was deep in the heart of sorrow. There he found a faith with which to face life and this is what he said, "Then Job answered the Lord, and said, I know that thou canst do everything, and that no thought can be witholden from thee. Who is he that hideth counsel without knowledge? therefore have I uttered that I understand not; things too wonderful for me, which I knew not. Hear, I beseech thee, and I will speak: I will demand of thee, and declare thou unto me. I have heard of thee by the hearing of the ear: but now mine eye seeth thee. Wherefore I . . . repent in dust and ashes" (42:1-6).

The adversaries of Job challenged him to give them his best explanation of God in order to justify his adversities. Job is now satisfied with an experience. He came to God in the darkness and accepted the burden without asking a reason for it and he goes away in the light. He did not ask to comprehend and now he is able to apprehend. He accepted the mystery and now he is given the mastery. Now he triumphs over his adversaries as well as his adversities.

The turning point in Job's adversity came when two things took place. First, when he was able to say of himself, "I have heard of thee by the hearing of the ear: but now mine eye seeth thee. Wherefore I abhor myself, and repent in dust and ashes." And again, when he was able to pray for his adversaries for then it is said, "And the Lord turned the captivity of Job, when he prayed for his friends." There would be no triumph and no victory so long as he was self-contained or self-contaminated. He could not be well and healthy and spiritually vigorous so long as the animus and virus of hatred were in him. There must be a cleansing before there can be a healing. Wounds never heal over inner infections.

When this came to Job God brought about an abundant restoration of substance and home even to the extent of multiplying it twofold. In this restoration we find the complete vindication of Job.

# 14
# Isaiah
## The Conquest of Despondency

ISAIAH'S LIFE AND ministry revolved around a great experience. That experience gave him a true estimate of himself by giving him a vision of God. It was the day of Isaiah's new beginning.

The record of Isaiah's life does not begin as records usually do, by telling where and when he was born but rather where and when he was born again. To Isaiah the real beginning of life was his spiritual awakening. All of us have two beginnings and the second is more important than the first, although without the first we could not have the second. Nonetheless, our second beginning prepares us for life by correcting what is wrong about the first beginning.

In Isaiah's case we find him the victim of despondency. He was despondent over personal and national conditions. Nationally the people of Israel were very religious but also very unrighteous. They were busy keeping the Sabbaths, observing the new moons and going about their feasts. In the midst of all this religious activity Isaiah is directed by God to ask a question for Him of the people: "To what purpose is the multitude of your sacrifices unto me?" (1:11). These were but the cloak of pretense with which they tried to cover up their national iniquity. Sacrifice without sanctity is a mockery. Religion without righteousness is hypocrisy. Altar prayers without closet prayers are vain repetitions. God required more than burnt offerings and Isaiah was instructed to say this: 'Wash you, make you clean; put away the evil of your doings from before mine eyes; cease to do evil; learn to do well: seek judgment, relieve the oppressed, judge the fatherless, plead for the widow. Come now, let us reason together, saith the Lord: though your sins be as scarlet, they shall be as white as snow: though they be red like crimson, they shall be as wool" (Isa. 1:16-18).

Isaiah's despondency was personal as well. It is revealed in the date mark of his great life-changing experience which is described in the sixth chapter. It is dated with the death of a king. That king was one of Isaiah's heroes and represented his hope. The king was Uzziah who had reigned for fifty-two years. His reign was highly successful but it ended tragically in the personal defection of the king who tried to usurp the priestly office and died a leper outcast. These happenings evidently had a despondent effect upon Isaiah who ponders them deeply and becomes concerned over his own and his nation's future. In this dark mood he makes his way to the temple where he sees vision. Instead of the vacant throne of his king there is the occupied throne of his God. Instead of an erring man whom he had idolized there is an unerring God in whom Isaiah may place his utmost confidence. It is this vision of God that changes both the character and course of Isaiah's life.

The surest cure for despondency is a transporting vision; not the kind that we often indulge in, although these sometimes serve a good purpose. Their deficiency is that they are only temporary. Sometimes when feeling blue and when in the depths of despondency we find ourselves carried on the wings of thought and we build castles and dream dreams. We find some relief, but it is only short-lived because when they vanish we are plunged back into our valley.

The vision Isaiah had was different. It was spiritual as well as mental. It was authentic because it was in God's house. There are conditions which govern our spiritual experiences and when these conditions maintain the experiences materialize. Isaiah was in a spiritual position and a spiritual atmosphere. He was where he could expect an authentic experience.

The result of this vision was a voice. It was the voice of God identifying His glory and speaking to Isaiah revealing his sin and shame.

What Isaiah experienced in the temple cannot be expected to be repeated either in its geographical or historical or splendorous details. None of us will behold the awe-inspiring sight of seraphic beings surrounding the Lord Jehovah on a throne high and lifted up. However, all of us do require an experience with God that will reveal His unblemished holiness and our sinfulness and unworthiness. Unless we have such an experience within our own soul we will never be what we ought to be.

First of all, Isaiah was where he ought to be. It was the place where God was to be found. Yet, it took a personal sorrow to bring him there. The Lord was always in his temple but Isaiah was not always looking. One day tragedy walked into his life and he walked into God's house.

It is often true today that we never stop to get our vision until sorrow stops us. We had been so satisfied with the secondary that we had no time for the primary. We were so busy with the things we could see that we did not see the things unseen. So it was in the year that our baby died, in the year the great depression came, in the year our health left us—it was then we saw the Lord. It was then we stopped to look and listen. It was then we had our great awakening and our new beginning.

What Isaiah saw resulted in a sequence of important events in his life.

*It made Isaiah conscious of sin.* When he saw the vision of divine splendor he became conscious of his own imperfections. He had been resting and trusting in a human king but now he was brought to trust in a divine king. His sense of God brought a sense of sin. Everyone of us must have a sense, a deep feeling of sin before there can be a true confession of sin. It can be truly said that no one has ever had a sense of God if he has not had a sense of sin. Every person whose experiences have been detailed in the Bible from Job through Daniel to Peter and Paul had this sense of sin because he was brought to a sense of God.

*It brought Isaiah to confess sin.* Before he confessed the sins of his people Isaiah confessed his own. We hear him say, "Woe is me! for I am undone; because I am a man of unclean lips, and I dwell in the midst of a people of unclean lips: for mine eyes have seen the King, the Lord of hosts" (6:5).

Conviction precedes confession and confession is necessary for cleansing. For us the New Testament formula of 1 John 1:9 is in dispensational order, "If we confess our sins, he is faithful and just to forgive our sins and to cleanse us from all unrighteousness."

Isaiah was to be dispatched upon a national mission but before that could be fulfilled a personal condition must be met. It was met in God's house in a life-changing spiritual experience.

Before Isaiah did anything about the condition of his nation he did something about himself. The way to make the world better is to begin with one's self. This betterment of Isaiah was not an effort of self-reformation. It was to be God's work of grace and it was related to God's house. It was here that Isaiah's preparation for life was made.

*It resulted in Isaiah's cleansing from sin.* Isaiah could confess sin but only God could cleanse it. No sooner had he made his confession than he received God's cleansing. The confession came as a result of Isaiah's vision of a throne while the cleansing came by means of an altar. There was both a throne of holiness and an altar of atonement. One brings conviction and the other brings cleansing.

One of the seraphic beings flew with a live coal from the altar and laid it on Isaiah's lips and said, "Thine iniquity is taken away and thy sin purged" (6:6). The lips are the expressive agents of the inner man. Their fruit comes from the root of the heart. They were to be the instrument of service in the prophet's office and hence they must be cleansed and fitted for service.

*It resulted in Isaiah's consecration to God.* This means one's whole and entire devotion to a great cause or task. In Isaiah's case it was to his nation. Isaiah heard God's voice saying, 'Whom shall I send, and who will go for us? Then said I, Here am I; send me" (6:8).

In the act of consecration we do the surrendering while God does the consecrating. This is a divine act by which we are set apart for service. It involves the surrender of our will, our ambitions and our desires as it also involves God's acceptance of us and the designation of our lives for the task to which we have surrendered.

*It put upon Isaiah a commission of service.* God said, "Go and tell this people." Isaiah had said, "Here I am" and God said, "Go." This was his commissioning. When a battleship is launched and passed through the process of fitting with instruments and armaments she is commissioned in what is quite an elaborate and impressive ceremony. When this is done in war it amounts to a simple direction, "Go." It is sent to the fleet and plays its part in the grand strategy of war.

Isaiah stepped from the temple into the great war of evil that raged in his nation. He was God's man for a nation's crisis. He went with "burnt lips" to which we might add the New Testament qualification of a "burning heart." Are your lips burnt and does your heart burn? Is there response within to God's voice and preparation for His service?

From this temple experience Isaiah went to conduct his great mission. He became God's voice to a wayward people. He was God's timepiece in evil times. He was a watchman on the walls. He drops the rags of despondency and despair and becomes a prophet of bold optimism. It was Isaiah who gave us our greatest prophecies of the coming Savior.

Despondency may arise from many causes. It may be natural to us. Many people are moody and are easily discouraged. Oftentimes sickness and disappointment are its causes, but it has its remedy. Isaiah lost his despondency in God's presence. While we cannot expect to see what Isaiah saw there is a place of vision. It may be the place of prayer in our closet of retreat where we see God "sitting upon a throne, high and lifted up." It may be the place of meditation before an open Bible where our vision comes. Or, it may be as it was with Isaiah, God's house, where in the company of His people we are transported by music and message into the place of vision and inspiration.

Despondency cannot live in the face of God's Word. It cannot exist in God's presence. Here the sigh changes to the song and the bowed head to the lifted face. It is here that we will thank God and take courage. It is here that we will "rejoice in the Lord" and find that we can leave this meeting place with God and face the world with faith and courage.

# 15
# *Jeremiah*
## *The Conquest of Frustration*

JEREMIAH IS COMMONLY characterized as a prophet of tears and melancholy, no doubt from the fact that he wrote Lamentations. To whatever degree this was true, it had a reason. The reason lay not alone in Jeremiah's nature which was timid, sensitive, shy and retiring, but also in the conditions of the people he served and the apparent lack of results in his ministry. He was the victim of frustration. He felt he was defeated and prevented from attaining his life's purpose. He felt that all his efforts were in vain and ineffectual and that his life was a failure. Many of us have felt the same way. We have been thwarted in reaching the place we set out to attain or in doing the thing we set out to perform. We have not been successful in achieving much success. We have been unable to largely influence the lives of those about us. It has resulted in a feeling of frustration which has produced discouragement and regret and a sense of defeat. Perhaps we have had our days of lamentation. Perhaps we have wished to give up. If we have ever been like that we have a certain relation to Jeremiah. We will meet ourselves in him.

Let us inquire and see what lay within and without the experience of Jeremiah that our own lives may profit from our findings.

It appears that Jeremiah was early aware of his life's mission as a prophet because, for one thing, he had a long public career of fifty years. He was God's chosen instrument from before his birth for God said, "Before I formed thee in the belly I knew thee; and before thou camest forth out of the womb I sanctified thee, and ordained thee a prophet unto the nations" (Jer. 1:5).

Jeremiah's first reaction was the common plea of unfitness. He said, "Ah, Lord God! behold, I cannot speak." This no doubt arose from his natural shyness but also from a sense of humility. Any proper person will shrink from a great place with a sense of unworthiness and unfitness. He will feel true reticence in finding himself God's choice. It is right when it is so for this shows genuine humility. But humility can be carried too far. When we use our weaknesses as an excuse for our responsibilities we are walking unworthily as the children of God. It is one thing to properly appreciate one's limitations, but it is quite another to allow those limitations to determine the limit of our usefulness.

God's answer to Jeremiah's complaint was both a command and an enablement. "But the Lord said unto me, Say not, I am a child: for thou shalt go to all that I shall send thee, and whatsoever I command thee thou shalt speak. Be not afraid of their faces: for I am with thee to deliver thee, saith the Lord. Then the Lord put forth his hand, and touched my mouth. And the Lord said unto me, Behold, I have put my words in thy mouth" (1:7-9).

For fifty years, this man of the shy and retiring nature carried on a most strenuous and dangerous public ministry. He lived in the most troublous times. His people were besieged, captured and enslaved by enemies. There were dissensions, and disorder in their own ranks. There were disturbing social problems in which there were the extremities of riches and poverty, plenty and want. Discontent, hatred, misery and envy filled the hearts of the common people. The land was filled with idolatry and apostasy. All of these conditions brought despair to the heart of Jeremiah but he did not allow his personal sensitiveness to hinder his ministry. He warned, condemned and judged his nation, but it seemed as though nothing would change the course of its iniquity.

In return for his faithful warnings Jeremiah received threatenings and persecution. He was exceedingly unpopular. He was opposed and condemned. He was ridiculed and scorned. On one occasion he was stoned out of his own native village. Again he was beaten in public disgrace. He was imprisoned. He was thrown into the stinking slime of a pit.

All of this made Jeremiah wonder. Was he personally mistaken about God's call? Was he in the right place? Was God with him? It led to a feeling of frustration and we hear him cry out, "Oh that I had in the wilderness a lodging place of wayfaring men: that I might leave my people, and go from them for they be all adulterers, an assembly of treacherous men" (9:2) .

Here was the human feeling of failure and the altogether human longing to leave it and get away from it all. Who has not had both the feeling and the longing? The housewife longs to leave behind her the monotony of the home. The husband longs to leave behind him the unthankful job. The preacher longs to leave an unworthy appointment. However, the remedy is never found in leaving.

Jeremiah's feeling of frustration arose out of the apparent failure of his life's work. He felt thwarted and hindered in his great life's mission. He had warned with tears night and day and yet his warnings went unheeded. He had counselled and advised without response. The tragedy or his life is this, "that he preached to deaf ears and reaped only hate in return for his love to his fellow-countrymen. He was lightly esteemed in life, and he sank into the grave of a broken-hearted man. From being of no account as a prophet he came to be regarded as the greatest of them all."

Frustration can come from two causes. It can arise from the sense of our own inability or it can come from the unresponsive circumstances in which we labor. It appears that Jeremiah had conquered the first and suffered the last, at least for a time. It was the failure of his people that now brought Jeremiah to his sense of frustration. He was unable to reach them and to win them. He said at one time, "A wonderful and horrible thing is committed in the land: The prophets prophesy falsely, and the priests bear rule by their means; and my people love to have it so" (5:31, 32).

At another time we hear him say, "The harvest is past, the summer is ended, and we are not saved" (8:20).

It was this apparent lack of success that caused Jeremiah to long for the wilderness and to leave his unfruitful place. Nevertheless, he did not go, he remained stedfast. He stayed to finish his half century of faithful service. He conquered frustration. What Jeremiah did, we may do also.

Jeremiah conquered frustration and remained at his prophetic post because of his faith in God. It is reflected in Jeremiah's own confession of faith concerning a man's trust in God. "Blessed is the man that trusteth in the Lord, whose hope the Lord is. For he shall be as a tree planted by the waters, and that spreadeth out her roots by the river, and shall not see when heat cometh, but her leaf shall be green; and shall not be careful in the year of drought, neither shall cease from yielding fruit" (17:7, 8). When Jeremiah looked at his surroundings he longed to flee to the wilderness. When he looked at God he was satisfied with his lot in life and convinced no matter what conditions prevailed, faith would bring fruitfulness.

This faith gave him an unshakable conviction in the truth of his message. This conviction was not lessened by the fact that there were many false prophets in his time. He had witnessed a long procession of these prophets come and go. They curried popular favor and cried, "Peace, peace: when there is no peace." Jeremiah remained true to God even though it meant his own depreciation and persecution.

There is nothing like a great conviction to steady one in moments of depression and frustration. If this conviction has its roots in our faith it will hold us stedfast no matter what the circumstances around us may urge us to do. No matter what pressure is laid upon us and no matter what the trend of opposition against us we will find ourselves held strong and steady.

This conviction of faith may not see the fulfillment of its hope as was the case with Jeremiah but faith does not need to see, for faith believes without sight. Faith knows that God will accomplish what is promised and prophesied when the time is ripe. Faith says, "Be not weary in well doing: for in due season we shall reap, if we faint not" (Gal. 6:9). Faith says, "He that goeth forth and weepeth, bearing precious seed, shall doubtless come again with rejoicing, bringing his sheaves with him" (Ps. 126:6). Faith says, Therefore my beloved brethren, be ye stedfast, unmovable, always abounding in the work of the Lord, forasmuch as ye know that your labor is not in vain in the Lord" (1 Cor. 15:58).

It was such faith as this that kept Jeremiah at his place for fifty years, through famine, pestilence, captivity and apparent failure. Although he failed to move his generation he has moved subsequent generations. Although he was judged a professional failure he has proved to be a personal success.

This lesson all of us must learn, namely, that true faith will always lead to faithfulness. Jeremiah was faithful. Although he saw no visible results, although he received no credit from his own generation, although he paid a great personal price, he was faithful. This was success of the highest order. This faith kept him true and keeping true was the most necessary attribute of his life.

It must be so with us also. We must keep true. We must remain faithful The feeling of frustration must never lead us to desertion. It must never be allowed to shorten our vision so that all we see is what happens today.

It is evident also that Jeremiah conquered frustration by his sense of duty. This was an outgrowth of his faith in God. To have fled would have vacated a place of service which his people could in-afford to be without. It was no matter that this place was not pleasant or that it was hard or disagreeable. Duty does not require ease or comfort. It only asks, Is this my place?

It has been true of all of us more than once in life that we have sought to flee from our lot in life because it was not pleasant or easy. The test is not how we feel but what is our duty. Those who have done the most in life for God and man have not consulted their feelings. Jesus did not stay on the cross because it felt good. Paul did not pursue his ministry because it felt good. It is not our feelings but our compulsions which count. Duty must never compromise with comfort.

Jeremiah's faith and sense of duty were supported by a third reason for his conquest of frustration. It was the power of God. Jeremiah had been brought up in "the great company of scholars, priests, prophets and students of God's teachings." This fact accounted for his early faith but when he was thrust into the maelstrom of turbulent times he needed something more than could be given him by this quiet company. He needed power and strength and such as he needed he found in the company of God. The very times in which he lived: the very persecutions and abuses he suffered forced him back upon God. Here he found strength and courage. Here he was nourished upon divine food. Here he was steadied and made stedfast.

Frustration, this feeling of having failed and having been thwarted and denied our place in life, is bound to come to all of us at some time in our lives. It is most prevalent in the forties when we have lived long enough to have tried our wings and tasted both success and failure. We may feel that the home is too narrow for our nature and too limited for our ability. We may feel that all we have tried has enjoyed only mediocre success or perhaps is a total failure. In any case, our feelings are never the best judge of our circumstances. There are two proper standards, our faith and God's Word. Measure life by faith rather than feeling and see the difference it makes. Judge it by God's Word and you will have the right standard of comparison.

In all this we should be careful not to be too severe or too lenient. We can be both. There is a sense in which we must be severe in our self-judgment, but too much severity is bad. We must be frank and open in our self-judgment. Perhaps we are right in concluding that we have not been as faithful or as zealous as we should have been. Perhaps our lack of success and results is as real as it seems. In that case we must not seek a false comfort and console ourselves with self-pity. We should acknowledge our sin before God and surrender our life to God in new faith and devotion.

On the other hand the feeling of frustration may be Satan's weapon of discouragement. It may be his way to distort life and unbalance us emotionally. We may see everything in the shadows and conclude that nothing is worth while.

Whatever it may be, let us remember our visit with Jeremiah and recall in all kinds of conditions, that it is faith in God, a sense of duty and God's keeping and sustaining power that will hold us fast and true. None of us escape the need and all of us may have the experience.

# 16
# Daniel
## The Conquest of Fear

MOST PEOPLE READ the book of Daniel for the sake of its prophecy; few read it for the help of its prophet. Most people read it to see if they can find out what is going to happen in days to come; few read it in order to find out how to live today. Most people are interested in speculation; few in consecration. The book of Daniel provides some of the Bible's greatest lessons in personal trial and triumph. It gives in chapter 9 among other things, one of the greatest examples of prayer to be found anywhere in the Bible.

The book of Daniel is twelve chapters in length and divided into two equal parts. The first six chapters contain subject matter dealing almost exclusively with Daniel's personal life, save in one or two instances. These six chapters contain three great experiences which provide, for us, the principles of conquest in personal life. These experiences reveal the preparation for a conquest of fear in an unusual way. Fears of many kinds meet us in life. There are fears that have physical consequences and fears that have mental effects. Some are real and some imaginary. Perhaps most are like the latter, but real or imaginary, they constitute a difficult problem.

Daniel mastered fear by courage. His courage was more than an animal bravery based upon brute strength. It was founded where all real courage must be found, faith in God.

The most courageous people in the world are not necessarily those who brave physical dangers or exhibit their danger before the eye of men. The bravest souls that ever lived are those who have had to suffer alone. A soldier can lose all fear in an instant, in battle. The sound of guns, the presence of his comrades all serve to crystalize and galvanize his physical and mental forces so that he loses all sense and feeling of fear, but, not all people enter combat as soldiers. Some must wage their warfare of life all alone. Some of the bravest and most courageous people in the world never set foot on a city sidewalk; they never mingle with a crowd; they are never known to the world. Their battlefield may be a bed of sickness. Their conflict may be within. They must fight where no eye can see and no applause can cheer them on. Because of these conditions their conquest is all the more noble and praiseworthy.

Daniel's life is within reach of ours because the principles it illustrates are practical for our own experience. Romance and greatness may be something which fiction ascribes with daring exploits but the Bible puts them within the reach of the daily walk and experience of each of us. The smallest person in the most obscure place may know greatness and have romance because they belong to character. In God's sight the first are sometimes last and the last first.

The three high points of Daniel's life came in the form of tests of courage. These tests cover the entire field of human experience; not every possible experience, mind you, but the entire range of experience. It was first spiritual, then mental and finally physical.

## 1. *The Spiritual Test*

This occurred under no strange or unusual circumstances. It was particularly a young man's test. Daniel appears before us as a mere boy. He was among certain choice captives taken from Jerusalem to Babylon. How choice he was is revealed in the king's instructions to the master of his eunuchs that "he should bring certain of the children of Israel, and of the king's seed, and of the princes; children in whom was no blemish, but well-favored, and skillful in all wisdom, and cunning in knowledge, and understanding science; and such as had ability to stand in the king's palace, and whom they might teach the learning and the tongue of the Chaldeans" (1:3, 4). Having these qualities Daniel was among the first to be removed to Babylon. He was but a lad of fourteen. Consider the tremendous uprooting which took place in this boy's life. At fourteen a boy is only in the second year of his teens. He had not yet begun to be a man, yet Daniel is early called upon to bear the sorrows of a tragic experience. He is torn from the arms of his mother and the sheltering care of his father. He is taken from the influence of a godly home and thrust into the most inhospitable surroundings. What transpires is a tribute to the importance and value of a godly home training. The prayers of his parents and the influence of his home bear abundant fruit in the life of this lad now taken captive.

For three years Daniel and three companions are trained in a royal seminary for special court service. Their introduction to this period of training put upon them a very severe test. It was required of Daniel that they should eat "of the king's meat, and of the wine which he drank." This was far more than a question of vegetarianism and even more than one that transgressed Jewish law about the eating of improperly killed animals. It involved a spiritual principle. The food associated with the king's table was identified with the gods of the land hence Daniel saw the danger of giving sanction to idolatry and so he "purposed in his heart that he would not defile himself with the portion of the kings meat, nor with the wine which he drank" (1:8).

From the standpoint of a careless world this would be considered as the foolishness of an over-scrupulous youth. It would have been thought of as very imprudent and foolish. Here were three boys endangering their standing for the sake of what they ate. Moreover, they were captives and any disobedience of the regulations of their captivity and purpose of the king would have put them in a very precarious position. Expediency would have done differently and perhaps great pressure was put on Daniel to change his position, but Daniel was convinced that it would be wrong and he would never transgress his convictions, no matter what the consideration or the temporary advantages.

God and circumstances proved Daniel to be right. He was vindicated and exalted for at the end of his three years of royal training, during which time he touched none of the food from the royal table with its idolatrous taint, Daniel and his companions had excelled and exceeded all the rest. God singularly honored their faith and courage and justified the position they took for of them it is said, "As for these four children, God gave them knowledge and skill in all learning and wisdom" (1:17).

One can be quite sure that this knowledge and skill was not the direct result of their diet. It does not prove that vegetarianism and temperance will make a person brilliant. Experience does not corroborate this at all. It does say that God gave them knowledge and skill and we may properly inquire how. Did God hand out these gifts directly or indirectly? Did He put these things in them consciously or unconsciously? They were the result of both a choice and a course. The choice was to put God first and suffer whatever consequences resulted. The course was three years of faith and faithfulness at the end of which the king found them ten times better than all the magicians and astrologers of his court. I am quite sure that Daniel studied and worked during this time but his efforts were under the direct influence of his communion with God. He had chosen to be true to God and God chose to bless Daniel. God's blessing was real but it came within the usual sphere of industry, work and faithfulness.

The choice that Daniel made proves that it is always right to do right. There are no circumstances where it is right to do wrong. Nothing is more urgent and more necessary than doing right. It is never necessary to sin. Even the most pressing circumstances cannot justify wrong. Death is never an argument in its favor. Promotion and advancement must not induce us to evil. Expediency cannot be an argument. None ever had more convincing circumstances to cause them to yield their position, than Daniel, yet they were not made an excuse for giving in to what he felt and understood was wrong.

What Daniel experienced proves that most fears are unfounded. We fear the consequences of living righteously and honorably only to find that our fears are not justified. We fear that honesty does not pay because we see evil men prospering but we fail to remember that temporary prosperity is not lasting success. God's Book says to us, "I have seen the wicked in great power, and spreading himself like a green bay tree. Yet he passed away, and, lo, he was not: yea, I sought him, but he could not be found. Mark the perfect man, and behold the upright: for the end of that man is peace" (Ps. 37:35-37). What counts in a race is being ahead at the end. What matters in life is your finish and the finish depends on righteousness and godliness no matter how much evildoers may prosper now. There is no permanent prosperity in evil.

It is not our fears but our faith which God honors. It was Daniel's faith which made him bold and courageous enough to defy royal regulations. It was faith which led Daniel to base the entire success of his life on doing right. Physical courage might come from the functioning of the glands of your body but strength of character comes from faith. Daniel discounted his circumstances and counted on God.

It will be well for us to remember the value of trusting God in daily life. As Daniel proved the power of faith and trust in God in doing right, we also will find that it pays. The housewife, the business man and like Daniel, the schoolboy, can all experience the practical and eternal benefits of courage by faith.

## 2. *The Mental Test*

Daniel was faced with the solution of a great problem. The king had dreamed a dream which troubled him greatly and he could not understand it. He then put upon the wise men of his court the impossible responsibility of both recalling the dream and interpreting it. It was beyond their ability and the penalty for their failure was to be death for the whole company of court astrologers. This would include Daniel and his three companions. To save the situation Daniel went to the king and offered to recall and interpret the royal dream. This was a daring thing to do. It was manifestly a venture of faith. Daniel must have been sure of his ground, for he immediately went to his three companions and got them to pray for the success of his mission. God answered prayer and Daniel was given wisdom for the solution of the problem. The result was an explanation of one of the most significant revelations in all the Bible. Daniel went before the king and recalled to him the fact that his sleep-drenched mind saw a gigantic image of many metals standing on feet of clay and depicting successive world empires of the Gentile nations. This great multi-metal image stood in its grandeur and magnitude and splendor until in its final phase of existence a great stone was cut without human hands from the surrounding mountain and falling upon the feet of the image completely destroyed it while the stone grew into a great universal kingdom which filled the earth and had no end.

The significance of all this is explained to Nebuchadnezzer and "the king made Daniel a great man, and gave him many great gifts, and made him ruler over the whole province of Babylon, and chief of the governors over all the wise men of Babylon" (2:48).

Daniel had human occasion to fear the outcome of his daring deed in going to the king and single handedly offering to solve the royal problem. Note, he had human occasion to fear. As a man it would have been a fool's venture but as a man of God it was different. Daniel had already proved the place of faith in his life. He had already had occasion to know what God would do when one dared to be right and to trust Him. It was this knowledge that gave Daniel the daring to assure the king he could solve the problem.

It took more than a conviction. Daniel went from the presence of the king into the presence of God for the first thing he did was to surround himself with prayer. He called upon his colleagues Hananiah, Mishael and Azariah to pray. They prayed and Daniel prayed and the solution was forthcoming.

Here was prayer linked with faith in God and human wisdom. Daniel's faith is revealed in his offer to solve the king's problem. Daniel's wisdom came as a consequence of his faithfulness to righteousness and God. Being wise he was not too wise to trust God. He was also wise in the simplicity of his faith and trust in God.

Daniel's experience reminds us of our need of the prayer help of others. Daniel went to his friends and got them to pray. He did not carry the burden alone. He knew the value of concerted prayer.

Not only was there value in praying together but cooperation is important in all things that pertain to our common needs. God never intended us to live alone or to work alone. Life is a cooperative enterprise both as regards God and man, and man and man.

> All have a share in the beauty;
> All have a share in the plan.
> What does it matter what duty
> Falls to the lot of a man?
> Someone has blended the plaster,
> And someone has carried the stone;
> Neither the man nor the master
> Ever has builded alone;
> Making a room from the weather,
> Building a house for the King;
> Only by working together,
> Men have accomplished a thing.

It is a noteworthy fact in Daniel's life to observe that when he was elevated to the high place to which Nebuchadnezzer promoted him, he did not forget his three faithful friends. After all, their fortunes were bound together. They were captives together. They were students together. They worked and labored together. In the crisis of Daniel's great need they prayed together. Now Daniel remembers them when he is honored and insists that they share his prosperity. This reveals the magnificent height of his stature and the true nature of his character. He was neither jealous nor envious. He rejoiced in the prosperity of others. He insisted on sharing his own. He remembered those to whom he owed the obligation of gratitude. In this Daniel exhibits what few people who achieve high places reveal. Most people are interested only in their own prosperity. They want to rise alone. They cannot bear to share their high place with another. Not so Daniel. He spoke for his friends. He shared his blessings. This is true of greatness.

In considering the conquest of Daniel in the light of human fears we are to remember the specific nature of his test at this point. It was a mental test involving the solution of the king's dream-problem. Daniel's fears were not hallucinations; they were not the phobias that come out of the mind. It is evident with Daniel in this case that he conquered fear before it became a disturbing factor. That may not be so in our case. We may have fears that control and dominate us and drive us into despair. Instead of peace that passes understanding we may have fear that exceeds description.

Fear takes many forms. As a normal emotion, fear is a physical and mental reaction to danger. It stimulates our glands and puts our body into a state of alarm and readiness to meet threatened danger. This is normal and beneficial.

In other cases it is the studied and considered anticipation of coming trouble. Perhaps it may be economic fear or the fear of impending disaster. In this case we are wise to respond to its warning and wisely prepare ourselves against the threatened thin.

Usually fear is a fictitious feeling or dread that seizes us with strong feelings of fright. There is built up in our minds a picture of great disaster of one sort or another. Our emotions are aroused; our whole body reacts and we live in terror and dread. Sometimes it is the fear of death. Then again it is the fear of life. Some fear the future; others the present. Some fear men; others fear God.

A condition of mental and emotional disturbance of this kind is not normal to a Christian experience. There is no doubt that it is very real and genuine. Fears are nothing to laugh at. They may be fancied but they are not fictitious.

The conquest of fear can be achieved through preventive or corrective measures. We can master it before it develops or destroy it after it appears. To begin with we mut remember the Christian's position. We are told that "God hath not given us the spirit of fear: but of power, and of love, and of a sound mind" (2 Tim. 1:7). In Timothy's case fear was not an affliction of the emotions but a natural timidity and a feeling of inferiority. He is being reminded that in Christian character God has made no provision for weakness. He gives power. Fear within means exaggerated fears without. Faith within means the destruction of these fears without. Not only is the Christian a person with power but also love. "There is no fear in love; but perfect love casteth out fear: because fear hath torment. He that feareth is not made perfect in love" (1 John 4:18). The primary reference of this fear is to the fear of judgment but its application to the ordinary fears of life is just as pertinent. Love and fear are incompatible. They cannot exist together. Where love reigns in perfection, fear must go. When the love of God floods the heart and controls the mind there is no place for fear to take root. The last quality of Christian character is a sound mind. This is the equivalent of sound judgment or discernment in which it should be possible to distinguish between truth and error, right and wrong and consequently to discriminate our feelings so as to banish fear.

The equipment for peace and the destruction of fear lies within us right now. It is God's gift to the Christian. It will be realized by the appropriation of faith, the application of the Scriptures and the operation of prayer.

In Daniel's experience the conquest of fear was preventive: in ours it may be corrective as well as preventive. If we are fearless we may be kept so. If we are fearful we may lose them and reach that stage that Paul describes in Philippians, "Be careful for nothing: but in everything by prayer and supplication with thanksgiving let your requests be made known unto God. And the peace of God, which passeth an understanding, shall keep your hearts and minds through Christ Jesus" (Phil. 4:6, 7).

Daniel's greatest weapon was faith.

> When faith in God goes,
>    Man the thinker loses his greatest thought.
> When faith in God goes,
>    Man the worker loses his greatest motive.
> When faith in God goes,
>    Man the sinner loses his strongest help.
> When faith in God goes,
>    Man the sufferer loses his securest refuge.
> When faith in God goes,
>    Man the lover loses his fairest vision.
> When faith in God goes,
>    Man the mortal loses his only hope.

### 3. *The Physical Test*

The final phase of Daniel's life and experience brings him to a den of lions. He is now an aged man well past eighty. When we first met him he was a captive, only fourteen. During his long life and varied experience he had met every kind of adversity, enemy and fear. Whether young or old, in Jerusalem or Babylon, under a Babylonian king or a Persian king, Daniel found problems and difficulties facing him.

We think that old age will bring relief from strife—perhaps a change of residence or a different climate or a change in government will do so. Like the poor which we always have with us, so are the problems of life.

Even Daniel's position brought him no exemption from trial. By this time he had become the equivalent of prime minister. Even prosperity has its perils. In Daniel's case he became the victim of jealousy. Jealous of his rise to prominence a certain faction set out to destroy him. They considered their problem well and came to this conclusion, "We shall not find any occasion against this Daniel except we find it against him concerning the law of his God" (6:5).

In modern times religion is regarded as a weakness. It is so socially, educationally and militarily. Religion is something to keep still about. It is all right for Sunday but not for Monday or Saturday. It is all right for the church but it has no place in the office or the store. We must limit it and give it a restricted sphere. Not so with Daniel! His enemies made the discovery that his religion was the strength of his life. As a youth or an old man Daniel was the same. In training in the royal college or administering the office of prime minister he was the same.

To Daniel religion was more than a ceremony to be performed at stated times. It was his life because he lived with and for God. Religion needs a new definition. To us it has become a convenience but in reality it is a new character. To us it means anything we wish it to mean even to the manufacture of our own gods to suit our own wishes. In the true sense it is God's revelation of Himself through His Word and His Son. Daniel belonged to the great company who came in this succession of faith.

With their plan conceived, Daniel's enemies appealed to the conceit of the king and proposed that all prayer should cease for thirty days save prayer to the king himself. This was not an unusual occurrence for these Orientals often deified their monarchs.

Darius fell in with their scheme and made a decree, at their suggestion, that any disobedience would be punished by being consigned to the beasts. What of Daniel under these circumstances? Would fear cause an old man to tremble at so dire a fate as this? We can understand bravery in a youth but what about the aged? There is no difference with Daniel. He goes to his house and with the windows of his chamber open toward Jerusalem he prays, not only once, but three times a day. There is nothing secretive about Daniel. His enemies know exactly where to find him—at prayer.

There is something thrilling in the sight of this man at prayer. It was more than a religious habit: it was life itself. It was the man. It was not the urge of necessity and emergency that caused Daniel to pray, nor was it expediency that would have caused him to cease praying to escape the penalty of death that was pronounced upon all who prayed to God. It is said of Daniel that he "prayed and gave thanks before his God, as he did aforetime." Daniel was what he was everywhere and all the time. Decree or no decree, king or no king, death or life, Daniel would be true to God. So he prayed and faced the consequences, but not alone, for God was with him. We need never fear the consequences so long as we have faith in God because God will take care of the consequences. Take care of your faith and God will take care of you.

It is well to consider in this experience of Daniel, what one must ultimately face in life, that accusation and opposition are not always justly placed. No matter how properly we order our lives, slander may enter in. Even so, accusation is not necessarily an evidence of excellence. Some are martyrs to their own folly. Some suffer from their own mistakes. When injustice or unfairness is our lot then let us not think it strange nor let it embitter us. Learn from Daniel, learn from life and learn from God's Word where it tells us, "And who is he that will harm you, if ye be followers of that which is good? But and if ye suffer for righteousness' sake, happy are ye: and be not afraid of their terror; neither be troubled; but sanctify the Lord God in your hearts: and be ready always to give an answer to every man that asketh you a reason of the hope that is in you with meekness and fear: Having a good conscience, that, whereas they speak evil of you, as of evildoers, they may be ashamed that falsely accuse your good conversation in Christ. For it is better, if the will of God be so, that ye suffer for well doing than for evil doings" (1 Pet. 3:13-17).

The great heroes of the Bible and the great men of God who have blessed and moved the world have been men who said a resolute "No" to sin. They neither condoned it nor compromised with it. They did not hesitate or deliberate. Not for an instant did Daniel think of ceasing his practice of prayer because of the threat of death. Wherever conscience is concerned it is vital to act quickly and fatal to engage in second thoughts. Say "No" as if you meant it. Say it like Joseph did when in the face of enticing temptation he answered, "How can I do this great wickedness, and sin against God?" Say it like Moses when "he esteemed the reproach of Christ greater riches than all the treasures of Egypt."

It took courage to say "No" to the king but the root of Daniel's courage was Daniel's faith. He knew that the God to whom he chose to pray would either deliver him or sustain him. Daniel did not consider it necessary to live but he knew that some day he was sure to die. Death is more certain than life. Then he had better live so that when he came to die it would be without remorse or regrets. Better it was to live for God if even for only a few hours so that dying would be a glorious meeting with his Maker and Redeemer.

Daniel's faith exceeded his expectations and conquered his fears about the physical consequences of the lion's den. That night God made rendezvous with Daniel. Stones that could shut in lions could not shut out God. Kings might decree that a man must not pray to

God but no human power can keep God from coming to the aid of His children. The door has yet to be built, the chains have yet to be forged and the dungeon yet to be constructed that can exclude God from those who need Him.

What about the times when God did not answer prayer to close the lion's mouth or release the captive or save the dying or heal the sick? Is not Daniel's experience an exception and not the rule? Perhaps taking things all in all, it is, but it is the exception that proves the rule. Even if we are not now, in our age, seeing these wonders of the physical power of an invisible God, we can summon into court the mighty and tremendous evidences of the visible working of an invisible God. He is helping men to live and die, suffer and succeed. He is standing close by and walking alongside those in need. He is a "present help in time of trouble." He is a "friend that sticketh closer than a brother." He is one who can "be touched with the feeling of our infirmities."

Although the intellectual opinions of a sophisticated world of science and military might is decreeing that you should not pray, and makes a mockery of a practical religious experience it is our great privilege to do as Daniel did, to pray and "give thanks before his God, as he did aforetime."

> When for a purpose I had prayed and prayed
> Until my words seemed worn and bare with arduous
>     use,
> And I had knocked and asked and knocked and asked
>     again,
> And all my fervor and persistence brought no hope,
> I paused to give my weary brain a rest
> And ceased my anxious human cry.
> In that still moment, after self had tried and failed,
> There came a glorious vision of God's power,
> And lo, my prayer was answered in that hour.
> —Lowell Filmore

We salute Daniel the conqueror. We hailed him as a youth. We now bid farewell to an aged man who, having faced the foes of life, leaves victoriously. His life remains to be a constant inspiration to all who are put into situations of moral, spiritual and physical peril.

# 17
# *Jonah*
## *The Conquest of Willfulness*

JONAH IS THE Bible's example of a man who retrieved success after a miserable failure. With all that we hear of Jonah he is a man little understood.

To begin with, Jonah was not a coward. That is generally assumed by a superficial reading of the account of his running away from duty. The reason Jonah took to the sea instead of going to Nineveh was not his fear of duty but his willful attitude to God's will.

You see, Jonah was what we call a chauvinist, an extremely patriotic man. He was an intense nationalist. He believed that God limited His concern for the world to Israel and failed to see that God's interest in Israel was for the sake of the world, for He had chosen this people to be the depository of truth for the whole world and the channel through which He might bless all men even as He said to Abraham that in him all families of the earth should be blessed.

Jonah believed that the "kingdom of God was a Jewish kingdom. The providence of God was a Jewish providence. The triumph of God was a Jewish triumph." He was trained and taught to believe that the salvation of the world meant the salvation of Israel and that the climax of this salvation would be attained in the glory of the Jewish nation. He failed to see that Israel was a means to an end. The end was the enlightenment of the world and the salvation of whosoever will. The means to this end was the truth of God possessed by the Jewish nation which would ultimately reach its fullest expression in the incarnation, revelation and atonement of the Messiah.

Believing what he believed and feeling as he felt, Jonah found himself opposed to God's desires concerning the great Gentile metropolis of Nineveh over in Assyria. God proposed that Jonah "go to Nineveh, that great city, and cry against it; for their wickedness is come up before me." It was God's desire that with warning, the city would repent and live. Jonah hated Nineveh and he rebelled against the will of God and asserted his own will by fleeing by ship to Spain. Jonah felt that God was making a mistake in letting Nineveh off so easily. He was willing enough to go and denounce the city and to pronounce judgment upon its wicked people, but to go and give it a chance to repent so it might be spared the judgment was another matter. Jonah was unwilling to do this.

There is much of this same feeling among God's present people and modern prophets. They have a recriminative and retributive attitude. They believe that salvation by grace is too easy and that the world should be made to suffer for its sins. They believe a price should be put on salvation, the price of suffering or pain.

We have no right to dictate the terms by which God will deal with the world. Our position, like Jonah's, is that of a servant of whom one thing is required—obedience. Jonah was disobedient. He was willful and rebellious, yet at the same time he was not a coward. It was not fear that turned him from Nineveh. He feared God greatly and he believed in God intensely but he deliberately refused to be used in the proposed plan to spare a wicked and idolatrous people. Like the disciples of Jesus, he wanted spectacular action. They wanted fire to be called down from heaven and visited upon a Samaritan village, and Jonah wanted God to deal by force with this city of Nineveh

The alternative was flight. Jonah went down to Joppa and when a man takes the direction he took of running away from God he always goes down. When he arrived at Joppa he went down to the docks, down into a ship and was ultimately cast down into the sea. It was a progressive course of going downward. Away from God, one always goes down never up, never onward. He must reverse his direction, retrace his steps and retrieve his loss.

What happened to Jonah on his flight to Spain is a story of strange and awe-inspiring events. On the ship Jonah is awakened to see the folly and mistake of his life by a violent storm which threatens the entire ship's company. He sees himself a sinner. He who shunned to warn the sinners of Nineveh and thus save them from disaster now faces disaster because of his own sin of disobedience to God. In his predicament came an awakening and with that awakening a transformation. Jonah called upon the sailors to cast him into the sea as the only means to save the ship. It was vicarious dying but this was God's means to save the world. Jonah, by his own personal experience, was taught the lesson he had shunned before. Now he knew what it was to die for others. What happened to Jonah was the dealing of Providence that ultimately put him on land and right back to the place where he was before. God said, "Go to Nineveh." Jonah had to die to his own desires, his own will and his own plans.

There are many modern Jonah's who flee Nineveh for Joppa and God's will for their will. They have self-chosen ideas and plans. They propose to save the world differently than by God's plan of salvation.

We must not lose sight of the fact that Jonah was intensely orthodox. He was not a modernist by any stretch of the imagination. Jonah was so orthodox that he could not possibly conceive of God's mercy extending beyond the bounds of the Jewish nation to the wicked city of Nineveh. He had pushed his orthodoxy to the place of religious exclusiveness; God was exclusively interested in Israel.

Jonah's experience is a rebuke to this sin of orthodoxy. God had to judge Jonah. He had to allow him to go to the extremity of his willfulness and finally end up in disaster. God had to bring him down in order to lift him up.

Here is Jonah refusing to go to Nineveh to warn it of impending judgment in order to save it because he felt a sinful city was unworthy of this evidence of God's grace. At the same time he represented the spirit of religious exclusiveness. He drew his hypocritical skirts close about his orthodox regularity and would have nothing to do with that kind of dealing with Nineveh. At the very moment Jonah was refusing God's will in the spirit of religious exclusiveness, his own people were guilty of a far greater sin. Nineveh was a heathen city without a witness but Israel was a people with a long heritage of privilege. It had many prophets but it was at this very moment rejecting God and living in sin. It had seen God's mighty works in its behalf but had rejected all that. God had pleaded and warned but it had failed to heed God's voice. Yet here was Jonah refusing to go to Nineveh with a message of mercy while his own nation was violating the laws of God.

The sin of modern orthodoxy is much like this. It demands the letter of the law while it transgresses the spirit. It denounces the sins of the world while it has sins of its own at which it works. It would call down judgment on a wicked world but asks mercy for itself. And all the while it is nourishing the spirit of exclusiveness. There is denominational exclusiveness that makes the way to heaven the way of a certain denomination. There is fundamentalist exclusiveness that makes the final understanding of God's Word rest upon the interpretation of some hair-splitting theory of doctrine. The story of Jonah is a rebuke to this spirit of exclusiveness and a reminder that God will deal in grace with all who will heed His way.

There is but one way for Nineveh and Jerusalem, for Jew and Gentile, for religious and non-religious. It is God's way. It has been the same in the Old Testament as in the New. It has been the same yesterday as today. On God's side it is the way of grace and on man's side it is the way of faith. God's grace was manifest in His Son and our faith exercised in Him will bring salvation no matter what our nationality, position, race or crime.

The result of Jonah's experience on the sea was a reconsideration of God's will. Down in the bowels of a great fish he could see what he had refused to see before. Here he said, "When my soul fainted within me I remembered the Lord." Remembering the Lord he remembered what the Lord had wanted him to do and when he placed his feet once more on solid earth, "the word of the Lord came unto Jonah the second time, saying, Arise, go unto Nineveh, that great city, and preach unto it the preaching that I bid thee" (3:1, 2).

Jonah was willing the first time to go to Nineveh if he could have preached what he wanted to preach but he was unwilling to go if his message would result in their repentance and God's mercy upon them. Now God specifically tells him to go to Nineveh "and preach unto it the preaching that I bid thee." Jonah knows now that God means business and not wanting another experience in the sea he goes to Nineveh. It is a city as famous for its magnificence as for its wickedness. It was surrounded by walls at least 100 feet high which were so broad that three chariots might drive abreast of each other. Jonah walked up its streets, entered its public buildings, stood on the steps of its temples and preached passionately about the impending judgment of God. The inhabitants of the city were deeply moved. They believed in God and its king proclaimed a fast. Nineveh repented in sackcloth and ashes and God graciously spared her. Jonah was still greatly displeased, though he should not have been. Although his own nation heard his pleadings and warnings they remained hardened; yet this pagan city was brought to its knees in repentance by just one warning. Here was a man disappointed with his own success. Here was a preacher regretting the sight of a whole city of penitents.

Jonah apparently had not fully conquered his willfulness. He still retained his narrow nationalistic ideas and the spirit of exclusiveness.

Jehovah had given Jonah one lesson from the sea. Now He gives him one from the soil. It is the parable of the gourd. When Jonah saw the city turn to God he was "very angry and he prayed unto the Lord and said, I pray thee, O Lord, was not this my saying, when I was yet in my country? Therefore I fled before unto Tarshish: for I knew that thou art a gracious God, and merciful, slow to anger, and of great kindness, and repentest thee of the evil. Therefore now, O Lord, take, I beseech thee, my life from me; for it is better for me to die than to live" (4:1-3).

The burden of Jonah's bitter lament was just this. Nineveh's preservation after his proclamation of its judgment made Jonah appear as a false prophet. How could he now return to his own people with integrity and expect them to hear and heed him. He had depended on God's mercy when he fled from duty and went to Tarshish and made him pay the price for it, but here is a wicked, pagan, Gentile city repenting of its sin and not reaping any of God's threatened judgment. It is too much for Jonah. He wants to give up. He wants even to die.

Now comes the lesson from the soil—the parable of the gourd. Jonah remembers an arbor outside the city which he can go and find comfort under the shade of a gourd producing plant of large leaves.

He goes to see if after all some judgment might not come to Nineveh. God proposes to discipline Jonah and take all the willfulness out of him. Jonah's refuge is short lived, for a worm, perhaps a cutworm, cuts the root and the plant quickly withers and Jonah is left to the mercy of the elements.

He is greatly solicitous for the well-being of the plant that gave him comfort and when he considers what had happened, his anger knows no bounds. He is angry at the enemy that destroys the gourd. He is angry at a world that can be despoiled by unseen enemies.

Jonah was not angry with the gourd, but for it. He was defending its right to live and provide shade and comfort. How ironical for a man of God to condone a gourd and condemn a city; to be angry when a gourd dies and disappointed when a city lives.

Into this incongruous and inconsistent situation steps God and He says to Jonah, "Thou hast had pity on the gourd, for the which thou hast not laboured, neither madest it grow; which came up in a night, and perished in a night; and should not I spare Nineveh, that great city, wherein are more than sixscore thousand persons that cannot discern between their right hand and their left hand: and also much cattle?" (4:10, 11).

God was saying to Jonah that whereas he was pitying a plant that cost him neither toil nor labor, how much more reasonable it was for God to be concerned over hundreds of thousands of souls in Nineveh and how fitting that He should extend mercy after their repentance. If it was right for Jonah to want a plant spared, it was more just for Jehovah to spare a city. In God's sight one soul is worth more than the whole world and certainly one city is worth more than many worlds full of gourds.

Although the result of this parable is not recorded we must believe that it had its effect. We see in Jonah's experience four things that God used to get a man ready for life. God "prepared a great fish," and in this parable, He prepared a gourd, a worm and an east wind. Out of the combination of events thus arising came a man prepared for life. He came into a full conquest of willfulness and retrieved success from failure.

His life has many practical lessons. It teaches us that the path of selfwill is always downward; that in the hour of grief one may turn to the God he has left and grieved to find hope; that it is futile to resist the will of God; that the love of God and the concern of God is not bound up in any one nation or church or people; that God has granted repentance of life unto the Gentiles as well as the Jews; that our disobedience limits God's plans to bless the world and us; that true repentance may avert judgment; that one usually runs into a storm when he tries to run away from God. In that case we can thank God for the storm if it brings us to a realization of ourselves and a revelation of Himself.

## I MET GOD IN THE STORM

I met God in the storm
Where He found me all forlorn;
And He put His arm around me,
And I thank Him for the storm.

I met God in the dark,
Where I wandered stiff and stark;
And He caught my hand to guide me.
And I thank Him for the dark.

I met God in defeat
Where He followed my retreat
With a vision of new conquest;
Now I'm glad of that defeat.

I met God by a grave,
Where T braced me to be brave
But I failed, and then He caught me;
Yes, I thank Him for that grave.

I shall meet God when the night
Overwhelms my flickering light;
Then He'll lead me to the morning,
Far away from cloud and storming,
Where I'll praise Him for the night.

—Bishop Ralph S. Cushman

# 18
# *Peter*
## *The Conquest of Inconsistency*

IT IS VERY easy to understand why we should consider Peter as the first conquest character of the New Testament. There is no character more generally and universally loved than Peter. This is so, perhaps, because Peter is so representative of us and we see so much of ourselves in him. Perhaps, too, because inconsistency as well as inconstancy is such a prevalent human problem. We turn with great interest and expectation to Peter because more people are likely to meet themselves in him than in any other person in the Bible.

To begin with, Peter was a common man. He was, by trade, a fisherman. He had a humble birth and was without educational advantages. There is no evidence that he was more religious than the average Jew, hence it was not a natural consequence of events that put Peter among the foremost apostles. With these facts in mind we are prepared to look for a tremendous change and transformation in this man's life and to see much that will make our own lives more stable, liveable and consistent.

The secret of Peter's life is found in his very first meeting with Christ. At that time Jesus said to Peter, "Thou art Simon the son of Jona: thou shalt be called Cephas, which is by interpretation, a stone" (John 1:42). There is an implication in the name Jona that Peter was not naturally a strong man. Jona actually means dove-like, giving the idea of docility and weakness. That this was so is apparent for two reasons. First, because Jesus gave him a new name meaning a rock which refers to strength and stability. There would have been no purpose in this unless it indicated a change in Peter's character which was the opposite of his original condition. Second, because Peter's life reveals the inconsistencies of great extremes. He moves between bravery and cowardice, faith and doubt. At one time he boldly draws a sword to defend his Master and within a few hours he cowers before the accusation and identification of a servant girl and denies His Lord. Peter is full of inconsistencies. He was the first to confess the divine nature of the Lord for he boldly said, "Thou art the Christ, the Son of the living God." Yet, he was the first to deny the Lord among His enemies. He was the first to reach the tomb and observe the evidences of a risen Lord. He was also the first to suggest a return to former occupations and the abandonment of the cause of the kingdom. He was right in his attitude to the person of Christ but wrong in his attitude to the work of Christ, for when the Lord first spoke of His approaching death Peter exclaimed, "Be it far from Thee, Lord: this will not be unto Thee" (Matt. 16:22).

Even after Pentecost this fluctuation continues, but not to the degree previously true. At Antioch, on the question of circumcision Peter demeans himself by reversing a position formerly taken at the Council of Jerusalem. Once more he reveals this trait of inconsistency and is an example of the Christian's struggle between the higher and the lower nature, between the carnal man and the spiritual man.

Peter is not always like this. We have in the New Testament two letters by Peter written about thirty years after these earlier events of his life. They were not documents of doctrinal explanation but personal messages of encouragement to people who were suffering bitter persecution. They reveal that some great change has come into Peter's life. He is solid and steady and like a rock. He is no longer easily moved. He does not fluctuate and vascillate. He is confident and assured and he writes to his fellow believers scattered by persecutors throughout all Asia Minor. He speaks of "an inheritance incorruptible, and undefiled, and that fadeth not away, reserved in heaven for you" (1 Peter 1:4). He speaks of an intervening season of temptations and trial which is made bearable and endurable by the presence of the Lord Jesus, "Whom having not seen, ye love; in whom, though now ye see him not, yet believing, ye rejoice with joy unspeakable and full of glory" (1 Peter 1:8). He speaks of the solid and enduring virtues of Christian character such as faith, virtue, knowledge, temperance, patience, godliness, brotherly kindness and love and suggests that "if these things be in you, and abound, they make you that ye shall neither be barren nor unfruitful in the knowledge of our Lord Jesus Christ" (2 Peter 1:8). He prepares them for the future by saying, "Beloved, think it not strange concerning the fiery trial which is to try you, as though some strange thing happened unto you: But rejoice, inasmuch as ye are partakers of Christ's sufferings" (1 Peter 4:12, 13).

Simon Peter has matured. He is no longer a man of many moods. Suffering is now seen as one of the privileges of life. He counts it all joy. He glories and exults in the flame. Peter is the conqueror of inconsistency.

Since every effect has a cause we look for a reason for Peter's conquest. It certainly was not an accident. It lies in two things which appear to be extremes—one is love and the other is power. From the human viewpoint love and power are opposites. Yet they are two qualities which complete and crown Christian character. Love was the result of an experience with Christ while power was the result of an experience with the Holy Spirit.

There can be no doubt that Peter always had a deep love for his Master but there came a time when that love became the ruling passion of his life. It was at the time of the last interview with Jesus after the resurrection and before the ascension. Jesus is probing the depths of Peter's heart. He is searching the motives of Peter's life. Is it a cause Peter is interested in or is it Christ? What have the experiences of the past few years done to the man, this man who had just said to his fellows, "I go a fishing?"

Jesus asks the same question three times and three times He uses Peter's old name, Simon, son of Jonas. Three times a searching question, "Lovest thou me?" Did Peter love Jesus more than himself? Did Peter love Jesus? Out of the probing and searching of the questioning and the overpowering love of the Questioner a new affection was born. Peter had entered into a new era of life. Now as never before, it was Cephas rather than Simon. It was as a son of God rather than the son of Jona. It was something divine rather than human. It was an affection rather than an infatuation.

The second phase of the great transformation of Peter came at Pentecost. This meant power. On this day of Pentecost the disciples were all filled with the Holy Spirit in fulfillment of a promise which Jesus had made that they would receive power to become witnesses. Love is an attribute of character. Power is an equipment of ability. Love is a grace. Power is a gift. Love is for life. Power is for service.

Behold Peter after Pentecost. The man who had feared identification as a follower of Jesus stands up in the midst of a mocking mob and speaks of Christ. Pentecost completed Peter's transformation. Power and love account for Peter's conquest of inconsistency.

# 19
# *Philip*
## *The Conquest of Anxiety*

THE LIABILITIES OF yesterday and the possibilities of tomorrow are the two greatest handicaps of life. People carry with them the effects of their failures and they are burdened with the anticipation of their troubles. The remedy for the first is suggested in Philippians 3:13, 14, "This one thing I do, forgetting those things which are behind, and reaching forth unto those things which are before, I press toward the mark for the prize of the high calling of God in Christ Jesus." We are to forget the things which are behind. They are not to remain as liabilities for life today. This forgetting is not an effort to ignore the things which are behind, but it is to be based upon a proper dealing with them in confession to God. When our spiritual obligations are settled we are no longer to go back in remorse and regret but rather to go on without the handicap of previous failures.

The remedy for anxiety about what lies before is also suggested in Philippians. "Be careful for nothing: but in everything by prayer and supplication with thanksgiving let your requests be made known unto God" (4:6).

Unless we deal with these liabilities of yesterday and possibilities of tomorrow we are going to be weighted with so much anxious concern that we will be unfit for the responsibilities of today. It is today that matters. Today may have its full share of sorrow and trouble but these are not the hardest things to bear. It is the cares of tomorrow that bother and hinder us more than the cares of today. The greatest handicaps in life are the things that never happen. It is our worry about what is going to happen instead of our work with what is happening that wears people out.

One of the truest and wisest things Jesus said was in this direction. "Take therefore no thought for the morrow: for the morrow shall take thought for the things of itself. Sufficient unto the day is the evil thereof" (Matt. 6:34). This is a warning against borrowing tomorrow's troubles and the danger of anticipating trouble that never happens.

Jesus was not teaching us to be careless, but rather to be carefree and this carefreeness was in the good sense of being properly careful about our obligations, responsibilities and privileges.

A certain man carried a sack on his shoulder, under which he groaned and complained unceasingly. And as he slowly journeyed on, toiling under his heavy burden, the Angel of Knowledge came and spoke kindly, saying, "What carriest thou?" And the man made answer surlily, "My worries." Then the angel smiled upon him, and said, "Let us look into thy bundle and examine thy worries." And they looked, but lo the sack was empty. "Surely," cried the man, "there were two great worries, too heavy for man to bear. But, ah, yes, I had forgotten, one was the worry of yesterday, and it is gone" "And the other?" asked the angel. "And the other was the worry of tomorrow—and it is not yet here." Then the angel smiled with infinite pity. And the man took his journey and went swiftly on, and his heart and hands were free to relieve many other wayfarers of their burdens, and to pluck for himself sweet fruit and flowers along the wayside. And when he came at last to the setting of the sun, it was with a song.

Philip has the distinction of being the first one of whom it is recorded that Jesus said, "Follow me." It was the end for Philip, of an earnest and long search; for immediately upon accepting Jesus' invitation he finds Nathanael and says, "We have found him of whom Moses in the law and the prophets did write." Philip had been looking for the Messiah and he recognized Him when he saw and heard Him. The subsequent experiences which are recorded of Philip are not to be thought of as skeptical or doubt. It was anxiety arising from inquiry and concern. Most disciples' anxieties are like that. They are human concern about human things.

The anxiety of Philip is to be seen in two experiences. One was what we call the secular and the other was the sacred. One was physical matter and the other was spiritual. One was Philip's anxiety about the feeding of the five thousand and the other was his anxiety concerning Jesus' revelation of the Father.

Jesus had crossed the Sea of Tiberias and found great multitudes flocking to Him among whom were many pilgrims to the Passover at Jerusalem. These people created a problem for Jesus because having come a long way unexpectedly they are unprepared since none had food. Jesus deliberately posed a question to Philip because He must have sensed the anxiety and inquiry of Philip's mind. Jesus asks him, "Whence shall we buy bread that these may eat? And this he said to prove him: for he himself knew what he would do" (John 6:5, 6). In other words, these are our guests and we must take care of them. Have you thought of what to do? This was directed to Philip because of his overcareful attitude to his problems. It was a problem insoluble from the standpoint of physical means and natural resources. What would Philip do? Would he say to Jesus, you are capable of handling the situation, or would he do what over-anxiety and under-faith would do, send them away?

Philip's answer is that it is impossible to feed this great company. Why, even the entire resources of the disciples, two hundred denarii would not buy sufficient bread. A Roman denarius was worth at that time about fifteen cents which would make the equivalent of thirty dollars of our money.

Philip's attitude to the problem was based upon human resources and what they had was not enough. He was limited by what he saw. He had not yet, in spite of all the previous works of Jesus, been able to base his calculations and convictions on what Jesus could do.

This indicates a want of faith. All anxiety is a want of faith but a want of faith does not mean the presence of unbelief in the sense of active doubt. It is the case of passive doubt. It does not mean that we disbelieve God but that we do not believe that God can do the practical things. He belongs to the spiritual and not the physical. He belongs to the unseen and not the seen. Jesus shows Philip that He is close to life. He shows him this, not by unnaturally multiplying money, but by supernaturally multiplying bread. He takes the available resources and makes them meet the obligations they face. He showed Philip that the conquest of anxiety was by faith.

The other experience came at a later time. Jesus was giving His farewell message to the disciples. It was one against anxiety. He was saying, "Let not your heart be troubled: ye believe in God, believe also in me." It was about the future both as a state and a place. He was telling them that He was the connecting link between the present and the future: God and man, earth and heaven. He was telling them that He is the great I AM. "I am the way, the truth and the life: no man cometh unto the Father, but by me." Here is a profound utterance and, so far as human needs are concerned, the most important that Jesus ever made. What He said may be summed up in these three things: The way meant guidance; the truth meant intelligence and the life meant sustenance.

A little girl was lost in a big city. A passerby asked her where she lived. She told him the street and house number. So he proceeded to tell her to go four blocks ahead, then turn right two blocks, left half a block, across the street, and so on. By the time he got through she had forgotten the beginning and cried as hard as ever. Just then a gentleman came along and learning her plight said, "Give me your hand, my dear, I live close by your home and will take you there." The first man was a way shower the other man was the way. All her anxiety was gone. She did not have to remember the maze of directions. She simply put her trust in her guide and was brought home.

Jesus is the same thing to us. He did not come to give a lot of ethical directions, but to be in His person the way to God.

Upon the utterance of this great truth Philip makes his request,

"Lord, show us the Father, and it sufficeth us." Jesus had taught that He and God were one. He meant that He was more than a God-like man; He was a man-like God. He was God in the flesh. He brought God into the human sphere. Up to the time Jesus came God was Someone to see in a vision, but now in Christ, He was Someone come in the flesh.

Philip is still anxious and inquiring. He cannot bring himself to believe this and so he makes his request of Jesus, "Lord, show us the Father, and it sufficeth us" to which Jesus answers, "Have I been so long time with you, and yet hast thou not known me, Philip? he that hath seen me hath seen the Father: and how sayest thou then, show us the Father" (John 14:8, 9). The Christian revelation of God is not of a being to be spiritualized but of a Person to be materialized. In His character "God is a spirit: and they that worship him must worship him in spirit and truth." In His manifestation God is to be seen as a man. This manifestation of God was in Jesus Christ who lived a life of perfect love and perfect righteousness. He said He was God and then proved His words by His works for He did what only God could do. In Him men could see God. In Him they had all the vision of God they needed. It was not a vision of God in heaven, but on earth. It was a vision of God who was close to life.

All of this answers the anxiety of men. They want to know who God is and what He can do. Jesus satisfies this completely in these two experiences of Philip. He takes God out of the past and brings Him down into the present and He also takes Him out of the future and reveals Him in the present. If men want some visual and visible pledge of the future, that pledge is Jesus Christ. If they want some immediate sight of God they will not get it. God is not in the business of manifesting Himself in visions and wonders. This was the mistake of Philip who failed to see that for three years God had been in their midst as a man who was revealing God in love and righteousness, and although He had been so long time with them Philip had not known Him as such.

The importance of this experience cannot be over-estimated. Philip is putting into words what men have been pondering for centuries. Men have a natural capacity and curiosity for God. Where will they find Him and how shall they reach Him? The answer is, Jesus Christ. But how can people nineteen centuries away from Christ reach Him? The answer is, by faith. Faith is the means which God has provided to link us with Himself. It overcomes the limitations of time and space. It brings us into the presence of God. It recognizes the promises of God. It brings us the power of God.

Faith is God's answer to human anxiety. Faith will open the eyes to understand who Christ is. Like Philip, there are many who have been following Jesus for a long time and yet have never come to know Him. One never knows Christ until he sees more than a man and never until we come to this place can Jesus be the sufficient helper and sustainer that we need in our lives.

# 20
# *John*
## *The Conquest of Temper*

WE COMMONLY THINK of John the apostle in terms of gentleness and love because of the fact that he is called "the disciple whom Jesus loved" and because he was very close to His Master. His First Epistle is frequent in its mention of love. For these reasons we have grown to think of John in terms of tenderness and affection, but he was not always so. He was one of the "sons of thunder" so named by Jesus because of his vehemence and the impetuosity of his temperament. He was naturally explosive and volatile. He had little reserve and practically no inhibitions.

Do you meet yourself in John? Is it difficult to see a likeness of oneself in the intensely human person whom we have over-glamorized as some sort of angelic character. If there is one fault more common than another, it is an explosive temper.

Do not misunderstand what we have in hand. Temper is not a bad thing in itself. It is the use we make of it which makes it bad. Unless we govern our tempers they will govern us.

In metal, temper is its state of hardness and toughness. It is due to the mixture of certain qualities under heat. When a metal is given temper it is given durability and strength and its value and importance is thereby greatly increased.

In a human being temper simply means temperament. It is one's frame of mind or disposition. It can result either in equanimity and composure or else in passion and anger.

In its good sense it is a substance added to human nature to modify its natural explosiveness in order to achieve equilibrium and composure. This substance is the grace of God. In the work of regeneration a new nature has been implanted in our lives. This new nature has all the qualities of peace, love, longsuffering and patience. When it is in control the old nature which is selfish and explosive is brought into subjection and thus modified and neutralized.

In the tempering process nothing is ever destroyed. The old is still present but it is controlled and modified by the new substance which is brought in. So, grace does not destroy; it modifies and controls. Grace does not make people soft and weak but strong and stable. It is therefore not a weakening but a strengthening process.

It is a mistake to think that a Christian must be a spineless person without recourse to the expression of feelings of anger or temper. The Bible says, "Be ye angry and sin not." Temper, under control, may properly express feelings of indignation and justifiable anger. It is said of Dr. Andrew Bonar of Scotland that he was the man most like John in modern times. He was the incarnation of gentleness and love, yet on a train his anger was seen to blaze out like a very son of thunder. An intoxicated man came into the railway car where Dr. Bonar was sitting with a friend and began to swear at them and abuse them unmercifully. Dr. Bonar bore the personal abuse in calm silence until the man took the name of Jesus Christ upon his lips, then his whole countenance changed. His face blazed with anger. He called a guard and had the degenerate drunkard taken out. The man was cowed to silence and left without a word. Dr. Bonar's friend was amazed at the passion of indignation which had appeared so suddenly in one who under normal circumstances was the very incarnation of meekness. This was entirely praiseworthy and justifiable and it exhibits the value of temper in a well-rounded character.

The conquest of temper should begin at the moment of conversion. It may be the immediate result of our experience with grace, but usually it is the result of a sanctifying process. Whether sudden or slow, it is to be an expected result of conversion. If we are as passionate, resentful, sullen, morose and explosive after as before, what does conversion mean? If it does not affect our dispositions it does not affect anything. To settle the future without helping the present, or to affect the soul without affecting the nature would indicate a very inadequate salvation.

Let us not decry the fact we have tempers. Let us rather realize what they are and why we have them and then understand the means of grace by which they may be brought under control and used for their legitimate purpose.

It was Jesus who identified John as a man of temper. He it was who called him and his brother James, "Boanerges, which is, The sons of thunder." How picturesque such a title! What a booming, noisy disposition John must have had. Yet, behold, how gentle and loving he became, but this becoming was not an instantaneous experience for John. Called from his fishing nets John follows Jesus. He became one of the inner three which included, besides himself, his brother James and Peter. In the course of his companionship with Jesus we see repeated evidences of his thunderous disposition.

For one thing, John was very intolerant. He came to Jesus and complained of one whom he saw casting out devils in His name and whom he forbade "because he followeth not with us." This was the spirit of narrow sectarianism. This was the stuff bigots are made of. John was at serious fault and Jesus instantly revealed that He had no sympathy with John's intolerance. Jesus said, "Forbid him not: for he that is not against us is for us." Later on, Paul expressed the same thing in different words, "Notwithstanding, every way, whether in pretense, or in truth, Christ is preached: and I therein do rejoice, yea, and will rejoice."

Jesus was intolerant with sin, hypocrisy, unbelief and all forms of unrighteousness but He could easily tolerate and even commend a man who was doing right, even though he did not conform to all the outward forms of so-called religious regularity. Jesus knew that it was not the clothes a man wore or the name he subscribed to, but what was in his heart. If truth were there, and right, then Jesus was for him. Apparently this was all true of the man whom John rebuked for Jesus said, "He that is not against us is for us."

John was also very impatient. He once proposed, when a Samaritan village shut its heart and its gates against his Master, that He should call down fire and utterly rid the earth of the ungrateful and unbelieving people. To this Jesus said, "Ye know not what manner of spirit ye are of. For the Son of man is not come to destroy men's lives, but to save them." John thought that rejection merited destruction and that correction would only come by immediate judgment. He was here taught that Jesus' persuasion was one of love and faith rather than of force. He was not going to frighten men into believing. Beyond a certain point judgment would be a mark of justice but up to that point Jesus would show mercy and display love. The world was to be wooed by love and love does not go about its wooing with a club.

No doubt John's violence was the result of his impatience. It was the thunder in him. He wanted to sweep men into the kingdom like a storm sweeps over nature. Men are not to be driven, they are to be led. Jesus said, "Follow me." He did not say, flee into the kingdom before I strike you dead. Justice has its place and so does judgment but mercy and love always come first.

These traits in John show us that even while John followed Jesus and was one of His inner circle of confidants, he was not a perfect man. He had bursts of temper and moments of passion. Love had not yet been perfected in him and grace had not fully controlled him.

It was not long after the previous events, however, that John faced a crisis in his life. He had asked for a front seat in the kingdom. He was ambition in a selfish way and desired of Christ the foremost place in the expected kingdom. Perhaps he was playing politics, but whatever it was it was unworthy of a true Christian and was certainly not a compliment to Jesus if indeed he supposed that Jesus would play favorites.

As for the *place* Jesus had this to say, "To sit on my right hand and on my left hand is not mine to give; but it shall be given to them for whom it is prepared" (Mark 10:40). In other words, it is for the one who is fit for the place. Jesus win not fit the place to the person but rather the person to the place. Heaven in general is a prepared place for prepared people. Jesus Christ has gone to prepare the place and the Holy Spirit is here to prepare the people.

As for the *people* Jesus had this to say, "Whosoever will be great among you, shall be your minister: and whosoever of you will be chiefest, shall be servant of all. For even the Son of man came not to be ministered unto, but to minister, and to give his life a ransom for many" (Mark 10:42-45).

The places in the kingdom are not to be had by favoritism but by merit. It will be the merit of progress in grace and service. Mind you, the kingdom itself is not by merit but by grace. However, our place in it will reflect our progress in grace and service in life.

Apparently this was the turning point in John's life for after this we find none of the things that marked his previous years. Perhaps shame brought him to his senses. Certainly and surely it was what Jesus said at this time that had its abiding effect and left its permanent mark. From now on, John would give rather than demand; he would love rather than judge and save rather than destroy.

While love mellowed John it did not weaken him. It gave him a new expression for his life. Instead of John's thunderous expression of John there was the compassionate expression of Jesus Christ. It strengthened John because it gave him something besides himself to live for.

John was the bravest of the disciples at the crucifixion. After Pentecost he suffered imprisonment. Through the subsequent persecutions which threatened the extinction of the Christians, John remained true to Christ and his convictions.

This trait of his life and quality of his character is plainly reflected in the contents of his First Epistle. He speaks of life and love. Love is the manifestation and expression of life.

A story or legend has persisted through these many years that when he was an old man and too feeble to preach, John used to be carried into the company of Christians and there would say one thing every time, "Little children, love one another." His people always rejoiced to see him and lived to hear him preach to them and consequently were disappointed to hear this one thing from him. Someone ventured to say to him, "Master, won't you preach something else to us today." To which John replied, "It is the Lord's command, and if we fulfill this we have fulfilled all things."

The simple secret of John's mastery of temper and passion was Christ's mastery of John. When we understand what this meant we will see how desirable and important it is for us. The temper of metal is achieved by adding another ingredient, plus the energy of heat. The tempering of a life is achieving of control, equilibrium, constancy and all the other virtues of strength by both grace and love.

# 21
# Thomas
## The Conquest of Doubt

THOMAS HAS BEEN held up for both praise and blame. Many have risen to his defense but more have spoken against him. He appears to be neither a skeptic nor a saint but a man like most men who have their beliefs and their doubts. Thomas made the mistake of doubting his beliefs and believing his doubts. His interrogations soon outweighed his affirmations.

Thomas was more of an egotist than a skeptic. He did not doubt Jesus' resurrection for want of evidence, although he demanded it, or for want of opportunity, but because of the spirit of inquiry. It was inquiry carried too far because it led to personal egotism. He was an exacting egotist who said, "Unless I" see so and so, and "unless I" do so and so, and "unless I" touch so and so, "I will not believe."

We must remember Thomas' place. He was on the inside and not on the outside. He was one of Jesus' disciples which would indicate that he had the approval of Jesus and was essentially a man of faith. Apparently Thomas never lacked faith in the sense of believing implicitly in the Lord Jesus Christ, either as to His person or His work. Undoubtedly Thomas believed that anything was possible with his Lord. So long as the Lord was personally and physically present Thomas was satisfied, for he could see. Now that Christ had died and left the disciples, it was a different matter. Thomas wanted some evidences. He wanted to know how things could be.

There are people who can accept a thing on the basis of divine testimony: it is in the Bible and that is enough. There are others who have no less faith in what is in the Bible but they would like to know how and why. They may carry it too far sometimes, but their attitude is no more skeptical than Thomas'. Not everything in the Bible is within the range of reason. Some things must forever rest on faith. Man is finite and God is infinite but there is much that will yield to inquiry. Much ancient truth can be understood in the light of our advancing knowledge.

Some people's faith may be but a shield for their lazy minds. If it is immediate faith on reverent inquiry the end is the same. The man who accepts the testimony of the hands of a watch without asking what is behind them knows the time just as well as the man who gets back of the watch face into the works and tears them apart to see how they work. In the last analysis, faith is the answer to life.

By contrast with Thomas the rest of the disciples were not men of great faith. The meeting from which Thomas was absent when Jesus made His appearance was attended by all the other disciples. Why did they go to the upper room? Scripture says, "Then the same day at evening, being the first day of the week when the doors were shut where the disciples were assembled for fear of the Jews." It was fear which brought them together and while this fear does not mean necessarily the absence of faith, it at least reveals that their fears were more urgent than their faith. They did not go to this place as one does to a rendezvous, to await their Risen Lord. They went in their own interests because they feared the Jews might harm them. In the light of this fact Thomas does not appear as bad as he had been made out to be. One form of fear may not be any worse than another. If Thomas feared Jesus was not risen it was not worse than the other disciples fearing what might happen to them.

Thomas does not deserve the name nor the reputation of a skeptic. He was no more skeptical than his colleagues who, when the women reported earlier that day what they saw at the tomb in the rolled-back stone and the undisturbed grave clothes and the angel visitors, said these were "idle tales, and they believed them not." This had happened on the morning of the very day when Thomas later expressed his so-called doubts. The only difference between the disciples and Thomas was the form of their language. The disciples did not say, "Unless we walk inside the tomb, unless we see the door rolled aside, unless we see the place vacant where He lay and unless we talk to the angels, we will not believe" but they certainly were guilty of not believing.

When Thomas found out that Jesus had appeared to the disciples during his absence his natural spirit of inquiry became an unhealthy state of arrogant egotism for he retorted, perhaps because of petulance and disappointment at what he had missed, "Except I shall see in his hands the print of the nails, and put my finger into the print of the nails, and thrust my hand into his side, I will not believe" (John 20:25).

It may be as has been intimated that this was an outburst of petulance because of disappointment that made him say this. Certainly we cannot charge Thomas with a skepticism like the world's. The scientific skeptic says unless God will climb down into his test tube to be analyzed or between his calipers to be measured he will not believe. The philosophic skeptic says unless God win come within the limit of his ideas to be humanized he will not believe. The religious skeptic says unless God will divest Himself of the mystery of deity and the wonder of miracles and come within the limit of his rationalistic creed he will not believe. God is not in the habit of accommodating Himself to human demands. He refuses to be measured, weighed and understood by our standards. He demands faith for "he that cometh to God must believe that he is, and that he is a rewarder of them that diligently seek him."

Just why did Thomas express himself as he did? It was not that he doubted the resurrection of His Lord and Master because he feared it could not be so. It was not what had happened but how it had happened that bothered Thomas. Perhaps it was the desire for material signs and physical evidences yet "faith is the substance of things hoped for, the evidence of things not seen." It appears it was more an inquiry into how it took place than a doubt that it did take place. If it was both it was the first that caused the second, but essentially it was not skepticism as we know it.

Twice we read of Thomas in action when he exhibits this spirit of inquiry and both are practically about the same things. The first time was just a few days before Jesus was crucified. It was in the upper room, perhaps the very room where Jesus appeared after His resurrection, and Jesus was telling them about going to His Father. After telling them of His Father's house Jesus said, "And if I go and prepare a place for you, I will come again, and receive you unto myself, that where I am there ye may be also. And whither I go ye know, and the way ye know." At this point Thomas broke in and said, "Lord, we know not whither thou goest: and how can we know the way?" This was characteristic of Thomas. In one case he demands to see the evidences of wounds. In another he wants to have some tangible evidence of the way. Perhaps it was the "show me" attitude. He wanted to get out a map and have the way pointed out.

We should not be too hard on Thomas because of this question. It was not doubt in the sense of unbelief; it was the spirit of inquiry. Thomas would like an explanation. He would like to know how.

What happened to satisfy Thomas in both cases is very significant, for he was satisfied, you know, both times. In the first case, Jesus replies, "I am the way, the truth and the life: No man cometh unto the Father but by me. If ye had known me, ye should have known my Father also: and from henceforth ye know him, and have seen him." In the second case, Thomas saw Jesus in person. In both instances the answer to Thomas' demands was the person of Christ. He was the way to God and He was all the evidence needed of a resurrection for when Jesus appeared a week later Thomas did not bother to examine His wounds.

There are two reasons to explain this doubting of Thomas.

1. He was absent when Christ was present after the resurrection. Having missed the experience of seeing Jesus he wanted the explanation. Much of our trouble would be liquidated in the personal satisfaction of a spiritual experience.

2. He had to get his information about the resurrection secondhand. He might have been irked by the knowledge of what he had missed and thus might have been prodded into the attitude of demanding proof. Had they not all doubted the testimony of the women in the morning? Did they not say the women were telling idle tales? What right had they now to tell him that they had seen the Lord? Thus Thomas wanted some justification for what they said. He wanted reality down even to nail prints and spear wound.

Thomas discovered that he did not need that which he demanded. He found Jesus exactly where he missed Him. It was in the same room and under the same circumstances. When Jesus stood in his midst and said, "Peace be unto you." He turned to Thomas and offered the evidences he had been demanding. By then, Thomas did not need them. All he needed was Jesus and he cried out, "My Lord and my God."

Notice how Jesus treated Thomas. He was not angry with him. He did not scold him or condemn him. He did not humiliate him before his fellow disciples. He gently and calmly said, "Reach hither thy finger, and behold my hands; and reach hither thy hand, and thrust it into my side: and be not faithless but believing" (John 20:27). All Thomas needed was a sight of his Master. He did not need the evidence he had demanded. He did not need a demonstration. Jesus Christ will be all any of us need. He will be the satisfaction of our inquiries and the answer to our doubts.

How different our attitude would be. We would condemn and expose. We would berate and denounce. We would figuratively consign him to the rack and burn him at the stake. Were we honest with ourselves and fair in the estimate of the so-called faithful orthodox, we would have to say with the poet, that there is "more faith in honest doubt than in half the creeds." Thomas had the honesty to acknowledge his misgivings and Jesus came to him with the answer.

The incident ends with a significant statement, "But these are written, that ye might believe that Jesus is the Christ, the Son of God; and that believing ye might have life through his name." Believing brings life but believing involves two things, faith and trust. Faith is an act of the mind in which we acknowledge the truth about Jesus Christ while trust is an act of the will in which we accept the person of Jesus.

Years ago there lived a famous tightrope walker named Blondin, who performed most astonishing feats. On one occasion he walked from one end of the center transept of the Crystal Palace, in London, to the further side, along a rope stretched across at a tremendous height and not only so, but he stopped in the middle and cooked an omelet.

On another occasion a rope was stretched across a shipbuilding yard, also very high, and Blondin, at this dizzy height, carried a man across on his back, thousands of spectators gazing with awe and wonder at the remarkable performance.

When he had completed his perilous journey and descended to *terra firma* he noticed a boy gazing at him in speechless amazement and admiration. So, approaching the lad, he said, "You saw me carry a man across safely. Do you think I could carry you?" "Certainly you could, for I'm only a little fellow, and he's a big man." "Well, then," returned Blondin, "jump up, and I will take you." Whereupon he suited the action to the word, and bending down, said, "Well, jump up." But the boy instead of doing so, speedily disappeared in the crowd. He did not care to trust himself to him; he was afraid to do so.

Perhaps now, you have reason to think better of Thomas and perhaps you can see something of yourself in him. Surely, if we are honest with ourselves we will recognize our own proneness to doubt and our own weakness of faith. If this be a genuine spirit of inquiry, remember that as Jesus treated Thomas, so He will treat us and if our attitude is as genuine as that of Thomas it will end with one of the Bible's most noble confessions of faith, "My Lord and my God."

We owe a debt of gratitude to Thomas for his inquiry has furnished us with indisputable evidence concerning the resurrection. His experience teaches us a great lesson of faith and as has been said, "Thomas doubted that we might have no reason to doubt." Let us go away believing.

# 22
# Mary and Martha
## The Conquest of the Important

WITH THE ADVANCE of civilization, life becomes more and more complex. We have lost simplicity and find ourselves in a synthetic world created by mechanical inventions the effect of which is not to relieve us for better things, but to make life more burdensome. We find ourselves neglecting the important and occupied with the unimportant. Like Martha we are "careful and troubled about many things."

We should "beware of the barronness of a busy life." Any true view of life will recognize that activity without a purpose is pure folly.

This means that we must have a new value of time and things. Valuing time we will use it as our most valuable commodity of life. Cecil Rhodes, the great Englishman, looked about him and wrote, "So much to do, so little done." The things that are done are what count, not what we intend to do. In that case, we must make up our minds what should be done and then say with the apostle Paul, "This one thing I do" (Phil. 3:13).

There are many books to read, but which is the most important book? There are many things to do, but which is most urgent? There are many meetings to attend but which is the most necessary? There are many people we might visit, but who needs us most? There are things we must leave undone if we are ever to do what must be done.

Little may we realize at the time what great things rest in a small deed. A word spoken may change the world. Back in 1880 a United States revenue cutter put into the harbor at Wilmington, NC. As they lay in harbor the captain of the cutter whose name was Charles Jones, took the opportunity to tell a little Chinese cabin boy the story of Christ and the gospel. What that boy heard that day proved to be the turning point in his life for as the result of the captain's faithful witness he became a Christian. His name was Soong, the head of the

Soong family of China which included Mei-Leng, now Madame Chiang Kai-shek. What a great day's work that was! Yet it might not have been had Captain Jones despised speaking of Christ to an insignificant Chinese cabin boy. What appeared unimportant became the most important.

We must also put a new value on things as well as time. The money we put in the bank, the food we put on the table and the clothes we put on our bodies may be so all-important that their attainment may consume all our effort. The most important things are what outlast life and what death cannot take from us. What we can take with us when we die is more important than what we must leave behind.

In a little village lived a lawyer famous for drawing wills. On the passing of a certain respected neighbor, there was much speculation as to the value of the property, and the village gossip undertook to find out the facts.

"I suppose you made out the will?" He asked of the lawyer.

"Yes," the lawyer answered.

"Then you probably know how much he left. Would you mind telling me?"

"Not at all," answered the lawyer deliberately; "he left everything he had."

If he left everything it was because he lived for the things a man must leave. Jesus suggested another motive for life. "Lay not up for yourselves treasures upon earth, where moth and rust doth corrupt, and where thieves break through and steal: but lay up for yourselves treasures in heaven, where neither moth nor rust doth corrupt, and where thieves do not break through nor steal" (Matt. 6:19, 20).

In judging the difference between the sisters, Mary and Martha, we must not go to extremes. Martha was by no means a materialist, nor does she represent the person who lives for just one world. Martha was as spiritual as Mary, but not as intensely or extensively as Mary. Martha was not less consecrated or devoted to Jesus but she failed in the discernment of what was important. She failed to judge what she should do and what she should leave undone.

Martha represents the practical Christian who can allow herself to be carried too far in that direction. For this she is worthy of no more censure and criticism than spiritual Christians who allow themselves to be carried so far in that direction that they are no longer sensible of their practical obligations. Spirituality is no reason for the neglect of the proper care of one's person, home and family.

To be like Mary does not mean all sitting and no serving, an praying and no working. Mary had the same obligations as Martha but her timing was correct. She sensed a great occasion when it was time to do one thing more needful than another.

There was no injustice in Jesus' rebuke to Martha when He said, "Martha, Martha, thou are careful and troubled about many things:

But one thing is needful: and Mary hath chosen that good part, which shall not be taken away from her" (Luke 10:41, 42). It was Martha's complaint about Mary which led Jesus to say what He did. Martha had complained to Him that Mary had left her to make an the preparations alone. He was just as critical and perhaps more so, of Martha's attitude to Mary. Jesus would not have criticized if Martha had not complained, indicating that Martha's spirit was wrong. She no doubt felt that as long as she was working, Mary should do likewise, when in all probability anything that needed to be done could have been accomplished without Mary.

It is the old problem of human nature. Some feel they are being ill-treated if they have to do all the work. A division of work is always necessary. If Mary had been taking advantage of Martha it would have been a different matter, but that was not her motive. She recognized a great opportunity and seized it. Jesus was there and she must make the most of it. Where Martha was chiefly wrong was in her attitude to Mary. Had she gone about her work without complaint, perhaps everything would have been well and maybe she would have realized how unnecessary much of her activity was. Her envy of Mary clouded her view of Jesus as all material and physical anxiety is bound to affect our spiritual appreciation.

There is a time for everything and the time to work was not when Jesus stepped in to make His visit. Mary had sensed it but Martha had not. Moreover, Martha had not sensed the fact that Jesus was not interested in overdoing preparations for Him. His needs were few and He was not interested in an elaborate display. She put "many things" in the way of "one thing needful."

What Jesus was trying to check in Martha was a tendency to excessive care and over anxiety. Martha's anxiety was exacted at the expense of spiritual calm and blessing. Mary was far better prepared than Martha to discharge her obligations because of the moments spent in Christ's presence. Such moments are never lost. Mary assumed the attitude of a learner when she "sat at Jesus' feet and heard His word." Learning is essential to living. Jesus said, "Take my yoke upon you, and learn of me, . . . and ye shall find rest unto your souls." We have to learn to rest and rest to learn. Learning to rest, we must rest in order to learn.

Mary had made her conquest of the unimportant by reason of her spiritual perspective. She saw things in their true light. She knew the time to rest and the time to work the time to learn and the time to be busy.

Perhaps there is some indication here why women generally seem to be more appreciative and sensitive to spiritual things. It is true that Martha did not but the fact of Mary's resting at Jesus' feet may be a true indication of a woman's recognition of her spiritual need. She seems to be more sensible of this than man, perhaps because her sphere is the home and it is more conducive to these things. Perhaps also, because of the nature of her lifework in bearing and rearing children there may be a greater sense of need and dependence upon God. When a woman does not have this sense it always seems far worse because she is the heart of the home.

What happened at Bethany may happen anywhere. Our homes may become the guest houses of the Son of God. He may be the silent listener to every conversation and the unseen guest at every meal, but, He needs recognition. Martha in the kitchen missed Him, but Mary made His visit the occasion of great blessing. The kitchen has its place but also its time. Jesus was not rebuking Martha for her attention to home duties, but rather for her preference for these over the more important things and at the wrong time.

# 23
# *Nathanael*
## *The Conquest of Prejudice*

OUR VIEW OF life can be sadly warped by prejudice. Prejudice means prejudgment or opinions made without sufficient grounds or arrived at before one has sufficient knowledge. It is the cause of much misunderstanding and sorrow in the world.

Among Christians prejudice is the sin of criticism. It is one thing to appraise a person or thing but another to condemn without grounds or evidence.

So far as Nathanael is concerned it does not appear that his prejudice came from a warped and undeveloped character. He was a man of transparent sincerity. Jesus called him a man without guile. This does not mean he was without fault so much as that he was a man of sincerity. In this case his prejudice sprang from other than narrow and warped convictions. Apparently Nathanael was seeking with the most sincere motives, signs of the coming Messiah and when Philip rushed in with his breath-taking and almost breathless exclamation, "We have found him, of whom Moses in the law, and the prophets did write, Jesus of Nazareth the son of Joseph," Nathanael could hardly believe it. He would not have been disappointed to see the Messiah but he seriously discounted that He could have such an origin as Nazareth and Joseph. It was Nathanael's prejudice against Nazareth, for he exclaimed, "Can there any good thing come out of Nazareth" (John 1:46) .

We do not know all that lay behind Nathanael's prejudice of Jesus' origin in Nazareth. One reason may have been the fact of his own origin. Nathanael was from Cana in Galilee and it might have been local jealousy. Often our own prejudices arise from jealousy. We are prejudiced against another because he is successful in a large way and we only moderately so.

National prejudices often arise from this cause. Nations live in rivalry because of prejudice. One is larger and more powerful and more prosperous. She becomes the object of envy and opinion is distorted by jealousy which leads in time to strife and war. Much of the prejudice against the Jew is of this nature. It has been ingrained for centuries. Anti-Semitism is not a new thing; it only breaks out in new forms.

Besides jealousy of others, prejudice is often inspired by pride in ourselves. Pride is simply an over-emphasized opinion of our own excellence and importance.

Our pride leads us to prejudice of people because of their circumstances. Our community is better than theirs, or our house is better than theirs and with a self-chosen feeling of superiority we view others with prejudice. With Nathanael we say, "Can there any good thing come out of Nazareth?" Of course the geography is different but the spirit is the same.

Our prejudice of people is often because of their appearance. We judge them by the appearance of their clothes which is always a very superficial judgment. The latest fashions may cover a vile character while style may be absent from the choicest saint. I think it was with this in mind that Peter, under divine inspiration, wrote "whose adorning let it not be that outward adorning of plaiting the hair, and of wearing of gold, or of putting on of apparel; but let it be the hidden man of the heart, in that which is not corruptible, even the ornament of a meek and quiet spirit, which is in the sight of God of great price" (1 Peter 3:3, 4).

Appearances may be and often are very deceiving. The appearance of countenance may hide an altogether different spirit. Beneath an ordinary appearance there may be transpiring an extraordinary experience. Something like this is expressed in the book of Job where this great man retells his bitter experiences. He suffered much at the hands of false friends who totally misjudged Job because of his adversity. They read in his calamities the judgment of God for sin, whereas nothing of the sort was true. Job was not in the fires of judgment but in the crucible of character. To his false friends he cries out in these words, "I have heard many such things: miserable comforters are ye all. Shall vain words have an end? or what emboldeneth thee that thou answerest? I also could speak as ye do: if your soul were in my soul's stead, I could heap up words against you, and shake mine head at you" (Job 16:2-4).

How truly Job spoke when he said, "if your soul were in my soul's stead." The point of view which we take is always determined by the place from which we look and speak.

### IF I COULD KNOW THE AGONY OF PAIN

If I could know the agony of pain
   In which my brother wrought, yet gave no sign,
His bungling work would take on graceful shape,
   And glory would illumine every line.

If I could know the heartache bravery hid
  Beneath the smile of courage, day by day,
I'd not withhold the kindly deed and thought
  To cheer my friend upon his lonely way.

If I could know the struggle to do right,
  Of that poor fallen one so sore beset,
Not 'Shame,' but 'Bravo,' would I say to him:
  Thou fightest foes whom I have never met.

If I could know the longing pressing close
  Beneath derision's sneer at holy things,
A friendly hand I'd stretch across the gulf,
  And know the thrill which world-wide kinship brings.

And I can know. Come, Son of man, Divine,
  Flood all my soul with sympathy benign,
Until my very life is love impearled,
  And pulses with the heart-throbs of the world.

—Selected

Appearance is never a proper basis for judgment of people. The Lord does not look on the appearance. He looks on the heart. The only true test we have any right to apply is the test of character and experience rather than appearance. This takes time and observation.

Jesus said, "Judge not according to the appearance, but judge righteous judgment" (John 7:24). Even so there are many things that are going to remain outside our ability to understand or appropriate in which case we must not allow prejudice to embitter us and our relationships. Nathanael's prejudice almost shut him out of the richest experience of his life. If we permit it to control us it will lead us into many sad experiences.

Prejudice not only results from the superficial judgment of appearances and conditions but it comes also because of ignorance. Ignorance of another's background or struggles or true character can give us a very warped view of one's life. This may have been true of Nathanael. Here was a man who had been stedfastly looking for the Messiah and when He came Nathanael looked at Him through the village that nurtured Him. Perhaps he was entirely ignorant of Nazareth when he contemptuously asked, "Can there any good thing come out of Nazareth?" Anyway the Messiah was bigger than Nazareth. Nazareth did not account for His nature nor for His power. Jesus was from heaven, not Nazareth.

Even today, many people are still judging Jesus by Nazareth. They use different terms but they mean the same thing. They judge Him by antiquity and say that He belongs to the ancient age. They cannot see Him riding in an automobile or walking down the streets of a modern city or riding the elevators of a skyscraper. They see Him only with his flowing first century robes and cannot think of Him in terms of modern clothes. They think of Him as a Palestinian Jew forgetting that God meant Jesus for the whole world. They are forever pushing Jesus back into the past and clothing Him with ambiguity and shutting Him up in Nazareth

Again we must say, Jesus was bigger than Nazareth. He is not dated merely by the first century. Remember Jesus lived before Nazareth. He belongs to heaven and eternity. The nationality of his flesh was Jewish but his Jewish nature was merely the vehicle through which he could come to all the nations of the world. God was His Father, deity was His nature, heaven was His home. You must get back of Nazareth to God before you can judge Jesus properly.

How can one conquer and overcome prejudice? Certainly not by argument: only by evidence. Nathanael was at first opposed to Jesus because of inadequate evidence. He judged Jesus by circumstances. He looked at Him through Nazareth. Philip did not argue the case with him. He simply said, "Come and see." Philip wanted Nathanael to see Jesus for himself. All he needed to do was to give Jesus a chance. That is all anyone needs to do. Do not judge Jesus from where you stand; if you do you are sure to be wrong because to begin with human judgment about divine things is at variance for "the natural man receiveth not the things of the Spirit of God: for they are foolishness unto him: neither can he know them, because they are spiritually discerned." One must "Come and see." One must get where Jesus is. One must get close to Him. He must stand upon redemption ground, otherwise he will forever make Jesus wear "Jewish old clothes" and tuck Him away in Nazareth with prejudice.

The result of Nathanael's coming and seeing was the complete loss of his prejudice. Immediately as he walked into Jesus' presence he heard Him say, "Behold an Israelite indeed, in whom is no guile." Nathanael is taken aback and asks, "How do you know me?" Jesus replied to say that He knew Nathanael even before Philip called him to tell him that the Messiah was come. This was not the power clairvoyance. Jesus was not a mystic involved in Oriental magic. He was showing Nathanael that He did not belong to Nazareth. He was revealing what Philip wanted Nathanael to see and hear—His deity. Nathanael had judged Jesus by Nazareth but Jesus judged Nathanael by heaven. Nathanael had measured Jesus by human standards but Jesus measured Nathanael by divine standards. His judgment of Nathanael did not make of this man some kind of sinless creature who did not quite belong to this world. Guileless Nathanael meant a man of sincerity. He was sincere in his prejudice of Jesus but in that sincerity he was wrong. There are many sincerely wrong people and there are many sincere sinners. Sincerity can be a liability as well as an advantage.

Nathanael's sincerity had not made him *right* nor would it make him *righteous*. It would not save him but what it did was to bring him to the place where he could see who Jesus was. And when Jesus gave evidence of being someone greater than Nazareth and one who was, in truth, the long looked for Messiah Nathanael no longer stood in the place of an inquirer or questioner but became a believer and confessor and cried out, "Thou art the Son of God: thou art the King of Israel." This was more than religious attitude to Jesus. Nathanael was confessing his faith and surrendering his life. He was admitting how wrong he had been about Jesus and everything else. He had seen a man bigger than Nazareth and he proposed to follow Him.

Nathanael settled his destiny that day by surrendering his soul to Christ. He never went back on his word and never looked back to Nazareth.

Upon this confession of faith Jesus gave Nathanael a vision of the future. He said this to him, "Because I said unto thee, I saw thee under the fig tree, believest thou? thou shalt see greater things than these. And he saith unto him, Verily, verily, I say unto you, Hereafter ye shall see heaven open, and the angels of God ascending and descending upon the Son of Man" (John 1:50, 51). This was to be the fulfillment of Jacob's vision, for he had seen a ladder set upon earth and reaching to heaven with angels ascending and descending. It was a means of contact between earth and heaven, man and God. This is what the world needed. It was cut off from heaven and shut off from God by reason of sin. It lost both relationship and fellowship with God. Now that is restored, for Jesus Christ becomes a ladder to God. He becomes man's means of reaching God and God's means of blessing man.

Nathanael was promised the sight of "greater things." If Jesus could see Nathanael under the fig tree and appraise his character He would do greater things. If by His life Jesus could inspire men to forsake all and follow Him, by His death He would do greater things. By both life and death He would combine deity and humanity in the greater work of redemption. He would be a ladder set upon the earth, which meant humanity, yet which would reach heaven, thus revealing deity.

This divine-human ladder would perform for the world a twofold service.

## 1. It Would Be a Ladder of Salvation

This is what Jesus meant by "greater things." It meant more than being able to tell what a man's character was. It meant power to change that character. It meant power to do something for man's greatest need.

There had been attempts made to set up other ladders of salvation in the world. Great religions had come and offered various ways to God. When Jesus came He was not another human effort to find God. He was God's means of finding man. As such His way to God was exclusive for He said, "I am the way, the truth and the life, no man cometh unto the Father but by me."

The fig tree revealed what Jesus knew about us but the Cross revealed what Jesus could do for us. Jesus found Nathanael under a fig tree and saw a man "in whom is no guile" but that was only a negative and a passive righteousness. Nathanael needed the greater work of the cross with its positive and active righteousness.

The fig tree needs that other tree that was planted on Calvary. We need the power of Christ. We need His healing for our ailing. We need Him to make us right as well as to tell us what is wrong.

> He took our suffering human race,
>   He read each wound, each weakness clear;
> And put His finger on the place
>   And said, "Thou ailest here, and here."

It is Christ and the cross which gave promise of the "greater things." It meant before anything else the means of salvation.

### 2. *It Would Be a Ladder of Ministration*

Upon it could be seen the angels of God. These are the divine ministers and through the Lord Jesus Christ they would be benevolently concerned with earth's needs. You will notice that they do not descend and ascend, but rather ascend and descend. They began with early needs and brought a heavenly blessing. To our present knowledge all of this is of a mystical nature. We can neither understand it nor explain it but there can be no doubt that in the spiritual sphere of Christian experience there is this ministration of divine things. There is evidence in the lives of God's people of the effects of the unseen ladder. Upon it we ascend in prayer. By means of it we receive the blessings of life for this ladder is none other than "the Son of Man."

Nothing further is said of Nathanael but we can be sure that prejudice turned to praise and suspicion turned to assurance. It is thought by some that Bartholemew of later mention is this same Nathanael. Be that as it may, we can be assured that Nathanael was a different man after he met Jesus. His superficial opinion of the Messiah turned to deep devotion and reverence. None can have Nathanael's experience and be the same afterwards.

# 24
# *Andrew*
## *The Conquest of Insignificance*

HAD ANDREW, BROTHER of Simon Peter, not performed certain nonspectacular services he would have done nothing and been nothing. He was not a man of great gifts that brought him public notice and prominence. Had he not been willing to be just Andrew neither his name nor his place in life would have been important.

Andrew is very important to us because most people find themselves in likeness to him more than to most other Bible characters. They do not possess the dynamics of Peter nor the brilliance of Paul nor the oratory of Apollos, but they do resemble this man Andrew. Few are leaders; many are followers. Andrew was a follower but that was no reason why he could not be useful. He did not despair because he did not have the gifts of his brother. He did not quit because he was not great. He did what he was capable of doing.

There is a mistaken notion current among us to which we often address ourselves with wistful longings, that all of us are supposed to be great. We have been led to believe that when the Holy Spirit fully and completely controls us we are going to do great things. This will not necessarily occur, for each of us has his place in the Body of Christ. "For the body is not one member, but many. If the foot shall say, Because I am not the hand, I am not of the body; is it therefore not of the body? And if the ear shall say, Because I am not the eye I am not of the body; is it therefore not of the body? If the whole body were an eye, where were the hearing? If the whole were hearing, where were the smelling? But now hath God set the members every one of them in the body, as it hath pleased him. And if they were all one member, where were the body? But now are they many members, yet one body . . . Now ye are the body of Christ and members in particular. And God hath set some in the church, first apostles, secondarily prophets, thirdly teachers, . . . Are all apostles? Are all prophets? Are all teachers? . . ." (1 Cor. 12:14-29).

Did it ever occur to you that not everyone of the twelve apostles was famous and outstanding? Each had his place but that place was not necessarily prominent. Each had his place and each was to be himself. We, too, must learn to be ourselves and fill our place. This does not mean there is no room for betterment, advancement or improvement but it does save us from the feeling of not mattering as well as from inordinate ambition and greed.

Andrew mustrates the conquest of wrong attitudes. With us it may be the attitude of jealousy, pride, hatred, greed or envy. With Andrew it was the attitude of insignificance out of which he arose to overcome any thoughts of jealousy ar envy of his brother Simon Peter.

Andrew suffered what might be termed the misfortune of being Peter's brother. Yet we must not forget that had it not been for Andrew, who brought Peter to Christ, Peter would never have been known to us. Then having brought Peter to Christ, Andrew must witness his brother taking the larger place. He must say what John the Baptist said of Jesus, "He must increase, but I decrease." Andrew was largely eclipsed by his brother's prominence. He did not belong to the inner circle. He was not among those who went with Jesus to the Mount of Transfiguration nor to the olive grove in Gethsemane. He was not chosen to be the spokesman for the Christians at Pentecost. While Peter walked in the limelight Andrew finds a place in the shadow.

Andrew overcame any feeling of envy or jealousy he might have had for his brother's gifts and prominence. He refused to permit himself to be gripped by the futile feeling of insignificance. Had this happened Andrew would have lost the usefulness God intended him to have in his own right.

While Andrew did not have Peter's gifts he had his own, and who will say they did not matter? Peter could move multitudes, but Andrew could move Peter. Andrew could not be Peter but God never intended him to be; He only intended that he should be Andrew and he was humble enough to be himself by the grace of God.

The Scriptures do not tell us in what specific way Andrew conquered but it does tell us what he became. He became an introducer. He is probably the Bible's best example of the personal worker, apart from Christ Himself.

Three times we see Andrew introducing someone to Jesus. These three times are the only ones in which Andrew appears except his mention as one of the Twelve. What Andrew could do he did with great faithfulness and success as the record of his service reveals.

## 1. He Introduced His Brother to Jesus

"He first findeth his own brother Simon, . . . and he brought him to Jesus" (John 1:41, 42). There is something very important about those first words, "He first findeth his own brother." This was *prior work* as well as *personal work* and with the results that followed it became *eternal work.* The best days work Andrew did in all his life was the day he went to find his brother in order to bring him to Jesus. It may prove to be true in your life, too. The winning of a single soul may mean more than the doing of a hundred thousand other things.

We notice that it was at home that Andrew began his work. This may prove to be the most difficult thing we can ever attempt. Few dare to speak their convictions among their own family. No matter, it is best and right that we begin at home. I am sure that is what it means when it says, "Ye shall be witnesses unto me both in Jerusalem . . ." Our Jerusalem is at home. It means those near at hand and who are nearer than our brothers and sisters? To whom do we have a better right to speak about Christ than those who are at home? To whom is it more logical to speak than to those who are home? Here all professional aspects are lost and one speaks from heart to heart which is the greatest attribute of personal witnessing.

Not only is all this true from the standpoint of the listener but also to the speaker, because the home is the best place for the Christian worker to try his wings. It is the most natural and the most familiar of all places to him and it affords him the best opportunity for his first efforts.

There is much that needs to be said about the precedent which Andrew established in doing personal work. After all, Christianity is something which has its basis in the person. It began with the person of Christ. It is the reception of Him as a Person. It is not the belief of ideas or doctrines as such but only as they are related to and through the person of Christ. It is a personal experience which must come to us as individuals and is something apart from nations or families. It was established by the personal witness of believers to whom the experience of the Holy Spirit became the credential for service. These people were the men and women who were called from an walks of life to follow Christ. Upon them rested the task of carrying the message of Jesus Christ to the world. This meant one thing, namely, that it was a layman's task. Christianity is very distinctly a layman's religion. It is not the religion of priests and preachers but of laymen. It is not a system but a fellowship. It was through the personal witness of the common people that Christianity was to spread and multiply.

It is altogether fitting then to re-emphasize the work and place of Andrew, for his work is ours. In this work there can be no excuse of inaptitude or insignificance. It does not require great gifts nor brilliant knowledge. It is the work of common people who have had a personal experience of regeneration. It is reporting what one has found and knows. It is being a witness to an event. For Andrew the event was finding Christ in person as the Messiah. For us, the event is finding Christ in a personal experience as the Savior who satisfies the needs and longings of the human heart.

## 2. *He Introduced a Lad to Jesus*

"One of his disciples, Andrew, Simon Peter's brother, said unto him, There is a lad here, which hath five barley loaves and two small fishes: but what are they among so many?" (John 6:8, 9). The occasion of this introduction was the feeding of the five thousand. Philip had raised the question about feeding so many hungry people. Even two hundred pennyworth of bread (about $30.00) would not be enough to provide food for so many. But Andrew, filled partly with hope and partly with despair, partly with faith and partly with doubt, thinks he has a solution. The only hope he sees is in a lad whom he introduces to Jesus. Now, if he had looked at the lad alone he would have no reason for hope, for how could his meager lunch suffice for so many? It was not the lad nor his lunch that could save that situation, but what the Lord could do with the lad's yielded lunch. In the boy's hands five barley loaves would be nothing more and the the fish would remain just that, but in the hands of Christ they would become enough to meet the need of that crisis.

The link between the lad and the Lord was this man named Andrew who is spoken of here as "Simon Peter's brother." He is not spoken of in his own right but must bear the handicap of being the brother of a very famous and important man. Yet Andrew became important in his own right. It was not Peter who introduced the lad to the Lord. It was not Peter who was important to this occasion. It was Andrew. Peter is not mentioned as doing anything worthy of remembrance in this incident, but Andrew is.

Andrew's importance was not in himself as a multiplier of bread. He could not break the lad's lunch into enough to feed a multitude, but he saw a boy who had something Jesus could use. The boy had no idea that Jesus could use what he had, and that is where Andrew came in. Perhaps Andrew himself was somewhat skeptical and did not completely understand how so little could feed so many. Nevertheless, he brought the boy to his Master. It was Jesus' problem now, not Andrew's. Andrew had done what he could; he saw a boy, noticed what he had and believed that in some way His master could use it.

Suppose Andrew had not done his part? It is conceivable that the multitude would not then have been fed. Humanly speaking, Christ would have been impotent without the lad and the lad would have remained unnoticed without Andrew.

We can be modern Andrews. Ours is not the power to perform miracles. We may never have in our possession that with which a miracle can be performed, but we can be middlemen. We can see great possibilities in small things. We can see a boy's place in the world's affairs. We can be eyes for Christ even if we do not have His bread-multiplying hands. We can supply Him with the human elements for His necessary work.

Quick eye had Andrew. He it was amid
    The thronging multitudes, that marked the lad;
    And what his basket and how much it had,
Two fishes small and loaves of barley five,
Rewarded eye, to trivial things alive;
In that poor basket, what rich mercy hid!

A brother's heart had Andrew. Joy beyond
    All joy to him, the promised Christ to find,
    But heavenly joy may not to duty blind.
He cannot rest, his bliss is incomplete,
Till Simon sits with him at Jesus' feet;—
His brother then, by more than natural bond.

O happy they with Andrew's eye to heed
    A lad and his scant business, in the throng;
    Nor by high scom to do his efforts wrong:
And happy they with hearts that win not rest
Till in their bliss a brother too is blest.
What joy a Peter to the Lord to lead!

### 3. *He Introduced Some Greeks to Jesus*

"And there were certain Greeks among them, that came up to worship at the feast: The same came therefore to Philip, which was of Bethsaida of Galilee, and desired of him, saying, Sir, we would see Jesus. Philip cometh and telleth Andrew: and again Andrew and Philip tell Jesus" (John 12:20-22).

Once more Andrew plays the part of a middleman. Even Philip needed his help while Andrew here does not play the sole role of introducer. They go together.

The Lord is approaching the great hour for which He came into the world. The shadow of a cross falls across His path. What he would do that mattered most for the world He would do on that cross. The Greeks were a sample of that world. They were seeking Him and He is about to tell them how they will see Him; not as a mighty king nor as a great philosopher, but as a dying Savior. When Andrew and Philip tell Him of the inquiring Greeks Jesus tells them of the hour that is come in which "the Son of man should be glorified." Those who see the importance of that hour and those who go with Him from that hour to bless the world will be like seeds sown in the soil. Only by death can they live in the hearts of men. Up to this moment the life eternal, the life divine which He had was His own. Like a seed it could not be multiplied unless it died. So He died. He died that we might live and only by identification with His death can we live. Hence He said to those who inquired of Him, "He that loveth his life shall lose it: and he that hateth his life in this world shall keep it unto life eternal. If any man serve me, let him follow me . . ." (John 12:25, 26).

The Greeks had come from the land of religion and philosophy, for Greece was full of both. Apparently they were dissatisfied and disaffected because they were seeking something else and had come to worship at the feast. Here they had heard of this new leader of men, perhaps thinking of Him as so many think of religion, as something to think and something to do. They found instead a Person who spoke of dying, like a seed in the sense that it might spring forth into new life; that it might populate the world with a new kind of people. If Christianity has a place for worship, remember it is more than a religious feast. It is a life from God. It is life out of death. Whoever would have it must die to himself. To love one's life is to lose it while to lose one's life is to save it. This is Christ's new law of life. It is the law of the sown seed. It is only when a seed falls into the ground and dies that it lives. It is only when a soul is identified by faith with the Cross that it lives.

Here is the heart of the gospel. Andrew had a part in bringing this great truth to the attention of strangers. He did not create the truth or even explain it. He simply brought these men to the source of all truth. His part was very unspectacular. There was nothing loud and noisy. It was quiet and away from the public gaze, but it was effective, for knowing the power of Jesus, we have every reason to believe that the Greeks whom Andrew introduced to Him, became His followers.

Andrew, the introducer, is an example for emulation by all, but particularly by those who do not seem to have a large place in life and who do not seem to be endowed with spectacular gifts or to be capable of outstanding performance. Andrew's conquest lay in the realm of willingness to be who and what he was. He did not try to be his brother nor did he despise being what he could be and doing what he could do. This required both faith and humility which will merit a reward equal to that of his illustrious brother. We are to remember that rewards are for faithfulness and not for greatness. They are for service and not for so-called success.

Andrew's conquest lay further in the fact that he had a real and satisfying experience in Christ. He could say, "Eureka! I have found the Christ." Having found Him he could now help others to find Him. Acquaintance is the first requirement of an introduction. In fact, it is really the only requirement. It does not require eloquence or brilliance but acquaintance. Andrew found Christ and told his brother and it became the beginning of a fruitful ministry of introduction which later led him to discover the possibilities that lay in a lad and to bring some anxious inquirers into the presence of Christ.

# 25
# Matthew
## The Conquest of Reputation

ALL OF US have reputations. Not all are the same kind, nor had in the same way. Some reputations are made; some are acquired. Some are deserved and some undeserved. Some are true; some false. Often reputations are given by those who deliberately, and for reasons of their own, set out to spoil another's life. In such a case the reputation is beyond the control of the one on whom it is conferred.

While a good name may be taken away from us, a good character is solely up to us. There is a difference between reputation and character. Reputation is what is said about us while character is what is true of us. Reputation is what people know while character is what we know. Reputation is variable, often subject to gossip, jealousy, rumor and misinformation, whereas character is a fixed and settled quantity before God. With Him character counts far more than reputation.

Even Jesus acquired a bad reputation. They called Him gluttonous and a winebibber and charged Him with being one with publicans and sinners. They judged Jesus by appearance but it was such judgment as was inspired by jealousy and hypocrisy. His answer to His critics was not an attempt at self-justification but a caustic estimate of the critics themselves. He said, "But wisdom is justified of her children."

It is comforting to realize that we are not judged by God or going to be judged, on the basis of what people say about us. On the other hand neither will we be rewarded for our reputation. A preacher, for instance, may have a fine popular reputation and be well thought of by men whereas God's opinion may be otherwise. It can be so with any of us. We may put on a proud and pretentious front while our real self is despicable and unrighteous. Before God, we will receive credit for what we do and not for what we pretend to do.

There is a quaint Scotch story of a certain penurious lord in Fife, whose weekly contributions to the church never exceeded the sum of one penny. Yet he was immensely rich. It was the custom in that church to drop one's offering in the plate that was held at the door as one passed into the sanctuary for worship. One Sunday, by mistake, he dropped a five-shilling piece. Discovering his error before he was seated in his pew, he hurried back. He was just about to replace the silver piece with his usual penny when the elder who kept watch over the plate challenged him. "Stop, my lord," said he, "ye may put what ye like in but ye must not take anything out." After some discussion, in which the elder turned a deaf ear to the wealthy man's plea, the latter said, "Aweel, I suppose I'll get credit fir ut in heaven." "No, no," said the elder, "ye'll only get credit fir the penny." And he was right. The manner in which the contribution was made marred the whole procedure and discounted the value of what was given.

Our credit before God is on the basis of the intention of our performance. What we do before men is not necessarily what we are before God.

Matthew is not the only one in Scripture who suffered badly from his reputation. He had company in a man named Zacchaeus. They were both publicans who were a company of tax gatherers. In those days taxation was a form of political graft. There were Master-publicans who farmed out to lesser publicans the gathering of taxes in the various localities under Roman jurisdiction. These tax gatherers levied upon the people whatever they thought they could collect, and would keep for their own profit what was over the legal tax stipulated by the government. It is no wonder that they were hated and despised by the people as parasites upon the public.

While we have no right to think that Matthew was different from the rest of his kind, neither should we arbitrarily attribute to him any excessive and unjust sin of his calling. He at least suffered a bad reputation for he was classed with the rest of the publicans. Yet it is not thought that Matthew was as bad as his reputation pictured him. In Zacchaeus' case his reputation was evidently true, for when he followed Jesus he gave evidence of the sincerity of his conversion by making restitution. He said, "Behold, Lord, the half of my goods I give to the poor: and if I have taken anything from any man by false accusation, I restore him fourfold" (Luke 19:8, 9). Whereupon Jesus said, "This day is salvation come to this house." Zacchaeus was not saved because he made restitution: he made restitution because he was saved.

We mention this simply to point out the contrast in Matthew's case. He made no restitution and we believe it was because he had no need to, for it is unbelievable that the Lord would have required of Zacchaeus what He did not expect of Matthew. There are no favorites with God and no exemptions from righteousness all of which would point to Matthew's innocence of specific crimes. While a general accusation might be laid against Matthew that he was a bad Jew for having a part in this iniquitous system and lent himself in hypocrisy to further the aims of the oppressor, it was not apparent that he was like Zacchaeus. Had he been it would indeed have been strange that Jesus called him to be one of His disciples without some visible evidence of great change in both his character and conduct.

If Matthew was suffering justly from a bad reputation and if he was equally as guilty as Zacchaeus, then his response to Jesus at the seat of customs was not the first contact he had with Him. In any case he must have had previous contacts with Christ for his conversion was not some kind of miraculous summons that suddenly changed Matthew from a racketeer into a saint. There is a spiritual value to his conversion and call that leads back to other circumstances. Matthew had heard of Jesus long before He challenged him to follow Him. He had heard His gracious words and had seen His mighty works. All this time Matthew was being moved. A change was taking place, imperceptibly at first but irresistably at last, in this man's life. He loathed his business in life. He despised the company he was forced to keep and when Jesus stood before his desk one day at the tax office and said, "Follow me;" Matthew followed.

Matthew's conversion involved two things, his decision and his confession (Matt. 9:9-13).

## 1. His Decision

When Jesus came without warning to Matthew's tax office He fixed His gaze upon him and said boldly and bluntly, "Follow me." This command and invitation of Jesus brought Matthew face to face with the most important moment of his life. Never before had he seen or heard Jesus like this. Before he had been part of a crowd. Before it was impersonal. Before Matthew had struggled with principles. Now all that is changed and Matthew is alone with the Master of men. Now it is a personal matter. Now it is a matter of doing something with a Person and that Person none less than the Son of God. Now it is imperative that he answer and his answer must be in the form of a decision. He cannot argue: he must decide. He can no longer go on as he was. He can no longer do what he had been doing. Matthew made his choice and followed Jesus and that was not without its price.

We often say that it costs one nothing to be saved. That is true so far as the provision is concerned. Nothing that we can do can provide salvation, but the practice of it is not without cost. It cost Matthew his business to become a Christian, for when he chose to follow Jesus he also chose to forsake his profession. He could not follow the one without forsaking the other. The two were incompatible. This does not necessarily mean that business and Christianity are inconsistent, but it does mean that when business is against the principles of Christianity it has no place in Christian profession.

It also cost Matthew his companions and social standing when he followed Jesus. We may be tempted to say that the standing he had was not very desirable and that is quite true. Yet, it meant something to Matthew, but he gladly surrendered it for a better standing in the company of the Son of God. No matter what one gives up for Christ, it is not a sacrifice because he receives in return something which is infinitely better. Matthew gave up far less than he gained. In exchange for the sinful company of publicans he gained the immortal company of the Son of God. For the customhouse of Capernaum he gained the Father's house in heaven. His sacrifice was immediate and his gain both immediate and ultimate.

This conversion of Matthew is described by the very simple action of following Jesus. There probably is no better way of stating the meaning of becoming a Christian. To be sure, on the divine side it involves the operation of the Spirit of God and the application of divine means, but I am speaking of the human side of the experience.

Following Jesus means first of all to accept Him as our Savior. This requires faith in Him as the Son of God. Following requires faith and faith is our attitude both to God and to self.

Then, following Jesus means standing up in recognition of His claims upon us. In other words it is taking our stand for Christ. We must be willing to stand up and be counted. We must be willing to declare our faith by our stand. None can walk who do not first stand.

Then, following Jesus means leaving something. We cannot carry our past with us. If we do, it will rise up to condemn us. Christian experience means a new beginning without an old past brought into the present.

Finally, following Jesus means a new direction. Up to a certain point Matthew and Jesus were going in opposite directions. Their moral lives were different. Their eternal destinies were different. Now this was changed because Matthew changed directions. He began following Jesus, hence his life took a new course and he was headed in a new direction because he had a new Master.

This new direction means a new destiny and our destiny is simply our destination. The destination of God's people is totally different from that of those who are not God's people. Jesus spoke of this different destiny when He told of life's two ways. He said, "Enter ye in at the strait gate: for wide is the gate, and broad is the way, that leadeth to destruction, and many there be which go in thereat: Because strait is the gate, and narrow is the way, which leadeth unto life, and few there be that find it" (Matt. 7:13, 14). One way leads to destruction and one way leads to life. These are the separate destinations of men. Following Jesus Christ means going in the direction that brings us to the destination of life.

## 2. *His Confession*

Up to this point Matthew's affair with Jesus was personal; it was a maker solely between himself and the Lord. Now it becomes public, for confession must follow conversion. Therefore we see Matthew giving a feast to which Jesus is invited along with Matthew's publican friends in order that he might make an appropriate announcement of his great decision.

It may seem odd and a bit untrue to say this but it is a fact that Jesus takes us and we take Him. It is not a one-sided affair, because while we follow Jesus He follows us. To explain it this way, notice that when Matthew followed Jesus out of the customhouse then Jesus followed Matthew into his house. Here Matthew had gathered his unsaved friends and proposed to tell them of his decision to follow Jesus. In so doing Jesus put Himself at Matthew's disposal and entered into Matthew's plan in order that Matthew might conclude his new transaction of life by making a public confession of his faith.

It has been noted that Matthew gave this feast for his friends in order that he might make an appropriate announcement of his decision to follow Jesus. There were some people then, as there are some today, who did not think a feast of this kind was an appropriate thing. In ancient times feasts were common occasions for announcing most every great event. They were common occasions to announce births and deaths, the coming of age of sons and marriages. Now Matthew makes a feast the occasion to announce his conversion. When the prodigal returned from the far country his father gave a feast to celebrate his return. When the shepherd found his lost sheep he called in his neighbors to rejoice with him, when the housewife found the lost coin she asked her neighbors to rejoice in her good fortune. It is further said in this connection that "likewise joy shall be in heaven over one sinner that repenteth." But when the prodigal's father made a feast the prodigal's brother found fault at such a demonstration. So it was when Jesus attended Matthew's coming out party. He was criticised by the so-called saints of His day for eating with publicans and sinners.

Perhaps Matthew weighed the propriety of this in his own mind before inviting Jesus. Would it be fair to Jesus to throw Him among notorious sinners like his publican friends? Would it be fair to expose Jesus to criticism in this way? Apparently Matthew concluded it was the right thing to do and certainly Jesus did because He put His approval on it by His presence. Whatever He did was the right thing to do. Wherever Jesus went was the right place to go. Whatever Jesus said was the right thing to say. If one is ever troubled about right and wrong, look at Jesus. Simply follow Him for He is going in the right direction.

As for the critics, they complained out of their apparent holy attitude that Jesus' dining with sinners proved His unfitness to be a Messiah. To them, this sort of thing was vulgar and anti-religious. To them religion was an exclusive thing that shut out certain people. If one did not belong to their religious group and perform their religious exercises they had no place in their religious circle. They expected Jesus to fit into their narrow scheme. That He did not proves how right He was.

People were continually shocked at what Jesus did and today we have somehow lost sight of the perfect naturalness of Jesus in so many ways. Unfortunately, we have built up a vast religious tradition about Him and have put Him into a strait jacket of artificially religious things. We associate Him in art with a person of death-like appearance. Almost every religious artist's conception of Jesus is that of an emaciated, anaemic and emasculated character. We associate Him with poverty and sadness. We are deathly afraid to think of Him sitting at a feast table or listening to music or smiling and laughing. We are careful to keep Him always in the company of holy people who would not touch a sinner. We seem to want Jesus kept in some exhibit case that is religiously air-conditioned where He cannot be normal or human.

If you are brave enough to take it and if you are honest enough to admit it just read the New Testament and see how many times Jesus disproves this false picture we have built up. Here He is at Matthew's house enjoying a feast, surrounded by publicans and sinners, the most despised class of people in Jerusalem, and those, remember, who perhaps never attended the synagogue or the temple. Before this, at the beginning of His public ministry, we find Jesus at a wedding feast where He supplies the nuptial wine. On the shores of the lake He turns a gospel meeting into a picnic and bids the people be seated for meat, while He multiplies a lad's lunch into enough for over 5000. Again, we see Him walking on the Sabbath with His disciples through a field of corn and says not one word when they pluck ears to eat which was contrary to Jewish law. We see Him at another feast in Bethany. And, at the close of His earthly career while the shadow of a cross falls at His feet, we behold Him at supper in an upper room. Do not misjudge that moment by saying it was merely a spiritual occasion. Remember that the Lord's supper was preceded by a love feast and while the Lord's supper is in no way to be secularized and made an occasion for a food feast, it signalizes the whole temper of Christian experience as being a life of joy and happiness. Almost the last picture we have of Jesus is standing at the door saying, "Behold, I stand at the door, and knock: if anyone hear my voice, and open the door, I will come in to him, and will sup with him, and he with me" (Rev. 3:20). He invites us to a feast of good things.

All the while that Jesus is doing these things He is the subject of criticism. He is criticised for not obeying the law. He is criticised for flaunting social standards and religious rules. At one time He is accused of being a winebibber and at another time of being a social crank for they said, "We have piped unto you, and ye have not danced." Nothing that Jesus did gained the unanimous approval of these people, but, thank God, Jesus was not to be regulated by what people thought. What does it matter what they think?

Even though Jesus took this liberal attitude He never transgressed moral or spiritual principles. He was not bound by the legalism of the past for He was establishing a new life called the Christian life. He was not going to be merely religious like the Scribes and the Pharisees. Instead He came to give men life and to give it in abundance. It was to be above the average. It was not to be bound by man-made religious rules yet it was to be based on the laws of the spiritual life. It was not national but international. It was not religious but spiritual. It was not selfish but selfless.

The justification which Jesus gave for His presence at Matthew's feast was that physicans are usually among their patients. When a man is sick his physician goes to him and sits down with him. He does not stay aloof in some hygienic place fearing contamination but makes himself personally available to the sick. So Jesus said, "They that be whole need not a physician, but they that are sick." The inference was that the publicans needed Him while the Pharisees did not. So far as the Pharisees were concerned they needed Jesus just as much as anyone else, but they did not know it. Religion is not a substitute for regeneration. Religious people need Christ as much as the most sinful because human need is congenital, i.e., it goes back to birth. To put on good clothes over a diseased body does not heal sickness. Neither does the putting on of religious robes over a fleshly and sinful nature bring salvation. The Pharisees were sinful in spite of their profession and place and they were worse off than the publicans because the publicans realized their sinfulness while the Pharisees refused to see theirs.

Jesus was not making any apology for loving sinners but He was establishing an important precedent for all who follow Him. He said, "But go ye and learn what that meaneth, (the whole need not a physician, but they that are sick) I will have mercy, and not sacrifice: for I am not come to call the righteous, but sinners to repentance" (Matt. 9:13).

Jesus had a purpose in coming into the world. It was sick and He would heal it. He would give it a transfusion of new blood. He would not merely give a temporary relief from the pangs of conscience but would heal the disease itself. Therefore He went among his patients and when Matthew gave his feast of confession Jesus went not only to celebrate but to seek those to whom Matthew was going to speak. The feast was a means to an end and Jesus took that means to reach those who were sick and needed Him.

What do you suppose Jesus meant when He said to His pharisaical critics, "But go ye and learn what that meaneth, I will have mercy, and not sacrifice." It seems He meant this: Jesus was not interested in artificial religious rules and regulations. He was interested in men for the sake of their present and eternal welfare. He wanted mercy and not sacrifice because to these Pharisees sacrifice meant adherence to mere religious rules that were strictly artificial. These rules kept them so aloof from sinful men that they could not be in a position to help them lest they themselves become polluted. On the other hand mercy meant such compassion for all men that it would seek to lift them up and save them from their sins. In short, sacrifice concerned itself with rules while mercy concerned itself with men. By no manner of means did Jesus mean that we should experiment with sin in order to be in a position to know it and the sinner's need. It is always true that we are not to have any "fellowship with the unfruitful works of darkness" but this does not prohibit us from that normal and proper relationship with sinners in order to reach them for Christ. We cannot save the sinning ones by being like them. Our duty is to love them and seek them. This is mercy and Jesus wants it far more than He does sacrifice. He did not say that He wanted mercy without sacrifice as if He were releasing us from all righteous and holy standards and all proper, reverent and ordered respect for God. The sacrifice He wants is the kind that begins with God and not with man. It is not our kind but His kind.

There is one thing Matthew took with him when he left the tax office—his pen. But it was not such a pen as figured new burdens to levy on people. It was a pen which relieved people of the intolerable burdens which sin placed on them. It was used to write the first Gospel. While it was somewhat autobiographical, that was not its chief purpose. He wrote to give His own people, the Jews, an account of the life and death of the One whom he dared to follow.

He who follows Jesus never narrows his life and usefulness by doing so. Perhaps some of Matthew's publican friends sought to dissuade him on the grounds that he would be narrowing his life. They could see little practical value in surrendering his tax office franchise for a place with the followers of Jesus. But how wrong they were and how right Matthew was is proved by events. The receipt of customs at Capernaum is gone. The publicans are gone. Rome is gone. But Christ remains and the pen Matthew took with him has left an eternal monument for itself and him in the Gospel bearing his name.

What Matthew did with his pen should cause consideration in all of us. Matthew walked out of the revenue office a new man. Henceforth his future was determined by the Man he followed. He had a new life but he did not give up his old abilities. He took his pen and that old ability fell under the consecration of God and was used to write the story of life everlasting. Old abilities have new purposes. Consecration and sanctification can take them and put them to new and eternal uses.

Matthew took a pen and gave it to his new Master. What have you taken? Is it a needle like Dorcas'? Is it a scalpel like Luke's? Is it a rod like Moses'? Is it a tongue like Apollos'? Is it a mind like Paul's? Is it a house like Aquilla's? Whatever it is, give it to Him and He will give it back sanctified and consecrated for a glorious use.

# 26
# *James*
## *The Conquest of Zeal*

THERE ARE TWO persons named James in the New Testament. Both suffered the disadvantage of being brothers of more famous men. There is James, the brother of Jesus; and this James whom we are about to study, the brother of John, son of Zebedee. Neither James was by any means insignificant but they are overshadowed by their brothers. James, the brother of Jesus, was the author of the book of James and became the moderator of the first Christian assembly at Jerusalem. James, the brother of John, was one of the three disciples closest to Jesus. He ranked with Peter and John as the inner group whom Jesus so often took with Him upon important occasions.

There are two prominent occasions when James stands out before us. One was that time when he, through his mother, sought a prior place in the kingdom. The other was when Jesus came to a Samaritan village and James along with John asked Jesus to destroy it. Both of these instances reveal misguided and misdirected zeal.

Zeal is an admirable and a very desirable quality but it must be guided and directed or it may lead us into serious wrong. We must control our zeal or zeal will control us. Zeal is enthusiasm but enthusiasm must never be allowed to control us. Enthusiasm is the spirit of energy in which wo do things. It should not be the directive force of life. Enthusiasm often needs to be chastened and directed.

James was aptly called a son of thunder. It was a picturesque description of his zealous attitude to life. It revealed James' volcanic nature. He was eruptive and explosive. These eruptions were set off by the fire of zeal that burned in his soul. Like a volcano, James would be dormant and quiet just so long, but all the time the fires in his soul were gathering force and strength and when occasion arose he would erupt. He thundered against sin and evil. He spoke out against wrong and injustice. The energies of his soul were given expression in the eloquence of his lips.

But the enthusiasm of James was not always properly expressed.

There were those two occasions when it was misdirected. It got out of hand and led James into embarrassment which Jesus very graciously overruled.

Enthusiasm led James into two mistakes, *intolerance* and *selfish ambition.*

Enthusiasm's *intolerance* was in connection with that incident in the Samaritan village. It is described in Luke 9:51-56. "And it came to pass, when the time was come that he should be received up, he stedfastly set his face to go to Jerusalem, and sent messengers before his face: and they went, and entered into a village of the Samaritans, to make ready for him. And they did not receive him, because his face was as though he would go to Jerusalem. And when his disciples James and John saw this, they said, Lord, wilt thou that we command fire to come down from heaven, and consume them, even as Elias did? But he turned, and rebuked them, and said, Ye know not what manner of spirit ye are of. For the Son of Man is not come to destroy man's lives, but to save them."

This was intolerance at enthusiasm's worst. James' zeal for Christ could not conceive of anything less than complete and utter capitulation to him and such treatment as He was given in this village required the stearnest retribution.

Tolerance is a willingness to endure and be patient with other people's beliefs and ideas. It is the willingness to grant others the right of opinion and the privilege of holding a faith different from ours. But tolerance is never the willingness to accept that faith or belief. We can be tolerant without being compromising.

The more intense one's faith the more danger there is of intolerance. That is why those who believe in the fundamentals of the faith are often very intolerant and sometimes bigoted. They display little patience and less love toward those who do not believe precisely as they do. While they do not go to the extreme of James' enthusiasm they are very pronounced in their attitude of impatience.

Zeal for truth must be positive. When it concerns our attitude, let it never waver. Let us believe our beliefs. Let us be sure of our faith. Let us believe and know why we believe, but in too many instances intolerance with other people is a cover-up for our own ignorance. We know what, but not why, and we must make a big noise to silence the questions of others.

Intolerance has led to some of the worst crimes of history. It has led to bitter persecutions. It has brought cruelty in the name of religion. It has darkened the pages of church history. It began with James and his brother, John, and like most things it began with a good thing. It was a good thing carried to its extreme. James allowed his enthusiasm for Christ and right to become a thing of evil and a weapon of revenge and cruelty.

To avoid the extreme of enthusiasm's intolerance we should not go to the other extreme of supine and spineless acquiescence to everything. As Christians, we are not only expected to stand for somethng, but also to stand up for it. For this positive stand we are to take "the whole armor of God, that ye may be able to withstand in the evil day, and having done all, to stand. Stand therefore, having your loins girt about with truth . . ." This means a positive and uncompromising attitude and purpose of life. One can be against a thing without being bitter and cruel. One can hold the truth in love which means love for the truth and love for those who are against it.

Perhaps we can make an even closer observation of this matter and say that in our attitude we can properly distinguish between the thing that is wrong and the person who holds that wrong thing. Is it not a fact that God hates sin but loves the sinner? There is no tolerance of sin but a generous love for the person who sins, in spite of his sin. Our mistake is bitter rancor and hatred for the offending person. We fail to make the distinction. We also fail to be generous enough to understand the other person's background and viewpoint. We judge everything by the intensity of our faith and since we are as we are, we conclude that all should be such. A little more understanding on our part would soften the harshness of judgment of others while neither condoning nor compromising the thing that is wrong.

There is no doubt that Jesus was at times properly intolerant. He was intolerant of sin. He never excused it, but at the same time He never hated the sinner. He came to love and not hate, to save and not condemn and if we are to be as He is we must do as He did. He was intolerant of hypocrisy. Think of that occasion when He went into the temple and found it being desecrated by religious racketeers who were making it a place of merchandise rather than prayer. These He drove hence with a lash for He would not tolerate this abuse of sacred things; He would not compromise with them for an instant. Yet in all these things Jesus never lost sight of the sovereignty of the human will or the will of God. It was a man's privilege to choose his own destiny, subscribe to his own creed and lead his own life. But it was also God's purpose to save whosoever would be saved. The love of God was the all-inspiring motive. Jesus came as the personification of that love. He loved those who hated Him. He loved those who did not agree with Him. He loved even those who crucified Him for He said, "Father, forgive them, for they know not what they do."

While Jesus tolerated human sovereignty and gave expression to God's love it did not mean that all men were automatically saved by His attitude to them. His attitude is eternally unchanging but it is our attitude plus His that counts. It is men's faith and God's love that means salvation and life. Men are not saved simply because God loves them. The greatest expression on the love of God says this, "For God so loved the world, that he gave his only begotten Son, that whosoever believeth in him should not perish, but have everlasting life." The qualification is human faith. It is "that whosoever believeth in him should not perish but have everlasting life." God's love is the initiating cause; Christ's death is the executing fact while man's faith is the appropriating act in salvation and life.

Intolerance not only exists in Christian's attitude to non-Christians but, sad to say and lamentable in the extreme, among other Christians. Intolerance and ignorance and misunderstanding have divided more Christians than any other known cause. And, when sifted down it will be found that the issues at stake were relatively unimportant. We become intolerant of men about pin-point differences in doctrine about which we can afford to disagree. We can have differences without divisions but intolerance has crept in and we divide. At the same time we take such meticulous care about these little things we are often guilty of greater evils of tolerance. We tolerate sins and impurities that are far worse than the things we condemn. It is as Jesus said of the hypocritical Pharisees, they strained at gnats and swallowed camels. They condemned little things and condoned big things. They tithed mint and anise and cumin which was a small matter while neglecting the weightier matters of the law such as judgment, mercy and faith. Their virtues were little and their vices were big.

In many ways some believers are like the ancient Pharisees. But we hurry the thought quickly out of mind because we are not courageous enough to face it. Yet it is a fact for fundamentalism is too many times the ensign for contending cliques and parties who say, "I am of Paul, and I of Apollos, and I of Cephas." It is contending for the faith in a contentious manner. It is doing a right thing in a wrong way. It is straining at doctrinal gnats and swallowing moral camels. It is breaching the spirit while defending the letter. It is transgressing the law of love in its zeal to preserve the faith. In consequence the influence of its collective voice has diminished and its contentions are without much effect.

The mistake has been James' old error of misguided enthusiasm. He who wanted to defend his Master sought to do it in a manner unworthy of Christians. Jesus had to rebuke him and tell him he had the wrong spirit. Jesus was not interested in revenge or retaliation. He bore the spirit of love which builded instead of destroyed; which gave life instead of death for "the Son of Man is not come to destroy men's lives but to save them." All through His life He bore this spirit to the world in spite of its sin and evil and unbelief and hatred. He had to frequently correct His disciples, with their human weaknesses, in allowing their enthusiasm to be turned into intolerance. On one occasion John came to Him and said, "Master, we saw one casting out devils in thy name, and we forbade him, because he followeth not with us." But Jesus rebuked him, "Forbid him not, for he that is not against us is for us." You see how generous Jesus was. It was a generosity born of perfect intelligence and perfect love.

The Apostle Paul gave expression to the same generosity of spirit when he said, "Some indeed preach Christ even of envy and strife;

and some also of good will; The one preach Christ of contention, not sincerely, supposing to add affliction to my bonds: But the other of love, knowing that I am set for the defence of the gospel. What then? notwithstanding, every way, whether in pretence, or in truth, Christ is preached; and I therein do rejoice, yea, and will rejoice" (Phil. 1:15-18).

Enthusiasm led James also into another extreme. This time it was *selfish ambition*. Ambition is a good and necessary thing but it must have the right motives. A selfish ambition is a sinful ambition. The narrowest thing in the world is an ambition that thinks only of self. The world would be a far better and more prosperous place if our ambitions had a place for the consideration of others.

The account of James' selfishness reads like this, "And James and John, the sons of Zebedee, come unto him, saying, Master, we would that thou shouldest do for us whatsoever we shall desire. And he said unto them, What would ye that I should do for you? They said unto him, Grant unto us that we may sit, one on thy right hand, and the other on thy left hand, in thy glory. But Jesus said unto them, Ye know not what ye ask: can ye drink of the cup that I drink of? and be baptized with the baptism that I am baptized with? And they said unto him, We can. And Jesus said unto them, Ye shall indeed drink of the cup that I drink of; and with the baptism that I am baptized withal shall ye be baptized: But to sit on my right hand and on my left hand is not mine to give; but it shall be given to them for whom it is prepared. And when the ten heard it, they began to be much displeased with James and John. But Jesus called them to him, and said unto them, Ye know that they which are accounted to rule over the Gentiles exercise lordship over them; and their great ones exercise authority upon them. But so shall it not be among you: but whosoever will be great among you, shall be your minister: and whosoever of you will be the chiefest, shall be servant of all. For even the Son of Man came not to be ministered unto, but to minister, and to give his life a ransom for many" ( Mark 10:35-45) .

The wrong of this request was not necessarily in its aspiration to a right hand place but that James desired it by preference and not by merit. He and his brother wanted these places because they asked for them not because they deserved them. Preference plays no part in the assignment of honors and rewards. It does not come because a man happens to be an apostle or an archbishop or a minister. The choice kingdom places are not rewards for ecclesiastical service. They are open to all men and women. Jesus said, "to sit on my right hand or on my left hand is not mine to give; but it shall be given to them for whom it is prepared."

Here is the principle of a prepared place for a prepared people. The place and the people go together. The Lord Jesus is our advocate in heaven preparing the place, for He said, "I go to prepare a place for you." The Holy Spirit is our advocate on earth preparing the people for that place. Whatever distinctions there may be in the place, with one being before another, we will find this to be decided solely by the individual's fitness. Faith gives us a share in the place itself because it is only heaven that is given away; whereas faithfulness will determine the specific nature of honor of that place.

We know that there is much about this whole matter of rewards that is quite beyond understanding. How can there be differences of honors and rewards and yet have a living in perfect contentment and happiness? To look at it from the viewpoint of our present nature is to see difficulties but when we possess new natures they will be free from all such imperfections.

There is probably some mitigation in this incident so far as James and his brother are concerned. Jesus indicates this in his answer, "Ye know not what ye ask." That is, they did not fully understand what they were doing as if to say that it was zeal rather than greed that prompted their request. This is certainly the charitable view to take yet how few times we take the charitable view of others' acts and deeds. We lay the vilest implications against them and wish to see what is most wrong. When we understand a man, like James with his enthusiasm, we can easily see how he might have allowed himself to have made this request not so much from greed but because he always did things fervently and enthusiastically.

Ambition needs direction and control. In a life yielded to Christ there is the control of the Holy Spirit. Jesus said, "Whosoever will save his life shall lose it; but whosoever shall lose his life for my sake and the gospel's, the same shall save it." Ambition may save, yet lose while devotion will lose, yet save. There is here a law of sacrifice even as there is in nature. It operates by surrender and self sacrifice. The grapes must be crushed before there is wine. The alabaster box must be broken before there can be fragrance. The ore must be refined before there can be gold. The tree must be bruised before there can be sap. Life yields only when sacrifice makes it possible.

Because James was selfishly ambitious as well as intolerant was no hindrance to Christ's later use of him. All of us have our defects but in spite of the defects God can use us. Jesus took this natural propensity in James and sanctified it and used James for His glory. He can use us not because of ourselves but in spite of us. Remember also, that in God's use of men it is on the basis of natural and native ability which is redeemed and sanctified. Whenever a person comes to Christ he is given a new nature but this new nature does not destroy the old. The abilities we had in sin God can transform and employ in righteousness. Does it not mean this very thing when it says in Romans 6:13, "Neither yield ye your members as instruments of unrighteousness unto sin; but yield yourselves unto God, as those that are alive from the dead, and your members as instruments of righteousness unto God." The old members have a different use. Now they are regenerated and transformed and have a wholly different purpose. Thus when a person before his conversion had a certain aptitude and ability to do one thing, God uses this aptitude and ability in His service. It is each "according to his ability."

We hear nothing further of James until we have notice of his death. This does not mean that this man of zeal did nothing, but rather that what he did later was free from his previous errors. He did what he did without attracting public attention. He did not seek public preferment. He did not labor for the eye of men. Think of all who quietly but efficiently do their life duties without being noticed. Think also of those whose works are paraded for public notice. How much better to work for the work's sake rather than for self's sake. This purity of purpose should inspire all our service, for God will discount and count out all the selfishness with which we have wrought. It is far better that we do it now than that He should do it later when it is too late to be mended.

That James should have died a martyr's death was a great honor and a justifying climax to his life but that he died the first apostolic martyr was most significant. Jesus had earlier asked, "Can ye drink of the cup that I drink of? and be baptized with the baptism that I am baptized with?" to which James unknowingly replied, "We can," unknowingly perhaps, but sincerely. He did so drink and he was so baptized but little did he realize it when he said it. He became the first martyr of the apostles for it is recorded in Acts 12:1, 2 that "Herod the king stretched forth his hands to vex certain of the church. And he killed James the brother of John with the sword."

We often say with sincerity what we do not realize. Doubtless James did not realize what Jesus meant but it is to his eternal honor that he died faithfully. There is no account of weakness in his death. He does not falter but dies gladly for his Lord. He proves in death what he had lived in life. Even if his earlier life is marred by human mistakes his later life is filled with honor and glory.

# 27
# Paul
## *The Conquest of Handicap*

IT IS UTTERLY beyond human possibility that any tongue or pen should recount witb justice the measure of this man's life. We can easily recount its beginning but its depth and breadth is beyond words. In this case it is wise to focus attention upon one phase of Paul's life. But what phase shall it be? Shall it be his scholarship, his apostleship or his authorship? For us it had better be none of these for whereas few of us shall be scholars, none of us can be apostles or writers of Scripture. Why pursue a thing we never can reach? Why go back to a phase of life we can never fill? It is like chasing a rainbow to find its mythical pot of gold.

However, there is a part of Paul's life that touches all lives, it is his experience with suffering. A great handicap came to Paul which humanly would have been a very restricting barrier to at least one phase of his life's work. It is believed by many that his handicap was bad eyesight. He describes it in 2 Corinthians 12 as "a thorn in the flesh" divinely permitted but satanically produced.

Before we see what disposition Paul made of this handicap we must first of all see the man himself. To realize what he did we must understand who he was. Well, who was Paul? There are certain very illuminating autobiographical expressions in his Epistles which reveal the man to us, which in turn explain how and why he did conquer his handicap. You cannot defeat a man who holds such a view of life as Paul held. Anyone who takes the attitude of faith he did is bound to meet and master every obstacle. If you wish a philosophy of success here it is, all of which is of course based and predicated on his regeneration.

The very first expression is naturally in Romans where Paul recounts the struggle between Saul and Paul, between his old nature and his new nature. He exclaimsl "O wretched man that I am: who shall deliver me from the body of this death? I thank God through Jesus Christ our Lord (Rom. 7:24, 25). Jesus Christ was the answer to his problem and in the next chapter we read how he turns the conflict over to the indwelling Holy Spirit.

"But by the grace of God I am what I am: and his grace which was bestowed upon me was not in vain; but I labored more abundantly than they all: yet not I, but the grace of God which was with me" (1 Cor. 15:10). This explains the man—"By the grace of God I am what I am."

But this was not all one-sided. God did not seize hold of this man and against his will and without his cooperation thrust him into automatic action. God needed Paul as much as Paul needed God. What Paul yielded was as necessary as what God provided. God provided grace but Paul provided a life to manifest that grace. It came in the manner described in Galatians 1:15, 16, "But when it pleased God, who separated me . . . and called me . . . To reveal his Son in me, . . . immediately I conferred not with flesh and blood . . ." On Paul's part the secret was what we call consecration. It involved his immediate and complete surrender to this call. Without this part the grace of God would have been thwarted. It can be. Ultimately the divine purpose for the world at large will be fulfilled and in that sense God's grace cannot be thwarted or frustrated, but individually, we may oppose God's plan for us and miss His place for our lives. Not so with Paul.

What Paul did after his call is just as important as his response to that call. It was an attitude of continual humility. He never lost his perspective. He kept his place; he remained humble. This is revealed in Ephesians 3:7, 8 when he said, "Whereof I was made a minister, according to the gift of the grace of God given unto me by the effectual working of his power. Unto me, who am less than the least of all saints, is this grace given . . ." How Paul began was not more important than how he continued. He was willing to be less than the least. There was no ecclesiastical preferment here. He wished no hierarchal glory. Out of the limpid beauty and simplicity of this man's life came his great strength and power.

Paul never gloried in the greatness of his previous sins. He never advertised his former years nor capitalized on his previous experience. Yet he freely admitted how greatly he had sinned. "This is a faithful saying, and worthy of all acceptation, that Christ Jesus came into the world to save sinners, of whom I am chief" (1 Tim. 1:15).

Paul's continuance in grace never reached a higher level than when he wrote to the Philippians and said, "Brethren I count not myself to have apprehended: but this one thing I do, forgetting those things which are behind, and reaching forth unto those things which are before, I press toward the mark for the prize of the high calling of God in Christ Jesus" (Phil. 3:13, 14). This accounts for Paul's conquest of life more than anything else, save his new birth. He was perfected in his position but not perfect in his condition. His standing was complete but his state had yet to be completed. He was willing to see and admit this lack of apprehending and he set himself to the great task of laying hold of the prize.

Some of the autobiographical expressions came before and some after the great moment when he first faced the handicap which had come into his life. That moment is not described but it can easily be imagined. Here is a man busy with the greatest business in the world, the King's business. He is busy traveling and writing. He is busy preaching and working. From his pen came fourteen of the twenty-one New Testament Epistles. For this he could well use every faculty and ability of mind, heart and hand. Humanly speaking, these would have been indispensable especially in Paul's day with its absence of mechanical and scientific aids. However, a great handicap came into Paul's life. We are not specifically told what it was. So bad was this affliction that he needed an amanuensis. If he attempted to write his own letters or inscribe a personal greeting in his own hand he apologized for his writing. At the close of the Epistle to the Galatians he wrote, "Ye see how large a letter I have written unto you with mine own hand."

Without establishing the fact from the evidence found in Galatians we observe the presence of this physical handicap in Paul's life and ministry. He puts it in these words, "Lest I should be exalted above measure through the abundance of the revelations, there was given to me a thorn in the flesh . . ." (2 Cor. 12:7). This thorn in the flesh apparently was the handicap of impaired eyesight and with this disability one could easily understand how it could limit a man whose greatest ministry was writing.

There are numerous questions which gather around such a life experience as this. How did it come? How did Paul feel when he first faced it? What did he do about it? What did God do about it? What was the result ultimately, to Paul's ministry? These questions can be asked of Paul's distant experience and then transferred to our present experiences. While we are not in the same position as Paul with so much at stake, we nevertheless are subject to handicaps, disabilities, experiences, sicknesses and conditions that can either make or break us in life. But, we are to discover here that a disability does not necessarily mean a liability. We are to discover that we can find advantage in adversity.

I think we ought to begin with the beginning and see the causes from the very first. They lie in Paul's conversion and in his change from Saul to Paul the account of which is found in Acts 9. Here we notice three things. Paul's condition, Paul's conviction and Paul's conversion.

## 1. Paul's Condition

"And Saul, yet breathing out threatenings and slaughter against the disciples of the Lord, went unto the high priest, and desired of him letters to Damascus to the synagogues, that if he found any of this way, whether they were men or women, he might bring them bound unto Jerusalem" (Acts 9:1, 2).

His condition can easily be read in these words which describe the feelings and intentions of bitterness and hatred which he had against the Christians.

Paul's condition was that of a sinner. This included a number of things.

*It was an intellectual condition.* Paul was not an ignorant novice who did not know right from wrong. He was a scholar of high repute and brilliant mind, but intellectuality was not enough.

*It was a moral condition.* Paul was directed in these operations against Christians by his conscience which was regulated by his moral standards. It gave him a very high moral standing among men but it also made it possible for him to seek out innocent people for death whose only offense was their faith in Jesus Christ. In this he thought he was doing God a service. But, when Paul's morality was judged by God's standards it was seen in a far different light. No, morality was not enough.

Moreover, *it was a religious condition.* Paul was an intensely religious man. He boasted at one time of a proud religious regularity and a proud religious pedigree. "If any other man thinketh that he hath whereof he might trust in the flesh, I more: Circumcised the eighth day, of the stock of Israel, of the tribe of Benjamin, an Hebrew of the Hebrews; as touching the law a Pharisee; concerning zeal, persecuting the church; touching the righteousness which is in the law, blameless" (Phil. 3:4-6). This was his pedigree, but one can be a religious sinner just as well as an irreligious one. When Paul met Christ he had not a word to say about his intellectuality, morality or religion for then he saw the awfulness of his condition and the urgency of his need.

## 2. His Conviction

"And as he journeyed, he came near Damascus: and suddenly there shined round about him a light from heaven: And he fell to the earth, and heard a voice saying unto him Saul, Saul, why persecutest thou me? And he said, Who art thou, Lord? And the Lord said, I am Jesus whom thou persecutest: it is hard for thee to kick against the pricks. And he trembling and astonished said, Lord, what wilt thou have me to do? And the Lord said unto him, Arise, and go into the city, and it shall be told thee what thou must do. And the men which journeyed with him stood speechless, hearing a voice, but seeing no man" (Acts 9:3–7).

Here is a complete reversal of his previous ideas and opinions; not in words but in attitude. He capitulated in humility before Christ. He changed from a proud and imperious persecutor to a lowly penitent seeking mercy. He had no alibi. He offered no excuses. He simply gave in to Christ in the complete convicion of his soul that he was a sinner.

Conviction reveals us to ourselves and God to us. We come to know who we are and who He is. It is a revelation of need as well as a provision to meet that need.

We notice something supernatural and unusual about Paul's experience.

*There was a vision.* The light came, as we are told elsewhere, about noon and was of such brilliance that it outshone the natural light of the sun at its zenith. This was not a subjective vision which Paul imagined. Nor was it a case of sunstroke as frantic critics claim for the reason that it was something seen by those who were with Paul as well as by Paul himself.

While regeneration is always supernatural in that it is God's work in the soul we need not expect a duplication of these spectacular circumstances because in the first place Paul's conversion came in an age of miracles to give divine credentials to the apostles. Furthermore, conversion is not a standardized experience. Not all have the same emotional feelings. In each case it may be different because we are different and conversion fits our personality and condition.

*There was a voice.* The vision brought illumination and the voice information. The vision awakened and the voice explained. This is always true of conviction even though it may not be accompanied by either a vision or a voice. It awakens us to our true condition and in that awakened condition explains the purpose and plan of God for salvation.

### 3. His Conversion

"And Saul arose from the earth; and when his eyes were opened, he saw no man: but they led him by the hand, and brought him into Damascus. And he was three days without sight, and neither did eat nor drink. And there was a certain disciple at Damascus, named Ananias; and to him said the Lord in a vision, Ananias. And he said, Behold, I am here, Lord. And the Lord said unto him, Arise, and go into the street which is called Straight, and inquire in the house of Judas for one called Saul, of Tarsus: for, behold, he prayeth, and hath seen in a vision a man named Ananias coming in, and putting his hand on him, that he might receive his sight. Then Ananias answered, Lord, I have heard by many of this man, how much evil he hath done to thy saints at Jerusalem: and here he hath authority from the chief priests to bind all that call on thy name. But the Lord said unto him, Go thy way: for he is a chosen vessel unto me, to bear my name before the Gentiles, and kings, and the children of Israel: for I shall show him how great things he must suffer for my name's sake. And Ananias went his way, and entered into the house; and putting his hands on him said, Brother Saul, the Lord, even Jesus, that appeared unto thee in the way as thou camest, hath sent me, that thou mightest receive thy sight, and be filled with the Holy Ghost. And immediately there fell from his eyes as it had been scales: and he received sight forthwith, and arose, and was baptized. And when he had received meat, he was strengthened. Then was Saul certain days with the disciples which were at Damascus" (Acts 9:8-19).

Conversion means a spiritual, moral, mental and volitional change. It means to turn around and to change over. In Paul's case it was indicated in two ways.

*By what Saul said to the Lord.* He said, "Lord what wilt thou have me to do?" Paul recognized the Lord Jesus Christ as Savior and Sovereign. He admitted a new authority in his life. This is the change any genuine conversion produces. It is a profound change in the rule, the condition and the order of life. In fact it is a new regime.

*By what the Lord said to Saul.* He said, "be as a chosen vessel unto me." This indicated a new purpose for Saul's life. Henceforth he was to be in a new service. Conversion changes the purpose of life. Life is no longer a selfish engagement with pleasures sponsored by our sinful whims. It becomes a sacrificial outpouring of service for both God and man in which the highest happiness does not come from pursuing pleasure but in doing good.

The completed process of conversion, which is the human aspect of regeneration, transforms and fashions us into vessels of service. What a lofty conception of life this is and how different from the ordinary idea.

All of this describes the beginning of Paul's new relationship to God. It was the beginning of his Christian experience, the beginning of his apostleship and the beginning of his authorship. When, in the course of events, we find him struggling under the handicap of a thorn in the flesh we can then understand how he met and mastered that handicap. The basis of it was his new life in Christ. There can be no explanation apart from this experience.

Paul's handicap was not a moral one. It was common in its condition for people everywhere have afflictions, but in Paul's case he describes it as "the messenger of Satan to buffet me, lest I should be exalted above measure." In other words, it was a satanically produced but divinely purposed condition. Satan produced it which is not true of all sickness. They often come in the course of normal events. We can have sicknesses in which Satan has no part. They can be the result of accidents. They can result from the broken laws of nature. They can be natural weaknesses as in Timothy's case or from natural causes as with that of Epaphroditus, but in Paul's case it was diabolical. It was satanically produced under the permissive will of God. God had an immediate and specific purpose in Paul's ailment. It was permitted lest Paul "should be exalted above measure." It was a preventive measure for Paul had lately had a very exalting experience which is described in the previous verses of the chapter. He had been permitted a preview of a believer's experience after death. It was so exalting and so wonderful that words could not describe it. It might and could have become a source of great spiritual pride and had it been so it would have hindered and limited Paul's usefulness both as a Christian and as an apostle. So he says, "lest I should be exalted above measure through the abundance of the revelations, there was given me a thorn in the flesh."

Here is the fact of his handicap. How did he conquer it? God did not remove it in response to Paul's thrice offered prayer for healing. Paul had been God's instrument in healing others and later in his own experience was healed from the venomous bite of a viper, but here where so much was at stake, where his efficiency in God's service was involved, he was not healed. Naturally, we would ask, why? Just how did Paul meet it and how could he surmount the disability it created?

Paul conquered his handicap first of all by his understanding. He saw God's purpose in it. He recognized God's intention in permitting its occurrence. Understanding is the way to meet any problem in our lives. It is not well to close our eyes and try to grope our way out. That is folly. Paul had this condition come upon him and he gave it thoughtful and prayerful consideration. Where did it come from? What was it for? Was it the result of my own folly? Have I deliberately broken God's laws and is that the consequence? Paul found an answer in his case. He came to understand its source and its purpose. We should do the same but we seldom do. We seldom ask the Lord what it means. Usually, we complain and consequently fret and fume over the bitter injustice of God's dealings.

Let us be persuaded that in the scheme of Christian experience and in the realm of faith there is a pattern and meaning behind life. Even the most casual happening has a cause and the most pointless event a purpose. We are then, with that understanding, to be ready to have that purpose worked out in our experience.

The most natural and normal reaction was Paul's prayer for removal of the handicap. Three times he asked God to take this thorn away. God's answer was not as Paul had prayed, but God answered his prayer nevertheless. Instead of a cure He gave grace to bear his handicap. He said, "My grace is sufficient for thee; for my strength is made perfect in weakness" (2 Cor. 12:9). God did not remove the handicap but He did give grace. Grace was God's means, not merely to bear the thorn resolutely and patiently, or to suffer because it had to be so, but it was God's means to surmount the limitations which this handicap placed upon Paul. Not only that, it was also God's way of bringing two things into Paul's life and ministry.

It brought the *perfection* of strength out of weakness, for God said, "my strength is made perfect in weakness." It was Paul's weakness and God's strength. But what kind of weakness did this mean? Arthur

S. Way's translation of this passage illuminates it in these words, "It is in the forge of infirmity that strength is wrought to perfection." Paul's sickness was the forge of infirmity. Upon that forge lay Paul's life. It was being heated in a furnace of affliction. It was being brought to a state of malleability where it could be hammered and fashioned into the form of usefulness which God desired. Out of this experience would come a finer and better Paul. God has the pattern of a certain vessel in mind and Paul's sickness was the forge of infirmity in which it was being formed. His weakness is not to be mistaken for what we generally understand to be weakness. It was an attitude of mind and will to the purpose of God.

It brought *power* through suffering for Paul said, "Most gladly therefore will I rather glory in my infirmities, that the power of Christ may rest upon me." Whatever instrument God would fashion out of Paul in this forge of infirmity must be supplied with power and it would come out of this experience. Paul would be energized with the power of Christ.

There is a strange power in adversity and a wonderful strength in weakness. Not, of course, in the human side for if one passes through the normal experiences of adversity without Christ this is not so. But, in the processes of the forge new strength is fused into the metal and it comes out of the fire strengthened and shaped for a better life.

Paul conquered his handicap not only by understanding but, in that understanding, by a change of attitude. As we have already seen, his first reaction was to pray for its removal. Then with God's answer of grace to bear the handicap we observe a significant and important change in the apostle's attitude.

He first ceases to pray that God will heal him. Having prayed thrice he has proved that he is neither weak nor stubborn. He is not presumptuous and does not continue to insist upon his own will. Faith persuades him that God has a specific purpose in this experience.

In ceasing to pray for healing Paul does not lapse into a negative state of resignation. He does not accept it fatalistically. He does not determine merely to endure what God has denied. He takes a positive rather than negative attitude. It is expressed by two "therefores." "Therefore will I rather glory in my infirmities, that the power of Christ may rest upon me." And again, "Therefore I take pleasure in infirmities, in reproaches, in necessities, in persecution, in distresses for Christ's sake: for when I am weak, then am I strong" (2 Cor. 12:10).

Paul's emphatic "therefore" is based upon God's equally emphatic "wherefore." God was in it and Paul would get something out of it. This was a part of the divine plan for life and Paul would follow that plan. He would not groan over his thorn but glory in his infirmities.

In assessing the results we find that insofar as Paul's writing ministry is concerned he was unhindered and so far as his spiritual life is concerned he rose to greater heights than ever. The handicap was a constant reminder of his dependence upon God. It saved him from the danger for which it was given. Not once is Paul given to excessive pride and spiritual inflation over his apostolic privileges and experiences. God's wisdom is vindicated and Paul's life is richly enhanced.

As Paul conquered so may we. Our handicap or infirmities may not be of a kind with his. Ours may not be specific messengers of Satan. They may be the natural consequences of life under the permissive will of God. Yet none of these things need defeat us. We may conquer them as Paul did by two means, understanding and faith. These are two of the greatest weapons or forces at our command. Ignorance never mastered anything or advanced anyone. Let us study to be wise. Let us find that wisdom, not merely in knowledge, but in spiritual illumination. It is not worldly wisdom that is needed for we can have all that and yet not be ready to meet life. Look how worldly wisdom has brought the world into its present plight. God continually makes "foolish the wisdom of this world."

Let us treat our problems thoughtfully. Let us view them not through our prejudices or our feelings but through a wisdom made wise in the ways of life.

Paul's other great weapon was faith. Wisdom and faith go together. Understanding and trust are companions. Jesus put nothing beyond either the reach or the power of faith, but, it was always an enlightened faith. Any other kind of faith is presumption. There is no such thing as blind faith except it be utterly false.

Here we face life; either to be beaten by its adversities or to accept them as a challenge. Life need never be what it has been. It need never be useless and hopeless. It can be triumphant and fruitful and out of weakness we may rise to strength.

# 28
# *Christ*
## *The Conqueror*

NO STUDY OF this kind would be complete without bringing it to a close by thinking of the Lord Jesus Christ. We view Him as the Conqueror and through Him we can be more than conquerors.

If we have met ourselves in the Bible and have been able thus to better meet life it will only be because we have met Christ in the Bible. He is everywhere in this Book. He began it and closes it. When defeat came through temptation and brought sin He is immediately set forth as God's remedy for a defeated life. It was His business to bring life into the world and in doing so He brought God's life of which we may partake by faith. This life is designed for conquest. It is designed to conquer spiritual evil, moral evil and physical evil. It is designed to make us masters of life. By it we are able to meet the things that we encounter both outside and within ourselves. Outside lie adversities and inside adversaries. Outside is physical nature with its disease and disaster and inside is human nature with its temptation and unrest. The Christian life offers us victory over all of these.

First of all, who was Jesus Christ? Was He just a human being such as we, only on an advanced level? Is the best He can offer the inspiration of His example? Does He merely say follow Me if you can? That is what His statements would mean if He were only a man. But, thank God, He was and is more. He is God manifest in the flesh. Someone asks, does not that very fact make life hopeless for us? Because He was God He could live godlike while we are only human. No, it is not hopeless because the nature of His relation to us is what it is. If He being God came simply to live for His own sake it would be so, but, He came to live for our sake. His deity was manifest in flesh. He invested human nature with the divine nature. He chose voluntarily to limit Himself and subordinate Himself to the will of God in everything. Whatever He did or said was by the power of the Holy Spirit. He experienced temptation. He passed through suffering of every conceivable kind. He was not a stranger to sorrow. He touched life at every point. In fact, He was "in all points tempted as we are, yet without sin" (Heb. 4:15).

The very nature of His experience reveals how much He can help us for His deity was not something which kept Him from the actual experience of life. He came and identified Himself with the human race at the point where it suffered and sinned. The reason for this identification was to provide us with a new life so that we could meet our sufferings and sins.

Jesus Christ identified Himself with every part of life. He was "in all points like as we are." He felt what we feel. He saw what we see. He suffered what we suffer. All of this experience was as we experience it. It was not in some distant manner as might be true of a God who was not really human. Jesus bore the experiences in His flesh for "God sending his own Son in the likeness of sinful flesh . . . condemned sin in the flesh." Thus His contact with our suffering was real and personal. Likewise the issue of that contact was equally real and personal. When He was tempted in the wilderness it was not a mock temptation nor a sort of dress rehearsal. It was the real thing. He met that temptation on the basis of the life that He proposed to pass on to us. He did not meet it on some plane or by some means which would be out of our realm and out of our reach. It was the new life He came to bring into the world. It was the life Paul later spoke of when he said, "And the life which I now live in the flesh I live by the faith of the Son of God." It was Christ's life in Paul's flesh. Thus the same means by which Jesus met and faced temptation and adversity was provided for Paul and for us.

All this adds up to a significant fact. We are placed in the position of those who can draw upon a life which can be victorious and conquering. That life has already been tested; it has already been tried in every possible life situation. Nothing that we can experience escaped the test of this life which Christ lived and now offers to us.

It was in the knowledge of this all-inclusiveness that Paul wrote these thrilling words to the Romans, "He that spared not his own Son, but delivered him up for us all, how shall he not with him also freely give us all things? . . . Who shall separate us from the love of Christ? Shall tribulation, or distress, or persecution, or famine, or nakedness, or peril, or sword? As it is written, For thy sake we are killed all the day long: we are accounted as sheep for the slaughter. Nay, in all these things we are more than conquerors through him that loved us. For I am persuaded, that neither death, nor life, nor angels, nor principalities, nor powers, nor things present, nor things to come, nor height, nor depth, nor any other creature shall be able to separate us from the love of God, which is in Christ Jesus our Lord" (Rom. 8:32-39).

When we say that Jesus Christ met life in every conceivable situation just how extensive was it, or perhaps it is better to ask how specific was it? Can we get down to actual life-situations such as we will meet or must we deal in religious generalities and in a vague spiritual idealism? In other words, does Christianity get down to real business? Is Christ a practical Savior? Let us see.

The New Testament begins with the wilderness temptation. Here Jesus met Satan. Jesus met Satan as one person meets another person. This was not an imaginary combat with a fictitious foe. It was the recognition of spiritual evil in a spiritual personality who has the power and the presence to enter into our earthly life. This must be established as a fact of life to reckon with before we can face life. In preparation for life we are told to "put on the whole armor of God, that ye may be able to stand against the wiles of the devil. For we wrestle not against flesh and blood, but against principalities, against powers, against the rulers of the darkness of this world, against spiritual wickedness in high places" (Eph. 6:11, 12) .

Jesus faced life on the basis that the chief foe was a spiritual foe. He faced it at the place where the original battle of life was lost. Adam lost it at the place of temptation brought by this spiritual foe. Now Christ faces it at the place where it was lost. He does so victoriously. He proves the power of this new life which He has come to bring us. It was tested at its most important place and against its most impressive adversary. It met its historic, unseen spiritual foe and won. Satan is now a defeated foe and on the basis of Jesus' conquests we may conquer. His conquest was not some synthetic victory but a real victory. It was not a conquest which was beyond our plane or level of life. It was right where we live and just as we have to live it and on the very basis that we can now live it: for it is for us on the basis of faith.

When Jesus faced this temptation His physical strength was depleted. He had fasted for forty days and nights. Therefore it was not by superior physical strength that He met and conquered this foe. It is in a state of depleted strength that we must often face life. We must meet it in the physical weaknesses of sickness, of trial, of bodily defects, of daily labor and of a multitude of things that handicap us. Whatever our weakness, Jesus experienced it but He did it in the power of His new life which gave spiritual strength.

The wilderness experience of Christ touched every part of life— the physical, the moral and the spiritual. His was a token temptation of ours. He did not need to suffer every kind we suffer in the sense that He must pass through every detail. What He experienced was in the nature of our experience so that He escaped nothing that we must face. What He faced in the wilderness under great physical adversity is what we must face in life with all the weaknesses of the flesh. Likewise, His victory in the wilderness may be our victory in life. But how? Not by trying to emulate Jesus as a moral example or imitate Him as a religious ideal, but rather to partake of Jesus' nature by the birth of a new life. His temptation came at the beginning of His life but not until He died could that life which He had become the life which we need. When He died it was offered to us on the basis of faith. Faith is the link between God and man, the visible and the invisible. Paul said the life he now lived was "by the faith of the Son of God." It is on this basis that we, too, may face temptation in all its forms and conquer it.

In this manner Christ's temptation became the demonstration of our victory in life over temptation while His crucifixion became the distribution of the life of Christ by which this victory would be achieved. We cannot accept the Christ of the temptation as some sort of moral ideal and think to follow His example. It requires something within. It requires the Christ who loved us and gave Himself for us.

From the wilderness Jesus moved into life as we know it by everyday experiences. He had taken the measure of our common spiritual foe, the devil. He now can face the situations that were created by both spiritual and material conditions.

*Jesus faced sickness* almost immediately upon contact with the world after His temptation. He faced it in every conceivable form in those an about Him. Some were congenital i.e., from birth. Some were natural, just the effect of being alive. Some were retributive because it was the case of reaping what had been sown. Some were in youth. Some were in age. Some were organic. Some were neurotic. Some were mental. Some were physical. But all were real. They were not imaginary or illusory. They were not mental creations, they resided in matter and not in mind. What happened when Jesus faced sickness? In every case the sick ceased to be sick. He revealed His complete mastery over the physical ailments of life.

Now the question is, what about us when we have to face sickness? Having His life will we completely escape it? Having His life can we command the sick to be well or is this just another one of those things that is religiously impractical? We say Jesus healed the sick then why cannot we? If we can heal the sick why should we ever die? Why not go on living forever if we have the power of healing disease? These are real questions of real life. They must be faced.

To begin with, why did Jesus heal the sick? Was it to heal as many people as He could so in time He might be able to heal all the sickness in the world? We do not believe so. In the first place, when Jesus healed the sick He did not once heal the source of sickness so that the healed person never became sick again. He only healed the effect which disease produced which in one case was leprosy and in another palsy, and so on. If He set out to rid the world of disease by the art of healing, He had even for himself, an impossible task because He must be continually healing people of their recurring diseases. Jesus has a plan to rid the world of sickness but it is not by the incidental healing of our individual sicknesses. Moreover, every one of those whom Jesus healed ultimately died. If His purpose was that people should no longer be sick why not destroy disease or impart the means of overcoming it? He could have done both but he did not because disease is a part of the curse and so long as sin remains in the world disease will remain.

There was a deeper reason for Jesus healing of the sick than appears on the surface. The reason lay in the fact that His healing of the sick supported His claims of deity. The Jews had sought on one occasion to stone Jesus because He claimed to be God. Jesus made this statement, "If I do not the works of my Father, believe me not. But if I do, though ye believe not me, believe the works: that ye may know, and believe, that the Father is in me, and I in him" (John 10:37, 38).

These works of healing and kindred miracles had a meaning and purpose which we may confidently say was not intended to rid the world of disease. Jesus did not come as a physician to the world. He did not come primarily to be a healer. His healing were credentials for His claims of deity.

What about healing today? Do Christians ever get sick? Since they do what should they do about it? Should they go back to the Gospels and claim healing for all their sickness? Why not go back to the Old Testament and claim immunity from sickness for it was promised to Israel that if they would obey God. He would put none of the diseases upon them which had come on the Egyptians. Neither of these two goings-back would be right for the sphere of Christian experience does not lie either in the history of the Israelites or the history of the Gospels. The dispensational difference is great. Neither the experience of the Israelites nor of the disciples is a pattern for us. In the case of the Israelites they were living under entirely different circumstances. It was an age of law. In the case of the disciples they were living at a time when healings were performed promiscuously without regard to the faith of the sick person and entirely upon the power of Christ or the faith of the apostles. In the present case of the Christian, healing is a matter of two things, our faith and God's will. It is the prayer of faith which heals the sick according to the will of God. This is not the age of miracles. This is not time for promiscuous healing. Now it is done only when it is God's will to do so.

The dispensational pattern for Christian experience is Paul's experience with the "thorn in the flesh." It was genuine physical illness. He was a man of upright character. He was a Christian. He had faith. He prayed. Healing was denied, not because Paul did not believe or because God was reluctant but because God had a higher purpose than the healing of Paul's sickness. While the specific healing was denied his prayer was answered by grace sufficient to bear his disability and to cause him to rise above his handicap. This, we say again, is the dispensational pattern for Christian experience today. It is our recourse to prayer. It is our recognition of God's higher will. It is also our conquest of any kind of infirmity, liability or handicap by God's grace. Yes, we too can face adversity and have victory.

*Jesus faced death.* Three times he was face to face with death and was expected to do something about it. He did, and the dead no longer remained dead. He is the Lord of life. He is the master of death. Of His own death He had said, "Therefore doth my Father love me, because I lay down my life, that I might take it again. No man taketh it from me, but I lay it down of myself. I have power to lay it down, and I have power to take it again" (John 10:17, 18).

So far as death was concerned in Jesus' experience it held the same place as sickness. He was master of the body in life and death. The purpose He had in raising the dead was not to rid the world of death by these incidental ressurrections. He had another and greater purpose, namely, to reveal His deity and to establish His claims as the Savior and Redeemer. As the Redeemer He would ultimately destroy death for it is the last enemy on His list.

What are we to do about death? If we think the Gospel accounts give us the right to be healed every time we are sick then we have just as much right to think we can be raised when we die. Neither view is correct, much less the latter. There are healings today in response to prayer within the will of God but never raisings from the dead. Evidently a change has taken place in God's purpose. It has.

We conquer death not by having our dead restored to us. The best of us must die. Even those who seem so necessary to our happiness die and leave us. Are we to judge God for a faulty administration of our lives? God forbid.

Well then, what is the way to conquer death? The first thing is understanding. We must have a knowledge of what death means for a Christian. To begin with death came into the world as the penalty for sin. "Wherefore as by one man sin entered into the world, and death by sin: and so death passed upon all men, for that all have sinned." When Christ came and died He absorbed the penalty in His own body on the tree because "the sting of death is sin." When, then, we exercise saving faith in Him we do not suffer the penalty of death: we do not die because we are sinners. Yet, we still have to die and pass through the process of death which is dissolution; but its penalty which means the continuation of spiritual death into eternal death is no longer exacted.

When a Christian dies he merely changes location. He continues to live because when he believed on Christ he received eternal life. Death cannot touch that life so he continues in life in another place. That other place is described as being "with Christ." He has left a life in which a material body was the vehicle of experience for a life in which ultimately a spiritual body will be the vehicle of experience. But no matter what change in the vehicle, life continues.

The way to meet death when it comes to the Christian is by understanding what it is. Paul says, "I would not have you to be ignorant concerning them which are asleep, that ye sorrow not, even as others which have no hope." Then he goes on to give the basis for not sorrowing, "For if we believe that Jesus died and rose again, even so them also which sleep in Jesus will God bring with him." In this manner our conquest of death is based on Jesus resurrection. He was raised as the "first fruits of them that slept." His resurrection is the guarantee of our life.

When our faith is in Him we have a hope which survives the grave. That narrow cell of earth can hold only what is material and mortal. It cannot imprison the soul. He who lived in the body has gone where death cannot enter. So we look at death not as the end but as the beginning. It is not a conclusion but a commencement. It is not the last we shall see of our loved ones but the beginning of a varying interval after which we shall join them in the Father's house of life.

Whoever looks at death with this understanding and this faith has a new incentive for living. He knows now that the span of life is a time for investment. In it we invest our life, labor and talent. In it we make our contribution to the purpose of God. We look at it as but a brief part of God's plan. We listen to Paul saying, "Therefore, my beloved brethren, be ye stedfast, unmoveable, always abounding in the work of the Lord, forasmuch as ye know that your labor is not in vain in the Lord" (1 Cor. 15:58).

*Jesus faced selfishness.* It was not in Him but in man. He faced a world whose selfishness sprang from its sinfulness. Selfishness is essentially sinful. It is the desire for personal preference. It is rebellion against God's will. It is resistance against the claims of others about us. It causes all who are held by it to retreat within themselves and to think, live and work only for their own benefit. This makes life a competitive experience instead of a cooperative enterprise. We work for self instead of working with others.

The remedy for selfishness is sacrifice. Jesus said, "He that findeth his life shall lose it: and he that loseth his life for my sake shall find it."

Selfishness is hoarding. If a man hoards his money he becomes a miser. If a stream hoards its water it becomes a stagnant pool of scummy water fit neither for fish nor man. If then a life hoards itself it becomes lost for "he that findeth his life shall lose it." Finding means hoarding. It means keeping for self alone.

The way to conquer selfishness is by losing oneself. This is not throwing one's life away. It is committing it to a productive purpose. The farmer loses his seeds by committing them to the soil where they germinate and produce a crop. The investor loses his money by committing it to some enterprise where it increases itself by production. The student loses himself by committing his mind and time to the pursuit of knowledge. The lover loses his love by lavishing it on another and then finds it returned to him again. It is life's law that to get we must give, to find we must lose, to gather we must scatter, to go up we must go down. Jesus, being the Lord of life, was wise in the ways of life and said, "He that findeth his life shall lose it: and he that loseth his life for my sake shall find it" (Matt. 10:39).

Jesus faced all of the things we must face in life such as fear, unbelief, ingratitude, evil, error, persecutions and the future. In each case He met His adversary with success. So may we as Christians, for we have His life and having His life we have the basis and the power for the conquest of every one of life's adversaries.

The basis of this conquest is in His life and death. His life was lived sinlessly and victoriously. It proved that Christianity holds the answer for every human problem. His death gave His life to us so that we may live by His life.

The power of this conquest is in His death. It is the power of faith. Faith becomes the means of life. Jesus always revealed every failure of His disciples as being a lack of faith. It was usually in such words as these, "if ye had faith." Faith was to be the power of the new life. The power was not in faith as though faith was some kind of wonder worker. Faith was what released the power. The power was divine while the faith was human.

The Bible is a book of conquests by faith. A résumé is found in its great victory chapter in Hebrews 11.

"By faith Abel . . . By faith Enoch . . . By faith Noah . . . By faith Abraham . . . By faith Isaac . . . By faith Jacob . . . By faith Joseph . . . By faith Moses . . . And what shall I more say? for the time would fail me to tell of Gedeon, and of Barak, and of Samson, and of Jephthah; of David also, and Samuel, and of the prophets: who through faith subdued kingdoms, wrought righteousness, obtained promises, stopped the mouths of lions, quenched the violence of fire, escaped the edge of the sword, out of weakness were made strong, waxed valiant in fight, turned to flight the armies of the aliens. Women received their dead raised to life again: and others were tortured, not accepting deliverance; that they might obtain a better resurrection: and others had trial of cruel mockings and scourgings, yea, moreover of bonds and imprisonment: they were stoned, they were sawn asunder, were tempted, were slain with the sword: they wandered about in sheepskins and goatskins; being destitute, afflicted, tormented; (of whom the world was not worthy:) they wandered in deserts and in mountains, and in dens and caves of the earth. And these all, having obtained a good report through faith . . ." (Heb. 11:32–39).

# ADDITIONAL RESOURCES FOR YOUR STUDY OF BIBLE CHARACTERS

### Great Cloud of Witnesses
**in Hebrews Eleven**                                    **E. W. Bullinger**
A classic exposition including an examination of the great heroes of the faith. Full of rich, practical applications.

ISBN 0-8254-2247-7                    462 pp.                    paperback

### The Training of the Twelve                              **A. B. Bruce**
(Forewords by Olan Hendrix and D. Stuart Briscoe)
The monumental classic on discipleship and leadership training. A complete exposition of how Christ prepared His twelve disciples.

ISBN 0-8254-2236-1                    566 pp.                    paperback
ISBN 0-8254-2212-4                    566 pp.                    hardback

### Pontius Pilate                                         **Paul L. Maier**
Unlike most historical novelists who are strong on imagination but weak on fact, Paul Maier has invented a new literary genre, the "documentary novel," which aims for historical accuracy. In *Pontius Pilate*, the author unveils the colorful, untold story of Pontius Pilate and answers many questions relating to this famous historical figure.

ISBN 0-8254-3261-8                    384 pp.                    hardback

### Bible Portrait Series                              **George Matheson**
(Foreword by Warren W. Wiersbe)
Believers looking for fresh insights into Bible characters will find a rich treasure in Matheson's series on Bible portraits. Warren W. Wiersbe, says of this blind author, "No evangelical writer, including the great Alexander Whyte, surpasses George Matheson in this whole area of Bible biography . . . God has closed [his] eyes—only to open other eyes, which have made [him] one of the guides of men."

**Portraits of Bible Women**
ISBN 0-8254-3250-2                    264 pp.                    paperback

**Portraits of Bible Men** (1st Series)
ISBN 0-8254-3251-0                    384 pp.                    paperback

**Portraits of Bible Men** (2nd Series)
ISBN 0-8254-3252-9                    368 pp.                    paperback

**Portraits of Bible Men** (3rd Series)
ISBN 0-8254-3253-7                    368 pp.                    paperback